DISASTER!

ALSO BY DAN KURZMAN

Soldier of Peace: The Life of Yitzhak Rabin, 1922–1995

Blood and Water: Sabotaging Hitler's Bomb

Left to Die: The Tragedy of the USS Juneau

Fatal Voyage: The Sinking of the USS Indianapolis

A Killing Wind: Inside Union Carbide and the Bhopal Catastrophe

Day of the Bomb: Countdown to Hiroshima

Ben-Gurion: Prophet of Fire

Miracle of November: Madrid's Epic Stand, 1936

The Bravest Battle: The 28 Days of the Warsaw Ghetto Uprising

The Race for Rome

Genesis 1948: The First Arab-Israeli War

Santo Domingo: Revolt of the Damned

Subversion of the Innocents

Kishi and Japan: The Search for the Sun

WILLIAM MORROW • 75 YEARS OF PUBLISHING
An Imprint of HarperCollins*Publishers*

DISASTER!

The Great San Francisco
Earthquake and Fire of 1906

DAN KURZMAN

HarperCollins books may be purchased for educational, business, or sales promotional use. For information please write: Special Markets Department, HarperCollins Publishers Inc., 10 East 53rd Street, New York, NY 10022.

FIRST EDITION

Designed by Kate Nichols
Printed on acid-free paper

Library of Congress Cataloging-in-Publication Data

Kurzman, Dan.
Disaster! : the great San Francisco earthquake and fire of 1906 /
by Dan Kurzman—1st ed.
p.   cm.
Includes bibliographical references and index.
ISBN 0-06-105174-8
1. Earthquakes—California—San Francisco—History
—20th century. 2. Fires—California—San Francisco—
History—20th century. 3. San Francisco (Calif.)
—History—20th century. I. Title.

F869.S357 K87 2001
979.4'61051—dc21   00-053321

01 02 03 04 05 QW 10 9 8 7 6 5 4 3 2 1

For my dear wife,

Florence,

who, like the San Franciscans,

meets any challenge with

grit and grace

Contents

Acknowledgments   xiii

People in the Book   xvii

Map of San Francisco, 1906   xxi

Preface   xxiii

Prologue   1

1   Caruso and the Odor of Roses   7

2   Barrymore Slept Here   12

3   Sullivan's Nightmare   14

4   The Nectar of Corruption   21

5   The Banker and the Boy   29

6   Cook's Tour of a Cataclysm   32

7   The End of the World   37

8   Birth and Death   44

9   The Miser and the Melting Pot   49

10   The Accordion and the Cops   51

11	The Dishware and the Dragons	56
12	The Crackle of Terror	63
13	The Cruel Trap	69
14	Napoleon to the Rescue	72
15	Inoculating the Mayor	81
16	The Lord, the King, and the Executioners	89
17	Succumbing to Catastrophe	94
18	The Puny Millionaires	99
19	Not Even the Dead Were Safe	104
20	The Vengeful Demons	108
21	The Tongue of a Poisonous Snake	115
22	The Angel and the Newborn	120
23	Criminals in Uniform	124
24	Bringing Out the Best	136
25	The Case for the Fire	141
26	A Proud Ending	147
27	Ravagement, Racism, and Rats	151
28	The Persian Cat	160
29	Black News and White Tails	166
30	The Home Bank and the Burned Home	171
31	A Vow to Love and a Vow to Die	175
32	Misery, Murder, and Mastery	180
33	Running a Gauntlet	186
34	From Prayer to Action	190
35	Dynamite and Desperation	193
36	A Fruit Dish and a Cup of Tea	201
37	The Lure of Rare Wine	208
38	The Ghoulish Lion	212
39	The Deadline and the Doorknob	220

40	A Last Stand	223
41	Rise from the Ruins	228
	Epilogue	248
	Notes	257
	Bibliography	269
	Index	287

Acknowledgments

I AM ESPECIALLY INDEBTED to my wife, Florence, for editing this book with great sensitivity, helping to bring alive the cold facts of history. Her extensive research also contributed enormously to the human texture of this work.

I also wish to warmly thank my editors, Tom Dupree and Kelly Notaras, for their excellent editorial suggestions, and my dear old friend, Gladys Justin Carr, who, as vice president of HarperCollins, encouraged me from the moment I started on this book. Julian Bach and Sofia Seidner of the International Management Group deserve my gratitude, too, for their efforts on my behalf.

I am grateful as well to the following people for agreeing to interviews or facilitating the research in various ways:

Patricia Akre—photograph curator, San Francisco Public Library
Robert O. Appleton—son of survivor Abraham Appleton
Roger D. Borcherdt—scientist, United States Geological Survey, Menlo Park, California
Walter Brem—assistant curator, Bancroft Library, University of California, Berkeley, California
Philip Choy—president, Chinese Historical Society, San Francisco

Myrtis Cochran—librarian, Doe Library, University of California, Berkeley, California

Selby Collins—archivist, San Francisco Public Library

Emmet Condon—former chief, San Francisco Fire Department

Gerald C. Cullen—nephew of Fire Officer Charles Cullen

Alice Dowd—librarian, New York Public Library

Pat Dowling—United Irish Cultural Center, San Francisco

Franz Enciso—archivist, Bancroft Library, Berkeley, California

David Farrell—archivist, Bancroft Library, Berkeley, California

Faulhaber, Charles B.—director, Bancroft Library, Berkeley, California

Jeffrey M. Flannery—manuscript reference librarian, Library of Congress

Thomas S. Fowler—archivist, San Francisco Public Library

Calvin Fung—official, Chinese Historical Society, San Francisco

Herbert Garcia—archivist, Society of California Pioneers, San Francisco

Susan H. Garcia—public information officer, United States Geological Survey, Menlo Park, California

Susan Goldstein—city archivist, San Francisco Public Library

Susan M. Haas—registrar, Society of California Pioneers, San Francisco

Jean C. Han—assistant head, East Asian Library, University of California, Berkeley, California

Gary Handman—head, Media Services Center, Moffitt Library, Berkeley, California

Peter Hanff—director, Bancroft Library, Berkeley, California

Gladys Hansen—director, Museum of the City of San Francisco

Thomas Janora—official, Phoenix Society, San Francisco

Patricia Keats—director, library, California Historical Society, San Francisco

Rosemary Kennedy—archivist, National Archives, San Bruno, California

Kim Klausner—archivist, Judah L. Magnes Museum, Berkeley, California

Claire Knopf—researcher

Roberto Landazuri—librarian, San Francisco Public Library

Michael McCone—director, California Historical Society

Faun Minnis—official, San Francisco Public Library

Ann Moen—supervisor, Moffitt Library, University of California, Berkeley, California

Neil Orlina—librarian, Ethnic Studies Library, Berkeley, California

Edward J. Phipps—former chief, San Francisco Fire Department

Carol S. Prentice—scientist, United States Geological Survey

Ron Ross—founder, San Francisco History Association

Jennifer Schaffner—assistant librarian, California Historical Society

Rick Sherman—official, California Genealogical Society, Oakland, California

Xiaohong Shi—translator from Chinese

Susan Snyder—head, Access Services, Bancroft Library, Berkeley, California

Sue Stacks—secretary, Phoenix Society, San Francisco

Jim Stringer—clerk, San Francisco Superior Court

Malcolm E. Walker—author, *Three Fearful Days*

Wei Chi Poon—specialist, Ethnic Studies Library, Berkeley, California

Catherine F. Woesthoff—librarian, New York Public Library

People in the Book

George C. Adams—pastor who performed the Emersons' marriage ceremony

Dwight E. Aultman—army officer

O. D. Baldwin—real estate magnate

John Barrymore—actor

William Barton—orphan in a whorehouse

Jerome Bassity—king of the Barbary Coast

Phil B. Bekeart—employer of Charles Dray, who saved his dog

John Bermingham—intoxicated dynamiter

Fulton G. Berry—survivor whose home was dynamited

Gimpy Bill—legless survivor

Gordon Blanding—survivor who saved his home with a bribe of liquor

Thomas Bowes—boardinghouse owner who died in the fire

Raymond W. Briggs—army officer, dynamiter

Jack Brown—quadriplegic survivor

William F. Burke—assistant postmaster

Daniel H. Burnham—architect of San Francisco

Enrico Caruso—Metropolitan Opera tenor

George Chase—survivor who lost his candy box full of jewels

Fong Chong (Little Pete)—Chinese mobster

Bill Coffman—shanghaied sailor

Le Vert Coleman—army officer, dynamiter

William Collier—head of Barrymore's theatrical group

Antonio Compania—fisherman trapped in refrigerator

Jesse Cook—policeman who saw earthquake starting

Charles Crocker—railroad magnate

Aurelio Delbert (Del) Crespi—ten-year-old boy who loved his missing classmate Lillian

Ernest Denicke—army officer who witnessed a shooting

William Denman—lawyer who solved a logistical problem

Guion H. Dewey—Grand Hotel guest who narrowly escaped death

Jeremiah Dinan—police chief

John Dougherty—acting fire chief

Charles Nicholas Dray—boy who risked his life to save his boss's dog

John Drew—Barrymore's uncle

Bernard Dulberg—Rebecca's husband

Etta Dulberg—daughter of Bernard and Rebecca

Rebecca Dulberg—Bernard's wife, who gave birth during the earthquake

Jeremiah M. Dwyer—policeman in City Hall

George W. and Josephine Emerson—couple who married during the fire

Max Fenner—policeman who was killed

James Flood—tycoon

Mary Leary Flood—wife of James Flood

Frederick Newton Freeman—navy officer who pumped water ashore

Olive Fremstad—opera singer

Brigadier General Frederick Funston—army deputy commander, Pacific Division

Arnold Genthe—famous photographer

Amadeo Peter Giannini—founder, Bank of Italy (later, Bank of America)

Cliff Graves—bar patron who observed murder

Major General Adolphus Greely—army commander, Pacific Division

George Harrington—survivor who saved Ida and then married her

Ida Harrington (McMahon)—survivor who married George

Gus Hartmann—city supervisor who gave away liquor

Alfred Hertz—Caruso's conductor

Jimmy Ho—Hugh Kwong Liang's friend in a refugee camp

Mark Hopkins—railroad magnate
James Hopper—newspaper reporter
George and Amelia Horton—newlyweds who searched for each other
Collis P. Huntington—railroad magnate
R. Leonard Ingham—police sergeant who predicted earthquake
Rose Kane—matron, Emergency Hospital
Edna Ketring—fiancée of fire victim Bowes
J. W. Lake—relief camp leader
Franklin K. Lane—member, Committee of Fifty
Frank Leach—superintendent of the San Francisco Mint
Sol Lesser—child survivor who raided a candy store
Hugh Kwong Liang—Chinese survivor who was saved from suicide
Clifton Macon—Oakland minister
Charles Drummond McArrow—survivor who collected arms
Mary McDermitt—Holy Roller missionary
John McLean—policeman in Emergency Hospital
John McMahon—survivor who abandoned "wife" Ida during fire
Ruth McMahon—daughter of John and Ida
Mrs. John F. Merrill—owner of doomed home
Charles Miller—doctor in Mechanics Pavilion
John Moller—merchant killed by steer
Colonel Charles Morris—military commander
Joseph Myers—playground director who was murdered
Fremont Older—editor, *San Francisco Bulletin*
George C. Pardee—governor of California
Helen Huntington Perrin—elite citizen
James Phelan—former mayor of San Francisco
Edward J. Plume—policeman in City Hall
Osgood Putnam—head of relief work
William C. Ralston—builder of the Palace Hotel
William M. Ross—policeman who helped survivors
Rotary Rosie—intellectual prostitute
Abraham Ruef—corrupt politician
H. C. Schmitt—policeman robbed by a looter
Eugene Schmitz—mayor of San Francisco
Antonio Scotti—opera singer

Lester Sheeline—liquor store owner
Claus Spreckels—sugar baron
Rudolph Spreckels—son of Claus
Leland Stanford—former governor of California, railroad magnate
William F. Stehr—survivor in collapsed hotel
Jacob Steinman—militiaman who killed the playground director
Ashton Stevens—theater reviewer, *San Francisco Examiner*
Marshall Stoddard—survivor who wrote a note to his mother on a shirt
    collar
Dennis Sullivan—fire chief, killed in earthquake
Florence Mabel Sylvester—nurse
William Howard Taft—U.S. secretary of war
Tilton Tillman—surgeon in the Mechanics Pavilion
Rabbi Jacob Voorsanger—head of hunger relief
M. L. Walker—army commander
Harry F. Walsh—policeman who escaped maddened bulls
Edward Ward—police sergeant, tuberculosis victim
Jessy Wilson—survivor who saved her elderly mother

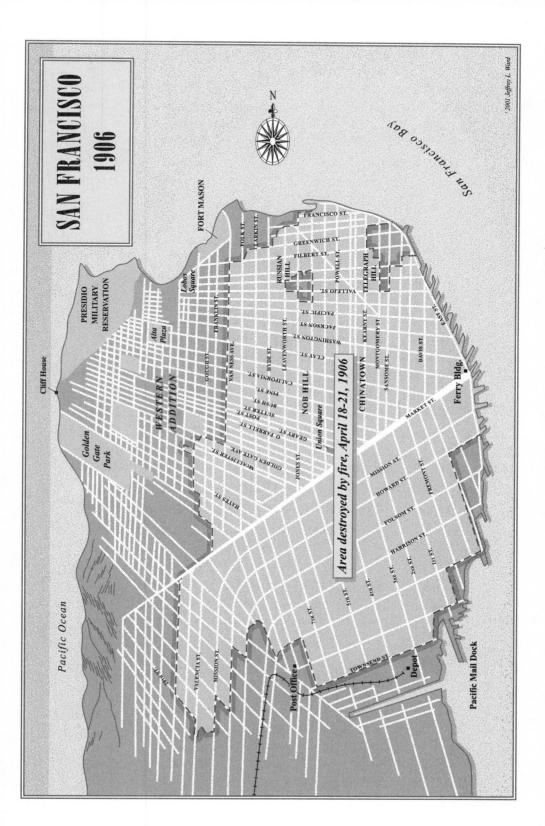

SAN FRANCISCO
1906

N

2001 Jeffrey L. Ward

San Francisco Bay

FORT MASON

POLK ST.

LARKIN ST.

FRANCISCO ST.

GREENWICH ST.

FILBERT ST.

RUSSIAN
HILL

POWELL ST.

VALLEJO ST.

TELEGRAPH
HILL

PRESIDIO
MILITARY
RESERVATION

Lobos
Square

FRANKLIN ST.

PACIFIC ST.

JACKSON ST.

WASHINGTON ST.

KEARNY ST.

MONTGOMERY ST.

EAST ST.

Alta
Plaza

GOUGH ST.

VAN NESS AVE.

LEAVENWORTH ST.

CLAY ST.

CHINATOWN

SANSOME ST.

DAVIS ST.

Cliff House

WESTERN
ADDITION

HYDE ST.

CALIFORNIA ST.

NOB HILL

Ferry Bldg.

Golden
Gate
Park

PINE ST.

BUSH ST.

SUTTER ST.

POST ST.

Union Square

MARKET ST.

O'FARRELL ST.

GEARY ST.

GOLDEN GATE AVE.

McALLISTER ST.

JONES ST.

MISSION ST.

HOWARD ST.

FREMONT ST.

HAYES ST.

Area destroyed by fire, April 18-21, 1906

FOLSOM ST.

HARRISON ST.

1ST ST.

2ND ST.

3RD ST.

4TH ST.

5TH ST.

Pacific Ocean

7TH ST.

VALENCIA ST.

MISSION ST.

14TH ST.

TOWNSEND ST.

Depot

Post Office

Pacific Mail Dock

Preface

S AN FRANCISCO HAS LIVED two lives—one before the 1906 earthquake and fire and one after. That massive disaster obliterated the city, which had to be rebuilt physically, economically, and socially—a feat miraculously accomplished in a few years. The story of San Francisco's destruction, with all its poignant drama, is important not only because it was probably America's worst peacetime disaster, but also because it mirrored the extraordinary spirit that drove people to survive and finally conquer under the most terrifying circumstances.

As a native San Franciscan, I have been intrigued from childhood by fantastic stories of the events of 1906, stories of heroism and horror that have been passed down through the generations. This book, therefore, is an attempt to explore the truth and reveal in a comprehensive way the bitter challenge that tested the heart and soul of a defenseless city under savage attack by a mindless, merciless enemy.

But as dramatic as many of the scenes here may be, none are fictionalized or exaggerated. All the facts I present are sourced and attributed in the notes, which reflect two years of extensive research supporting my reportage on how San Franciscans dealt with this catastrophe.

It was not always easy finding information about events occurring almost a century ago, especially since the earthquake and fire claimed the lives of so many people and turned many records into ash. In one case, I was only able to track down the descendants of a victim by finding her burial place.

In any event, I managed to unearth facts that confirmed many of the legendary tales. Some told of criminality and profiteering, but most reflected indomitable courage and extraordinary perseverance by citizens who lived up to the traditions of a tough frontier people, a people born in fire and hardened in the gold mines that financed the growth of San Francisco from a sleepy village to one of the world's greatest, most exciting cities.

Dan Kurzman
San Francisco

Prologue

FTER SUFFERING through a gray, drizzly winter, San Franciscans stoically endured yet another sullen morning on April 17, 1906. By afternoon the clouds surrendered to a dense fog that nearly smothered the city, slowing the pace of life in rhythm with the mournful wail of the foghorn. But as the day faded into dusk, a brisk wind dissipated the haze, and suddenly San Francisco glowed under a full moon. The people, optimistic by nature, rejoiced. Spring had finally come. The following day, many predicted, the city would bask in the sun, and they could savor the feel of its warm rays filtered through a cooling coastal mist.

George W. Emerson was especially optimistic. Could any day be sunnier than the day of his wedding? Tomorrow he would marry Josephine Hoffman and begin the ideal life he'd always envisioned. As chief accountant of the Union Gas Company, Emerson was already heading toward the top. Now he would share his success with Josephine, whom he had been courting for months. As he lay in bed that night, he could almost hear the voice of Reverend George C. Adams echo through the First Congregational Church as he pronounced their union eternal. And adding to the joy of the occasion, the sister of the bride would soon marry the reverend's son.

What a memorable day lay ahead.

Other San Franciscans also eagerly anticipated the dawn, if perhaps for less personal reasons. They could hardly wait to hear the mirthful cries of children on Easter vacation playing ball in the neighborhood park, the gravelly shouts of stevedores unloading crates of herbs, spices, and other exotic East Asian specialties from ships hugging the docks along the sea-wall, and the wily pleas of vendors at the beach selling trinkets with the help of trained canaries and monkeys.

Yes, tomorrow would be a fine day, a day that would suit the relaxed mood of this culturally mongrelized city, which, fittingly, was created in 1776—the year America was born, opening its arms to the unwanted of the world. No city's arms were spread wider than San Francisco's. Irish-men, Italians, Spaniards, Jews, Russians, Japanese, and Chinese arrived, and, despite lingering discriminatory problems, all drew on the energy generated in the adventurous past by a colorful assortment of pioneers—gamblers and gold miners, missionaries and merchants, vagrants and vig-ilantes. Many of the one and a half million foreigners expected to immigrate to the United States in 1906 were attracted by San Francisco's open, versatile, unvarnished character, and they would further contribute to the exotic makeup of the city, which author Robert Louis Stevenson called "the smelting-pot of the races."

If San Francisco would become a haven for the unwanted, early explorers, ironically, had almost rejected it as a desirable place to settle. In 1769, a party of Spanish monks and military men under Captain Don Gas-par de Portola, while searching for Monterey, discovered San Francisco Bay. Portola sent several men to explore the hilly, jewel-like tip of the peninsula poking into this grand inlet and pondered whether Spain should establish a colony there. After exploring the area and finding too little water and wood, the men reported back that it would be the worst place in all California to settle.

But six years later, in 1775, Captain Juan Bautista de Anza, who rec-ognized the importance of the discovery, led a party to the same region and planted markers that laid out the perimeters of a settlement. Soon a remote frontier outpost called Yerba Buena ("Good Herb"), later renamed San Francisco, sprouted in the wind-swept, shrub-embroidered hills, if with only a handful of dutiful priests and soldiers. They joined a sprinkling of raggedly dressed Indians and indolent whites braving the majestic wilderness that had intimidated Portola.

Until 1846, when an era of Spanish glory and religious chivalry came to an abrupt end with the arrival of the Americans from the East, the local government was directed from a tiny, dirt-floored, two-room adobe hut that was the home of the Mexican *comandante* at the army base called the Presidio. The *comandante* presided over what had become a good-hearted, lighthearted, crime-free hamlet of rancheros and adventurers who welcomed strangers into their unlocked homes and reveled at the fiesta, the bullring, and the racetrack.

But in 1848, two years after Captain John B. Montgomery of the American war sloop *Portsmouth* planted the U.S. flag in the village, the discovery of gold in the Sierras suddenly brought tens of thousands of fortune hunters from all over the world swarming into the area. The tranquility quickly dissolved in an explosion of greed and ruthless energy. But as the sleepy, trusting village expanded into a thriving, dynamic town, the frenzy for gold, with all its inherent evils, spawned a golden era of romance and heroism that would permanently shape the character of San Francisco.

NOW, IN 1906, 450,000 San Franciscans, more than double the population of Los Angeles at the time, resided in what had become the social, financial, commercial, and cultural capital of California. Carefree, prosperous, and proud of their idiosyncratic tradition, they viewed life with a lusty, almost passionate optimism, whether they were engaged in business, the arts, or the sinful pursuits that led the puritanical to prophesy terrible sanctions from heaven. San Francisco had been destroyed by fire again and again, yet each disaster had only sparked the will of its inhabitants to build upon the ruins a city more splendid than before.

Even in 1906 this city, though still imbued with a stubborn gold-rush rusticity, could claim a metropolitan status equal to some of the more urbane eastern cities and was constantly growing in importance. No longer dependent for its prosperity on gold extracted from the rocky soil of the Sierras and silver from Nevada's fabulous Comstock Lode, San Francisco now drew much of its life's blood from fertile farms and humming factories.

Such enterprises spectacularly generated trade with the Orient and helped to turn San Francisco into the busiest port on the Pacific Coast, served by huge, locally built steamers and the two great intercontinental railroads, the Southern Pacific and the Santa Fe, which terminated by the bay.

By 1900 San Francisco had become the headquarters for the coast's top financial, manufacturing, railroad, shipping, lumber, and distribution interests. And with people gradually getting around in gasoline automobiles, lighting their homes with electricity, and communicating by telephone, and with the wireless radio on the horizon, San Francisco's dynamic rush into the future would accelerate.

Huge office buildings and hotels were mushrooming in a bustling downtown area already sprinkled with stunning edifices, steadily changing the skyline of this once mountainous wilderness. There was, for example, the newly built James Flood Building, the largest office building in the West, and the still unfinished, Grecian-style Fairmont Hotel atop Nob Hill, a gleaming white, palatial tribute to San Francisco's new cosmopolitan grandeur.

Much of this grandeur, interspersed with islands of grubbiness, centered around Market Street, the broad main business thoroughfare, which diagonally crossed the city southwestward from the Ferry Building to Twin Peaks. All downtown streets—from the north, southeast, and west—converged on Market at wedge-shaped intersections. North of Market, Nob Hill, the kingdom of the rich, rose in opulent splendor. In its golden shadow to the south stood most of the great hotels, office buildings, expensive stores, theaters, and banking institutions, which dominated Montgomery Street, the Wall Street of San Francisco. And the splendor was enhanced by the green terraces falling away northward to a seafood-scented waterfront.

In unpretentious disorder south of Market, or "South of the Slot" (referring to the slot in the center of the cable car tracks running along Market), stretched the wholesale houses, factories, and railroad yards that reached westward into a shabby residential area of rickety wood-frame homes and cheap lodging houses, many catering to sailors. West of the downtown area, bordered by the glittering mansions of Van Ness Avenue, spread the Western Addition. This was a crowded middle-class residential section that petered off into windswept sand dunes leading to the Presidio and the Pacific Ocean, a stretch of desert monotony relieved by little more than the densely verdant lushness of Golden Gate Park.

It was evident in 1906 that the grandeur of San Francisco would spread. In fact, Daniel H. Burnham, an acclaimed architect, had been hired to draw up plans to remodel the whole city, with wider, winding streets replacing the grid pattern laid willy-nilly over steep hills and with a great amphitheater reaching into the heavens from Twin Peaks. The sand dunes were already dotted with some homes, and there were even a few paved streets crawling through this desertlike area.

The spirit of the bold and venturesome San Franciscans was futuristic, and one lived each day to discover the wonders to come. Especially in the spring, when young lovers like George Emerson and Josephine Hoffman would overwhelm the marriage bureau with requests for licenses that would permit them to share the joy of life in this city abounding with beauty and opportunity.

Still, not all San Franciscans found life as fulfilling. But even such residents could always find solace in the exhilarating embrace of the city itself with its unique charm and style, a city that pulsated with vigor and excitement, offering romance, mystery, and for the recklessly adventurous, license.

There were the steep hills swooping skyward—sometimes invisibly into a screen of fog—that resounded with the clang of cable cars because no horse-drawn carriage or automobile of the time could negotiate the grade; the sublime Golden Gate that sparkled like an entrance to paradise, cooling the land in summer and preserving a temperate climate throughout the year; the incongruous mix of intricate Victorian architecture with its regal spires that lent the city a touch of royalty, and the plain, stucco-covered adobe homes shaded by wide-eaved, red-tiled roofs that magnificently ratified its Spanish heritage.

San Francisco was, in fact, a city of contrasts, and as one writer would say, was "physically and morally . . . built on mud." Flowers of rare beauty grew out of this mud, a tonic for anyone's depression. But if the blues persisted, there were always the countless cabarets where glasses tinkled all night; the dank underground dens in Chinatown, where one could puff on an opium pipe or enjoy the favors of a young prostitute smuggled in from China; the bars along the infamous Barbary Coast, where the more daring might stop in for a drink— hopefully one that wasn't spiked, to render the drinker helpless as he was shanghaied and forced to swab the deck of a smuggler's ship. On this very day, the police barely saved a fifteen-year-old boy from such a fate.

For the wealthier and more conventional, the flowers in this merry capital of international society were always in bloom. They streamed into the lavish nightclubs and the theaters, many, on this moonlit night, into the Columbia to enjoy a performance of Victor Herbert's new musical, *Babes in Toyland,* or into the Tivoli to see *Miss Timidity*. People of more modest means crowded into the Orpheum vaudeville palace to savor clownish comics, jesting jugglers, and audacious acrobats.

The greatest number of pleasure seekers—three thousand, who would pay from seven to sixty-six dollars—gathered in the Grand Opera House for a special treat. Special, since it wasn't often that the Metropolitan Opera Company could persuade a performer to make the long, tedious train trip from New York. . . .

CHAPTER 1

Caruso and the Odor of Roses

ENRICO CARUSO, widely acclaimed as the world's greatest tenor, had been so persuaded. He would play the role of Don Jose opposite Olive Fremstad, a famed Wagnerian soprano, in Bizet's *Carmen* at the Grand Opera House on this warm spring evening of April 17. In truth, he needed little persuasion. He had been scheduled to appear in Naples, Italy, at this time but canceled the trip from New York to his native land right after Mount Vesuvius had erupted, with fiery ashes raining down on nearby villages and threatening to blanket the city. In one village market, 250 people died when the roof collapsed from the weight of the ashes. And though Americans were sending thousands of dollars for relief, who wanted to be close enough to extinction to be eligible for relief? Better to accept an offer to go with a Metropolitan Opera troupe to San Francisco, where at least he would be safe. On the train there, he told his orchestra conductor:

"Maybe it was God's will after all that I should come this far."

Still, who knew what dangers lurked in the Wild West? The region was still primitive, he had heard, and was not even fully settled yet. Indeed, Oklahoma had just been admitted to the Union. And so he had purchased a pistol and fifty bullets before boarding the train—just in case. And while crossing the western plains, he spent his time learning how to load the gun and draw it with a flick of his wrist, in time to thwart any bandit or would-be assassin.

On arriving in the Bay Area, Caruso learned from reporters that Vesuvius had made good on its threat, killing over 1,200 people in a massive eruption. He froze. If he had gone to his beloved Naples, the lava from Vesuvius might have caught him in the middle of an aria. Yes, God had chosen San Francisco.

Caruso moved into the thirty-year-old, world-famous Palace Hotel on Market Street between Second and Third Streets, a few blocks from the waterfront, where ships with red and green running lights rhythmically bobbed in the waves, as if affirming the city's placidly cheerful nature. Given the finest of the hotel's luxurious suites, once occupied by President Ulysses S. Grant, Caruso surveyed everything with a critical eye—the long, fringed green and gold draperies, the chairs upholstered in gold brocade, the great fireplace with carved marble mantel and gold-framed mirror, the furniture of California laurel, the native fir floor planking, and the carpeting from a prestigious New York firm, which had opened a San Francisco branch just to supply the hotel.

Not very elegant, he complained. But what could one expect in the Wild West?

The singer then directed his valet to unload his trunks, making sure his countless silk shirts, evening jackets, and pairs of Italian leather footwear were neatly put away. Was Caruso to wear a wrinkled shirt? He was in a sour mood, even when he learned the hotel was packed with guests, many of whom had come from distant places just to hear his voice. He was haunted by the thought of his narrow escape from Vesuvius. What if God had sent him to Naples?

On the evening of his performance, April 17, Caruso was still agitated, and not only by Vesuvius. He had an explosive confrontation with Madame Fremstad at rehearsal that afternoon in the Grand Opera House, which had been built in 1876 on Mission Street between Third and Fourth Streets and remained one of the few notable buildings to grace the largely shoddy south-of-Market district. Angered by the clumsiness of some of the locally hired stage hands, Fremstad had faltered in her aria. How, Caruso demanded, could he perform together with a woman who screeched her notes?

Get rid of the local workers! Fremstad cried. If Caruso were not paid so much, the company could afford to hire more professional labor.

Caruso was enraged. Yes, he was paid a record $1,350 a performance, but didn't he draw the crowd? Nobody would lose his job without Caruso's approval. Otherwise, he would not go onstage, and neither would Fremstad. Nor would he ever be in another opera with her again!

No one was fired.

The tenor had already been jolted earlier that day when he read the reviews of the previous night's performance of *The Queen of Sheba,* the company's first presentation, though he did not himself appear in it. The critics had relentlessly panned those who did, one of them calling it "the wrong opera [with] the wrong singers." Caruso felt his colleagues deserved the criticism, but he wondered if many in the full house who had come to hear him now would, in their cultural ignorance, show as little appreciation of his own artistry. And however great his voice, would they accept a pudgy, double-chinned man in the role of the dashing Don Jose? As if it were not enough that the two-hundred-pound Madame Fremstad would be playing the beautiful, passionate Carmen!

In any case, what could he expect from the progeny of the gold rush rabble, who lacked the sophistication of the more cultivated easterners? His distrust of this western audience was perhaps reflected in his nervous refusal to remove the pistol he hid under his stage attire. Actually, while the East was culturally more advanced, a large and vigorous middle class, nurtured by a golden past, had sprung up here, and the poorer class did not live in the squalor so prevalent in the East, being more willing to gamble on the future and to struggle up the ladder.

But the most important patrons of the opera, he knew, were members of a select, powerful community dominated by the millionaire heirs of crude, often ruthless gold rush pioneers, nouveau riche social lions who found opera a convenient cultural mechanism for appearing in public as people of substance as well as of wealth.

As if to make the point, in the audience were stunningly coiffured society matrons and their debutante daughters still glowing from their princess-for-a-night roles at the exclusive Cotillion Club ball that had recently opened the social season. Now, at this performance of *Carmen,* the social event of the year, they sought to cloak their provinciality in brocades, furs, and jewels. There was, for example, Mrs. Frederick Kohl, who wore a spangled black lace gown, a two-inch-wide dog collar of diamonds and pearls, a diamond tiara, and a jeweled American Beauty rose in her hair. There was Mrs. M. H. de Young, wife of the *San Francisco Chronicle* publisher, appearing in white brocade with a coronet of diamonds.

And there was Mary Leary Flood, who was married to tycoon James Flood; she seemed almost to light up with jewels. Her family had sold its beloved cow to pay for her trip from Ireland to the United States. Now she sat in a box seat, aglitter with diamond tiara, diamond shoulder straps, diamond dog collar, diamond stomacher, and diamond-speckled corsage—a far cry from her milking days. But a milkmaid was still a milkmaid in Caruso's mind. What could she know about music? Did cows sing? As Laura Bride Powers, the *Call* society reporter, would write:

"It takes what racing men call 'class' to wear a tiara, or even a wreath, and not make a comic valentine of one's self."

The opera management did its best to lend class to the valentines. "The house," wrote Powers, "was a terraced garden of orchids and narcissus and nodding roses, with fruit blossoms scattered between. And the odor of roses from the pit assailed the senses like the breath that blows from the flowery orchids of Santa Clara."

But to Caruso, the smell of the barn was more powerful than the scent of the rose—until the opera ended. For hardly had his voice with its strange pathos caressed the high vaulted ceiling with the final note when the audience jumped to its feet and with thunderous applause and cries of "Bravo! Bravo!" brought him back for endless curtain calls. Now Caruso could smell the roses. He had never been in better voice—and no one seemed to mind the tonnage of the principals.

Finally, Caruso, with other members of the cast, went outside, where scores of horse-drawn taxis were lined up waiting for passengers. Many opera patrons stepped into their own one-horse hacks or two-horse carriages, most of them driven by a top-hatted coachman, who with a gentle snap of his whip grazed the animals as if trying to flick off a fly. A second coachman sat stiffly beside him with arms folded, ready to hop off and stand at attention by the door when the passengers stepped down at their destination.

Caruso and his closest associates climbed into one of the newest model automobiles carrying the elite in convulsive, sputtering glory. About a block away on Market Street, they arrived at the Palace Hotel, and here in the gaily ornamented garden court, amid tall palm trees swaying in the cool sea breeze, they sipped fine wine at twenty-five cents a drink (ten cents more than at most bars) and wallowed in their triumph. Others watched from the eight crystal-chandeliered galleries overlooking the court, sharing this exhilarating moment.

Caruso and several others then went off to Zinkand's Restaurant for heaping portions of spaghetti served while a young woman—Elsa Maxwell, who would one day be a celebrated society hostess—sat at the piano playing operatic medleys. The tenor finished the evening by drawing caricatures of his friends on the tablecloth, to dispel any doubt that he was a multitalented artist.

At about 3 A.M., Caruso returned to the Palace, a few blocks away, still in an exuberant mood; even the provincials had been dazzled by his greatness. And as he climbed into bed, he could hardly wait to read the reviews, which would be printed during the night. They were not disappointing. Typically, the *Call* reviewer would write:

"*Carmen* rechristened itself for San Francisco last night. For the season, at least, it is Don Jose. Caruso is the magician."

And the reviewer for the *Examiner,* Ashton Stevens, even risked his job by rejecting his editor's demand that his rave review be toned down for publisher William Randolph Hearst who, bearing a grudge against the Metropolitan Opera, had no wish to glorify its presentation.

"Stevens," editor Charles Michelson warned, "no notice is as good as a job. And a job—well, isn't a good job at good pay more important than—?"

Stevens jumped up and roared: "Damn it! I've got three weeks of this Metropolitan season . . . I hope the goddamned opera house burns down!"

His review, he insisted, must be printed. And he brusquely turned in his copy, not suspecting the significance of his curse—or the fate of his review.

CHAPTER 2

Barrymore Slept Here

T ABOUT THIS TIME, a messenger brought Stevens a note from a visiting friend, John Barrymore, a twenty-eight-year-old actor who was hoping to replicate the success of older members of his famous thespian family with his appearance here in a play, *The Dictator*. The play had closed, and he was scheduled to leave with his theatrical company for Australia the following day. His note, written on the back of a menu, read:

"Dear Rock of Ages: Meet me at The Oyster Loaf instantly for an emergency conference. Bring pocketbook and a modicum of advice for the lovelorn."

Stevens walked to The Oyster Loaf, an all-night eatery jammed with theater people and journalists who shelled out $1.25 for dinner, including wine, and danced the bunny hug. Barrymore, dressed in white tails for a night at the opera, stood up and greeted Stevens at his table. The actor then sat down again, swallowed a fried oyster, and wasted no words.

"As you doubtless know, Ashton, I am sailing for Australia at high noon. . . . Do you happen to be in funds?"

Stevens knew Barrymore's reputation as a connoisseur of whiskey and women. In fact, the actor often boasted about his conquests, sometimes even about affairs that occurred only in his fantasies. Earlier that evening, he told Stevens, he had met a young woman at the opera, and he wanted to spend the night with her.

Why did he need the money? Stevens asked.

"For replacements," Barrymore replied, "in case I break some glassware."

Stevens claimed he had only a dollar on him, and Barrymore departed. Where did he sleep? This is controversial. He didn't stay at the St. Francis Hotel, where he was booked. He would later tell Stevens that he had stayed with the woman he met at the opera. But he would write in his biography that he slept at the home of a male friend who had invited him to look at his collection of old Chinese glass.

Wherever Barrymore slept, he hoped to oversleep. Why had he agreed to perform in Australia anyway? He dreaded the thought of spending weeks at sea. What if there were no women aboard? What if the whiskey ran out? . . . What if he couldn't be found before the ship departed? . . .

GEORGE HORTON, a young newlywed, was also going on a trip he wished he could avoid, though the journey would be short; he would be returning home the next day. Horton and his bride, Amelia, had little money and were forced to spend their honeymoon and start their life together in an inexpensive boardinghouse. But they were dreamers. They dreamed of buying a home of their own, and it soon seemed they might have one.

George had been offered a job in a prosperous business and had to leave on this evening of April 17 for San Jose to meet with a company official who lived there. He would stay the night at a friend's house. Though he would be gone only one day, this first separation was painful. The pain, however, was assuaged by the prospect that George would be returning with a figurative key to their dream house.

CHAPTER 3

Sullivan's Nightmare

FIRE CHIEF DENNIS SULLIVAN'S third-story apartment above a fire station on Bush Street, west of Kearny, was no "dream house," for the chief seldom slept long enough to dream. He climbed into bed shortly before 5 A.M., utterly exhausted after helping his men put out a raging blaze in North Beach. He had retired early in the evening but had been awakened at 1:30 A.M. when the alarm sounded, and he was soon rushing in his horse-drawn steamer to the scene of the fire.

Sullivan, fifty-six, was a physical giant whose toughness was reflected in his firm jaw and deep-set eyes that glowered under heavy brows. But after twenty-nine years in the fire department, the constant battle against fire and alarm-bell awakenings had taken a toll on his nerves, and he often seemed depressed. Yet he apparently went to bed now in a positive mood—with good reason.

For the thirteen years Sullivan had served as fire chief, he had been trying to persuade a reluctant municipal government that it must allocate him more funds to protect the city from being razed by fire. Though the city was bordered by water on three sides, it did not own even a single fireboat and had only 585 firemen. And if something happened to the water mains, he would have to rely on a relatively few 850,000 gallons of water—about

the quantity in an Olympic swimming pool—held in twenty-five old sub-
terranean cisterns that hadn't been used for more than fifteen years.

Sullivan had drawn up an intricate plan to reactivate the cisterns,
acquire fire-fighting equipment, build a supplementary saltwater system,
house high explosives, and train his men to use them in checking fires. He
had long foreseen what would happen if a fire raced out of control, especially after an earthquake, and threatened to ravage the city.

The water mains, he figured, would break, severing the regular water
supply. In that case, he would temporarily bypass the residential zones and
rush all engines and other fire-fighting equipment to the financial district
north of Market Street and the commercial district south of Market, and
pump salt water from the docks into these areas until they were saved.
South of Market, he would make a firebreak by dynamiting many of the
ancient fire-prone buildings to keep the flames from spreading east or
west. An intimate of Sullivan would explain: "It was his idea that the
money markets and wholesale business centers that formed the heart of
the city and were the fountainheads of its prosperity should be saved at all
costs even if great losses were thereby suffered in the residence quarters."

And the National Board of Fire Underwriters supported Sullivan's rec-
ommendations for enhancing the city's fire-fighting ability. In October
1905, it had warned in a report:

> In view of the exceptionally large areas, great heights, numerous
> unprotected openings, general absence of firebreaks or stops,
> highly combustible nature of the buildings, many of which have
> sheathed walls and ceilings, frequency of light wells and the pres-
> ence of interspersed frame buildings, the potential hazard is very
> severe.
>
> The above features combined with the almost total lack of
> sprinklers and absence of modern protective devices generally,
> numerous and mutually aggravating conflagration breeders, high
> winds, and comparatively narrow streets make the probability fea-
> ture alarmingly severe.
>
> In fact, San Francisco has violated all underwriting traditions
> and precedents by not burning up. That it has not already done so is

largely due to the vigilance of the fire department, which cannot be relied upon indefinitely to stave off the inevitable.

The report pointed out, for example, that engineers had found that the city's distributing pipe system "is inadequate to meet the demands for water flow necessary to fight a conflagration."

But Sullivan's pleadings were like whispers in the wind, even when the War Department in Washington offered to furnish a corps of engineers and sappers equipped with explosives that would be stored in the Presidio, the city's main army garrison. The War Department wanted only $1,000 to finance the building of a brick vault to house the explosives. But Mayor Eugene Schmitz was adamant: San Francisco would not "splurge" on what he considered an unnecessary expense. More needy, he felt, were the water and light companies, the United Railways, the Southern Pacific Railroad, and other cooperative firms—firms that realized licenses, contracts, and other "favors" came with a price. City leaders, they understood, had to make a living.

Finally, however, popular pressure forced the mayor to form a citizens' committee to assess Sullivan's needs for his fifty-five fire stations, which included thirty-eight engine companies, ten truck companies, and seven chemical engine companies. And Sullivan himself was to testify before the committee later on this morning of April 18, in just a few hours. No, he wouldn't miss the sleep, however weary he was.

At last, he hoped, money would be channeled to his department and he could make sure that San Francisco would not again be demolished by fire—a phenomenon that had occurred so often that during the gold rush years a phoenix rising from the flames was engraved on the seal of the city and county.

SAN FRANCISCO WAS, in a sense, born in the flames. In 1847, only a few days after the *alcalde,* or mayor, renamed the village of Yerba Buena after St. Francis, a brushfire threatened its fifty-three shanties and twenty-six adobe huts, which housed a population of some five hundred. Villagers hauling pails of water finally extinguished the fire and sparked the spirit of future firefighters, who would gradually build one of the nation's most skilled and dedicated fire departments.

The first great fire swept the city two years later, in 1849, shortly after gold was unearthed at Sutter's Mill in the Sierras, when the population suddenly leaped to six thousand. The new citizens were mainly scruffy-bearded men wearing soft slouch hats, trousers tucked into heavy rawhide boots, belts tightened around pistols or bowie knives, and dirty shovels angled, riflelike, over their shoulders. Men who had suddenly become rich—rich enough to buy from the auctioneers who hawked their wares for gold dust at a hugely inflated $16 an ounce, rich enough to shell out a dollar's worth of dust for a single egg.

The flames, whipped up the steep hills by brisk winds, quickly consumed the flimsy wooden shanties with their cramped dark rooms and shelf beds, not to mention the tents, some partly covered with blankets and the boughs of trees. These impromptu homes—built in a virtual swampland where pavements were constructed out of packing boxes, sacks of flour, and pieces of furniture—had been hastily set up by men too blinded by the gleam of gold to worry about comfort, cleanliness, or even security. Who would agree to keep watch during the day when there was such treasure to be found in the mountains?

This first fire was apparently set by gangs of bandits, mainly the Sydney Ducks, a group of former Australian convicts who swaggered into shops and saloons and demanded protection money from the owners. Why bother digging for gold when they could rob the diggers?

Before the fire, their intimidation often spoiled the fun of the young, rugged diggers who, in the bright, mirror-reflected light of the gambling houses and saloons, tensely gathered around tables heaped with gold bars, gold nuggets, and bags of gold dust, or in drunken abandon danced with one another to the tinny strains of a dilapidated piano; few women chose to endure the rough, raw, virtually lawless life here. It was a place where the victim could be as merciless as the bandit, where a killer like Joaquin Murieta was not only shot by vengeful miners but decapitated, his head displayed in a saloon for anyone with a dollar to spare. With shootouts and other violence increasingly common, however, few barflies would dare enter a saloon, even to see a severed head.

Of the few females willing to live in such an anarchistic, even savage society, prostitutes imported largely from Mexico, Chile, and France—many of whom worked the mines in men's clothing—outnumbered "respectable" women by an estimated twenty-five to one. Wives were as rare as aristocrats.

After the fire of 1849, San Francisco was rebuilt only to fall victim to three other criminally fueled blazes in 1850, and two more in 1851. Following each conflagation, the town rose anew from the ruins, with every spurt of reconstruction resulting in sturdier buildings. In the commercial areas, brick and stone structures thus replaced the more fire-prone wood frame ones, which would continue, however, to distinguish the architecture of almost all homes and other less exalted buildings. With people too busy searching for gold to look for the necessary bricks and stone, these items were imported from England, China, and Australia, each numbered so the building could be assembled almost as easily as an erector set.

The irony was that while bricks and stones were more likely to resist fire than wood, they were also more vulnerable to the city's frequent earthquakes. To save money, greedy builders constructed walls with nonreinforced brick held together, not by cement, but by less cohesive sand-lime mortar, permitting a quake to easily shake an edifice into piles of rubble. Municipal leaders, bribed handsomely by these builders, would pass few regulatory laws—until 1947!

Whatever the dangers, most San Franciscans ignored earthquake concerns, especially before 1906. Why worry about something that only God could control? As for fires, people could control them—especially the people of San Francisco with their phoenixlike tradition.

After each fire the city was rebuilt for a greater number of people. With gold-hungry miners pouring in, the population after the 1851 fire quintupled to thirty thousand within a period of four months. At the same time, after some three thousand buildings turned to ash that year, citizens struck back at the arsonists. They set up heavily armed vigilante committees that defied the "lax" authorities and took the law in their own hands, setting an odious precedent—massive public corruption, fraud, and kangaroo court justice. Meanwhile, the bodies of overt bandits piled up in the morgue.

In the following years, as new leaders took over, the public rode a seesaw of political reform and more corruption. Eventually, the violent crime rate plummeted as anarchy gave way to reasonably organized government. Thus, the men went back to the saloons, this time to dance with women, who were gradually joining them to share their life—and their glittery wealth. Though no major fires followed the purge of the bandits, San Franciscans, more than ever, came to accept fire as an inevitable nuisance, a fact of life, even an exciting challenge.

This challenge soon sparked the birth of the city's first fire companies, formed by wealthy, community-minded volunteers equipped with personal fire-fighting gear. Proud and vain, they vied with one another in parades for the honor of wearing the smartest uniforms, while fans cheered for their favorites, as if at a ball game. They also competed at glee club concerts, dances, and boxing matches held to raise money for their operations. In the 1860s, companies even accused one another of setting fires so they could be the first to extinguish them. At one fire, the Monumental Six and Social Three companies fought the Knickerbocker Five with fire tools, knives, cobblestones, and even firearms.

With public adulation of the volunteer firemen suddenly turning to disgust, the municipal government created a new, salaried San Francisco Fire Department in 1866. The official companies were also fiercely competitive, but their competition would energize the most exhausted firefighter and thus save many lives and much property.

In 1863, three years before the official fire department was established, firemen who had pulled hand engines to fires turned to a horse-drawn smoking steamer, creating a sensation as the horses pranced down Market Street. Horses used for fire fighting in San Francisco? How could they pull a fire engine up those hills? But the specially trained horses, picked for their size and strength, clip-clopped up even the steepest grades to permit firemen to snuff out fires before they spread.

His fire department, Chief Sullivan felt, had indeed developed into one of the nation's finest. And yet, the municipal government was depriving it of the tools it needed. Surely the citizens' committee would now listen to him. And he knew he had the unbounded confidence of his officers and men, who felt that no other man had the technical knowledge and administrative authority to save the city from possible disaster.

So dedicated was Sullivan that he often worried that he might die or be dismissed before achieving his goal. His assistant, walrus-mustachioed John Dougherty, was a fine gentleman, but he was old and lethargic and had neither the ability nor the temperament to spar with the bureaucrats for a refurbished fire-fighting system, or, certainly, to deal with a major conflagration if it should happen.

Without Dennis Sullivan, what would happen to San Francisco? Yes, he could sleep well, at least for a few hours. For he was on the verge of victory.

CHAPTER 4

The Nectar of Corruption

MAYOR EUGENE SCHMITZ, it seems, had a less peaceful night. He was not looking forward to the next day—a day that could determine whether he would soon be wearing prison stripes.

Five years before, Schmitz, a tall, imposing figure with a neat black beard and a warm, easygoing manner, had been a concert violinist and an orchestra conductor. One night in 1901 a shrewd, ambitious politician, Abraham Ruef, came to watch him wield his baton at the Columbia Theater and afterward went backstage to offer him another, if less genteel, conducting job.

With labor in increasingly violent conflict with employers, Ruef was forming a new Union Labor Party. And he hoped to persuade Schmitz, a popular figure in San Francisco, to join the party and run for mayor in the coming election. With the right puppet leader, Ruef was convinced, his united labor front could score a victory over the employers, investors, and agriculturists who supported the Republican and Democratic Parties in a struggle that would reflect the sharply polarized class conflict in San Francisco. The labor movement here was the most powerful in the nation, after all, and was holding its own in the rancorous transportation strike that was paralyzing the city.

Now Ruef needed Schmitz to tip the scales in favor of what would be the first union labor movement to enter politics as a separate party. Actually, Ruef felt no real affinity for labor; in fact, he was himself a landlord and investor whose derby and elegant waistcoat hardly suggested a man who soiled his hands. But since he had failed to grab control of the Republican Party, he saw labor as a stepping-stone to power.

The two men knew each other well. Ruef was Schmitz's personal attorney, as well as the attorney for the musicians' union, which the conductor led as its president. In fact, the two men, both thirty-seven, had known each other for fifteen years.

Ruef would later say that Schmitz was "a man of natural ability, of good intelligence and keen pretensions. He possessed a tenacious memory and an unsurpassable nerve. He could put up a better front than almost any man I knew. . . . I had often seen him assume a pretense which successfully covered up all deficiencies. . . . He was imperturbable. His face could completely mask his feelings."

Schmitz might be just the man to be Ruef's mayor. The conductor's German-Irish heritage would appeal to the two most powerful ethnic voter blocs in San Francisco. His father had come from Germany in 1849 to join in the gold rush, built the first brick house in San Francisco, and himself became an orchestra leader; his mother arrived from Ireland as an infant. As a Catholic and a native son, Schmitz would win over many other voters as well. True, he had no higher education and did not even finish high school, but his musical talent had already made him a cultural icon here. He was also seen as a model husband and father to his three children. Yes, just the man.

But when Ruef approached him, Schmitz laughed at the idea, replying, "I have no experience. I don't know anything about municipal affairs. I couldn't go through a campaign. I never made a public address. Besides, I haven't the means to make the fight. The whole thing is preposterous."

"You have as much experience and information as many men who have been nominated," Ruef countered, "and more than some who have filled the office. What you lack can easily be supplied. The speeches and the funds we can take care of. . . . Although you were on the Labor ticket, you could appeal to the conservative element who are tired of all the industrial warfare.

"Then, you are a man of fine appearance. . . . The psychology of the mass of voters is like that of a crowd of small boys or primitive men. Other things being equal, of two candidates they will almost invariably follow the strong, finely built man. . . . If you are nominated, people will turn naturally as you pass by and say, 'There goes the Labor candidate for mayor.' At the theater you will have a thousand people talking about you every night and advertising you who scarcely give you a glance now. Think it over."

Ruef, a man of striking appearance himself, with dark, curly hair and a handlebar mustache beneath his large, drooping nose, was born in San Francisco to well-to-do French immigrant parents. He graduated from the University of California at the age of eighteen, able to speak several languages fluently and to display a vast knowledge of art, music, and philosophy.

In his youth, Ruef was actually a reformer. His fellow students admired not only his penchant for melding wit with intellect, but also his idealistic, passionate plea for political reform: the corruption inherent in machine politics, he felt, had to be rooted out. But for all his zeal, he realized this task would not be easy, since the roots were deep. The gold rush of 1849, the rapid industrialization of cities after the Civil War, and the rise of powerful labor unions and corporations fed the political immorality of the day.

As conflict escalated among these economic forces and between each of them and the government, a shadowy figure emerged to broker their differences—exacting a steep price for a favorable ruling. The political boss, fat from bribes and booty, often became a supreme arbiter in shaping the city's political and economic life.

But Ruef was ready for the challenge. He would fight relentlessly to dismantle the machine.

After he had graduated from law school and passed the bar, remarkably at the age of twenty-one, the young zealot joined the Republican Party and helped to form within it a reform group that crusaded for better law and government. But the harder he tried, the more frustrated he became. As he trudged up the party ladder, he gradually came to feel that fighting corruption had little more effect than shadowboxing.

"The people were apathetic," he would lament, "and so I drifted with the machine. Whatever ideals I once had were relegated to the background."

Thus, the disillusioned lawyer, failing to fix the mendacious power structure, became part of it, diverting his political passion into more lucrative channels. Now he needed a front man to cover his tainted tracks. Schmitz agreed to think about it.

Schmitz would later say: "From boyhood, I had ever heard: Make money, no matter how. People will never ask how you made it, only get it. I had no money, no influence, no prestige. He [Ruef] had all these, and they were at my service."

Schmitz was earning forty dollars a week as a musician, much less than many politicians made. And the mayor, wielding the greatest municipal power, had the opportunity to earn the most, for did not power breed wealth—at least in San Francisco? Besides, a fortune-teller had read his future and prophesied that within a year he "would hold a high and mighty position in his native city."

Schmitz, as he had promised, thought it over—briefly.

"I'm not superstitious," he told Ruef, "but there's no use bucking a hunch like that, especially . . . when the case looks so good anyhow."

So Schmitz put down his baton, joined Ruef's party, and plunged into a hectic mayoral campaign. Ruef would observe:

Ordinarily, Schmitz lacked application. He was not fond of work, and always preferred to amuse himself. But he had a power of assimilating ideas and a gift of memory, and he developed a marvelous faculty of joining thoughts and sentences from many speeches, prepared for him, into new ones of his own. . . . He dressed well, but not extravagantly. He moved rapidly and everywhere. . . . He developed a remarkable self-confidence. If he sang a song, he did so with the impression that there was an entire operatic repertoire behind it. If he delivered one speech, it was as if he could deliver any kind at any time. Social attention was as nectar to him even in his first campaign.

And never was the nectar sweeter than when the returns came in. The winner? Schmitz by a large majority—in part because his friend William Randolph Hearst, then a Democratic member of Congress, vigorously backed him in his *San Francisco Examiner* in repayment for Schmitz's support of the publisher's earlier congressional candidacy. The musicians' union led parades in the new mayor's honor, and orchestras in the theaters joined them after their performances. Ruef and his puppet then stole away to a little hotel in Sonoma where the puppeteer instructed his ward in the art of making politics pay—big.

"We were the only strangers in the little village," Ruef would say. "There, in undisturbed peace, we talked and planned day and night. There in the tranquil Sonoma hills I saw visions of political power. I saw the Union Labor Party as a spark in California that would kindle the entire nation and make a labor president; I saw the Union Labor Party a throne for Schmitz, as mayor, as governor—as president of the United States. Behind that throne, I saw myself its power, local, state—national. . . . I saw myself United States Senator."

A *rich* senator, for the money soon started to pour into the bank accounts of the mayor and his Svengali, with Ruef's share siphoned into valuable real estate. Since any company wishing government help was routed to Ruef's law office, no contract was authorized without a kickback, no franchise approved without a personal fee. Illegal houses of prostitution sprang up, with the two men splitting a percentage of the take. In fact, Schmitz's brother-in-law was a partner in one whorehouse enterprise and, reports indicated, paid Ruef $250 a month in "protection" money, apparently to be shared with the mayor.

A plush-lined "boodle box" for Schmitz's bribe money was said to have been built into the bedroom floor of Schmitz's house, an imposing structure with gingerbread scrollwork. Schmitz admitted there was such a cavity in his floor, but he insisted it was only a repository for his violin.

The two city kingpins also pocketed a cut from the earnings of the telephone and telegraph companies and the city's public transportation system. And they tapped into public works, liquor licenses, French restaurant franchises, gambling, public buildings, road-paving contracts, construction permits, and even "municipal cigars" that private firms were forced to sell so kickbacks could be paid.

Nor was police corruption frowned upon, since some of the proceeds were funneled to the top. One seedy area downtown was nicknamed the

Tenderloin district—a name it still bears today—because policemen collected enough graft from whorehouses and gambling establishments in the area to dine in San Francisco's finest steak restaurants.

On the other hand, little public money was spent on vital needs if there was no opportunity for graft—accounting for Fire Chief Sullivan's frustration.

In 1903 and again in 1905, Schmitz's charisma and support of labor's causes paid off with new electoral victories. In the 1905 campaign, Ruef extolled the Schmitz administration as "the cleanest and most moral of any in the United States . . . as clear as the light of day, as pure as a mountain lake." And in ridiculing accusers, he would cynically begin a speech with "Ladies and Grafters. . . ."

"Three cheers for the North Beach hoodlum!" someone yelled, and Ruef responded to thunderous applause with a deep bow.

Everybody knew that Schmitz was lining his pockets with ill-gotten money, but strangely most people didn't care. He may have been the most corrupt mayor of all, but corruption was endemic in San Francisco politics. So why worry about it? What counted was that their mayor was charming, handsome, and exuded the dignity of a leader.

San Franciscans, with their innate affection for the unconventional, the outrageous, even the disreputable (if the person indulged in his indiscretion with a smile and a sense of humor), often skirted reality in a delusional acceptance of fantasy. In this case, the fantasy that Schmitz was a kind of latter-day Robin Hood—a man who helped the poor with the money he stole, or at least cared about them.

The people had made other flights into fantasy as a means of seasoning their lives. Joshua A. Norton, an eccentric Englishman, arrived in San Francisco in 1850 during the gold rush, made a fortune, and then lost it. As a result, he apparently lost his mind as well. For in 1855 he proclaimed himself Norton I, emperor of North America and protector of Mexico. Never seen without his blue, brass-buttoned, gold-braided uniform and plumed beaver hat, Norton I was just mad enough to please many San Franciscans, who considered *themselves* a bit idiosyncratic, if not quite as crazy as the emperor.

Norton traveled around the city, returning salutes everywhere while making sure that policemen were on their beats, that buildings were constructed properly, and that people were obeying local laws. The news media published his imperial proclamations, including an "incredible" demand that a bridge be built across the Golden Gate—a proclamation that was obeyed about seventy-five years later. When he needed money, he issued fifty-cent bonds, which were honored by banks and commercial enterprises. Whenever he arrived at the opera and other events, people stood up and applauded him. And ten thousand of them wept as they passed his royal rosewood casket when he died in 1880, while flags flew at half mast all over the city.

Like Norton I, Schmitz, a mesmerizing musician in mayor's clothing, added a touch of spice to the joy of living in San Francisco, whatever nasty habits went with the job.

Even headlines in the *San Francisco Bulletin* couldn't stop Schmitz and Ruef, though the paper exposed their corruption almost daily. Devastated when Schmitz was reelected in 1905, Fremont Older, the tall, lean, mustachioed managing editor of the paper, was obsessed with toppling him despite the electoral results, demanding that the two men be tried for extortion and bribery and thrown into jail. And to trigger an official investigation, he went to Washington, determined to persuade President Theodore Roosevelt to lend him two of his best federal special prosecutors. And the president, impressed by Older's proud humility, unpretentious manner, and crusading passion, agreed.

But Older now had to raise $100,000 to finance a full-scale investigation. Former Mayor James Phelan, a zealous reformer, strongly supported the investigation but could not afford to contribute that kind of money. But another reformer could—Rudolph Spreckels, a member of the house of Spreckels, sugar barons whose history was intricately interwoven with the economy of San Francisco.

A handsome man with a well-trimmed mustache, Rudolph first met Ruef when the lawyer came to him and requested his help in selling a city bond issue.

How could Ruef, Spreckels asked, guarantee that his bid would be successful when the sale of the bonds was open to competitive bidding?

Don't worry, Ruef replied, he would arrange for a paralyzing streetcar strike before bonds were put on the market to make sure that public confidence in the city government would be low at the time.

Could this proposal be serious? Spreckels asked in dismay.

Ruef suddenly flushed. He should have realized that his host was too straitlaced to agree to such a deal. He was only joking, he stammered. And he stood up, put on his derby, and hastily left.

This incident only confirmed in Spreckels's mind that the Schmitz-Ruef team had to go. Earlier, Schmitz had erred by refusing to see Spreckels to discuss a franchise to take over the city's streetcar system because the sugar baron was known to deplore kickbacks.

So when Fremont Older visited Spreckels, he was greeted with exceptional warmth.

"Older," Spreckels said, standing up and walking over to him, "I'll go into this! I'll put my money in this and back it to the limit."

And he did so, a decision that earned him bitter attacks by many leading businessmen who felt he was betraying his class by trying to deprive them of the profits that flowed from payoffs to Ruef and his puppet mayor. His social conscience would ruin them.

But Older was elated. With $100,000 and a couple of top prosecutors available, the glory days of Schmitz and Ruef were surely coming to an end. He was especially gratified when a hearing was scheduled for April 18, 1906, only a few weeks later. Nothing must delay the ignominious removal of the two men to a penitentiary.

Facing this fate, Schmitz could only wish he were still the respected orchestra conductor he had been before Ruef lured him into crime. Only a miracle, it seemed, could save him now.

CHAPTER 5

The Banker and the Boy

AMADEO PETER GIANNINI was one businessman who would never deal illicitly with the corrupt municipal government. He didn't need to, for he was prospering on his own. Miraculously, it seemed to many of his competitors. Giannini was the founder and first vice president of the fledgling Bank of Italy, the only one of more than forty banks in San Francisco that catered mainly to persons with lower incomes who needed money to launch small enterprises and were turned away by larger banks.

Bald, powerfully built, with heavy brows that bristled over gleaming hazel eyes, Giannini blended pragmatism with an idealism rooted in sympathy for these people, who were forced to borrow money from loan sharks at exorbitant interest rates. So he had stopped hawking farm products and opened up a bank. He knocked on doors, mainly in the Italian district of North Beach, selling not fruit now but an idea: Money under the mattress—a bit lumpy anyway, since only gold and silver coins were in circulation in California at the time—would not yield profits, but it would in his bank.

Only two years after the bank opened on the ground floor of a wooden building at Columbus and Washington Avenues, deposits surged to about $850,000, while loans amounted to more than a million. So prosperous had the bank become that in July 1905 it was able to disburse to stockholders more than $5,000, a hefty sum at that time. The directors voted Giannini himself a salary of $200 a month, starting in February 1906— almost covering his out-of-pocket expenses. The bank's capital was to be increased by $200,000. And on April 21, two thousand paid-up shares would be distributed.

Understandably, when Giannini went to bed in his San Mateo home on the night of April 17, he had few worries on his mind. Even so, he thought his bank could do better. There were still people who thought their money would be safer under the mattress.

AURELIO DELBERT (DEL) CRESPI, whose Italian family rented a house owned by Amadeo Peter Giannini's brother-in-law in North Beach, wished he had the money to put under his mattress. Though only ten, he was in love. His girlfriend, Lillian, was spending Easter vacation in the country with her parents, and he couldn't wait for school to start again. He decided he had to look his best for the occasion—if only he had $2.25 to buy that beautiful suit in the window of Rotten Jimmie's!

Never had Del suffered through so miserable a vacation. For one thing, his friends had all turned against him, calling him "teacher's pet" because he had skipped a grade, from the fourth to the fifth. Members of the gang he had once joined had even declared "war" on him, ostracizing him and threatening to beat him up. There was no one now to play marbles or mumblety-peg with on the wooden board floor of his backyard. And they wouldn't even let him play baseball anymore, though he was the best pitcher in his school. What could he do except sit at home reading *Dick Merrywell*? He was so tense that, like a soldier poised for battle, he sometimes hoped they would attack. Better to let fate determine the outcome than to cringe at every shadow. Especially since, he was sure, he wouldn't be the only one to get a bloody nose.

But even more disturbing to Del was his frustrated "love affair" with Lillian. She had stood by him against his tormentors and even told him to hide at home the "honorary card" announcing his promotion so his jealous foes couldn't get their hands on it. Del could not forget the last time he saw her. As he approached her house a few blocks away, she was standing at the front door. They smiled, sadly. It would be a lonely vacation. Suddenly, the door slammed shut. The girl's mother, it seemed, did not approve of their close relationship; her daughter should play with girls, not boys. And then Lillian was gone.

Del slumped away. In his depression, he returned home even before the streetlamp lighter came by at dusk and with a taper lit the light in front of his house—the usual curfew signal for every child in the neighborhood. He could not eat and had nightmares when he slept.

"The ominous sound of that door closing kept coming back to me and bothering me," he would say.

To relieve his tension—and prepare for "war" with his former gang—the boy pounded a punching bag and lifted dumbbells. He got a job delivering newspapers, hoping to earn enough money for the suit at Rotten Jimmie's. Thoughts of Lillian consumed him. Especially on the night of April 17. He would say later:

> I remember that the dogs went around whining and crying. I told my mother I wasn't well and went to bed without dinner. . . . When I lay down in bed I started to sweat. I had a terrible fear growing in me about something. I didn't know what. All I could hear was that peculiar slam of Lillian's door. My mother came into the room and caught me crying. She tried to talk to me and asked me if there was anything wrong, but I was ashamed to tell her, other than to say I didn't feel well.
>
> She put a cold compress on my head. All night I kept hearing that terrible door, and the fright kept growing. I tried to cheer myself up by remembering that school was going to open up in just five days and that I was to get paid Friday for delivering the papers. . . . Soon as I got my pay I was going to dash up to Rotten Jimmie's and buy one of those good suits. I was sure going to put the swell on for Lillian.

Shortly after 5 A.M., Del, having struggled through a sleepless night, heard the slam of the door echo once more in his reeling mind. But now it grew louder and louder. . . .

CHAPTER 6

Cook's Tour of a Cataclysm

POLICE SERGEANT JESSE COOK had been making the rounds all night in the harbor area north of Market Street and reported by phone to his superiors for the last time at about 5 A.M. on April 18. He then lumbered up hilly Washington Street toward headquarters as the dimming streetlights faded into the hazy blue of the dawn. Here in the produce district, which started bustling before most of the city awakened, he waved to people he knew from his daily rounds and breathed in the earthy scent of the onions, turnips, tomatoes, potatoes, and other fresh vegetables being loaded on horse-pulled carts.

The city was coming to life, and the cheerful chatter and haggling in many tongues seemed to reflect the prospect of a sunny day, with phonographs already blasting music from the brick buildings lining the streets. As Cook walked along, waving to a milkman here, a fruit peddler there, he met a fellow officer, H. C. Schmitt, whose beat was also the produce district. It would be a nice, quiet day, they agreed. Hopefully, there wouldn't be much action and they could enjoy the sunshine. The two men then went their separate ways.

A few minutes later, as Cook strode down Washington Street, he stopped to chat with a young man on horseback whom he knew from a produce house and noticed that his friend's horse was acting nervously.

"What's the matter with your horse?" Cook asked.

"I don't know," the man replied. "I never saw him act like this before."

Moments later, Cook heard a thunderlike rumble in the distance, almost loud enough to drown out a strangely growing chorus of barking dogs in the neighborhood. Suddenly, he realized why the horse was so nervous. Animals, unlike humans, could somehow feel the small, almost imperceptible waves ripping through the earth at lightning speed and recognize them as a vanguard to disaster. The rumble that followed was a familiar one—an earthquake. As one journalist would explain about San Franciscans: "They have become as used to these shakes as men in a besieged town to shell fire. They will tell you that the average earthquake is not half as terrifying to them as a thunderstorm in the East."

But would this be an average earthquake?

SAN FRANCISCO SPRAWLS between two faults, the Hayward and the more threatening San Andreas, the world's longest fault line. A ten-mile-deep gash in the bedrock of California, the San Andreas wends its way for more than six hundred miles from the Mexican border to the north of this city, passing eight miles from the center of San Francisco. It moves about an eighth of an inch each year.

An earthquake occurs along these faults when rock strata, or plates, lying on a layer of hot, soft rock, move as the coast range of mountains rises gradually, causing rock surfaces to violently abrade against each other. The softer the rock in a particular area, the milder the earthquake; the harder the rock, the more powerful the tremors as friction causes portions of the rock to crack up. Thus, with varied explosive power, the stress accumulated miles under the surface crust is released in a burst of repetitive energy, which travels through the earth as seismic waves.

While strong earthquakes had struck in 1836, 1865, and 1868, followed by many minor ones, great quakes occurred rarely. The last one to rock San Francisco before 1906 occurred in 1838, though only sixty or seventy people lived there in those pre–gold rush days. A writer who visited San Francisco Bay at the time would describe what was then a village:

"Beyond were dreary sandhills, with little grass . . . , and few trees, and beyond them higher hills, steep and barren, their sides gullied by the rains. [There] was a ruinous Presidio, and some three or four miles to the left was the Mission of Dolores, as ruinous as the Presidio, almost deserted. There were no other human habitations, except that an enterprising Yankee had put up a shanty of rough boards. . . . The entire region of the great bay was a solitude."

Thus, when an earthquake ravaged the earth then, there were few people to kill, few walls to collapse. The ground cracked open from San Francisco to San Jose, but the greatest damage was done to the giant redwood trees, many of which were hurled through the air.

Now, almost seventy years and more than two hundred relatively minor tremors later, the rock surfaces along the San Andreas fault that had been grinding against each other for so long gave way to irresistible stresses and slipped from nine to as much as thirty feet.

"There's an earthquake coming," Cook told his friend, "and it's going to be a good one."

OUT AT SEA, Captain Svenson could not understand why his steamer was lurching. The *John A. Campbell,* sailing off the California coast about 150 miles northwest of San Francisco, suddenly seemed to have hit something. But what? In dismay, he wrote in his log:

"Sudden motion, unexplained. The shock felt as if the vessel struck . . . and then appeared to drag over soft ground."

Soft ground—though his ship was floating in deep water? Svenson could not guess that his vessel had struck a seismic shock wave moving south.

Rending the ocean bed at a speed of two miles a second, the shock wave, like a rampaging super army, had earlier hit the deceptively peaceful, largely wooded California coast along the San Andreas fault at a spot two hundred miles north of San Francisco. It tore buildings off their foundations, splintered ancient redwood forests, and ripped the land open. When the ground closed again, millions of tons of displaced earth had transformed lowlands into hills, hills into prairies. The shock wave headed out to sea again, then struck shore once more slightly north of Point Arena, the epicenter of the earthquake, and continued plowing its way south toward San Francisco.

The vibrations of the seismic wave were felt along the Pacific Coast from Coos Bay, Oregon, to Los Angeles, and as far east as central Nevada. It toppled a train in Point Reyes and jackknifed a bridge over a suddenly narrowed stream at Paper Mill Creek. It redesigned a dairy farm at Olema—trees, gardens, and cowsheds were callously moved around. One unfortunate cow was crushed between the walls of a chasm near that town; the crack then closed, leaving only the animal's twitching tail to tell the tale. Virtually every brick building in Santa Rosa was decimated, sparking a fire that would burn down its whole business district. And the Stanford University campus was turned into a desert of ruins.

Perhaps the most tragic loss of life in this race to the ultimate catastrophe occurred at Agnew's state insane asylum near San Jose, where over a hundred inmates and attendants were buried in a mountain of debris. A police official would report:

"The moans of the dying were terrible. To add to the horror of the situation many lunatics had broken from the rubble and were trying to escape. They were wild and rushed to and fro, attacking everyone who came in their path. . . . There was no building nearby in which they could be confined, and as they were violent, it was necessary to restrain them in some way. A doctor suggested that they be tied to trees."

And they were, even as one of them cried: "I'm going to heaven in a chariot of fire!"

The earthquake would rupture three hundred miles of the San Andreas Fault. Finally, at 5:13 A.M., it struck San Francisco.

SERGEANT COOK gazed down Washington Street toward Russian Hill, the highest peak in San Francisco, where the cobblestones were suddenly undulating like ocean waves. The buildings on either side were precariously nodding and bowing to one another like ships caught in a storm. Wooden structures creaked and splintered as they twisted and fell, while those built with brick crumbled into piles of clay debris.

With thunder that might have been an overture to doomsday howling in his ears, Cook reeled like a drunk while people around him fell flat on their faces and could barely crawl on all fours. To people inside the buildings, as one would put it, it seemed as if a giant had lifted the structure to his shoulders, shaken it, and dumped it into eternity.

The sergeant was especially alarmed because the ground in this area, like in much of the eastern part of the city, was once marshland lying under bay water and was now "made ground." Over the years, the water-front in some places along the coast had moved about six blocks east of the original waterline, and in other areas creeks that had snaked through coastal land had completely disappeared. The fill for these tidal flats consisted not of hard rock but of garbage, pieces of wood, dirt, gravel, and other compressed material that might easily give way in an earthquake.

Cook dashed to the southwest corner of Washington and Davis Streets to escape cascades of debris falling from buildings in the area. But as he stumbled down the middle of Davis, the earthquake overtook him.

"Davis Street," he would say, "split right open in front of me. A gaping trench . . . about six feet deep and half full of water suddenly yawned between me and the east side of the street. . . . I took it at a running jump, and sprang up on the sidewalk at the southeast corner while the walls of the building I had marked for my asylum began tottering. Before I could get into the shelter of the doorway those walls had actually fallen inward. But the stacked-up cases of produce that filled the place prevented them from wholly collapsing."

Thirteen minutes after the first forty-second shock, another shock lasting twenty-five seconds rocked the area, fiercer and sharper than the first one. "The ground," Cook would later report, "seemed to twist . . . like a top while it jerked this way and that, and up and down and every way." He exclaimed to a man standing next to him in the doorway:

"My God, we're going into the bay!"

CHAPTER 7

The End of the World

JUST THREE HOURS EARLIER, James Hopper, a reporter for the *Call,* was strolling home after turning in a story about the opera crowd's reaction to Caruso's performance when he stared at the bay, not as a potential graveyard of the city, but as a vision of beauty, "with the red and green lights and the long silhouettes of ships at anchor, and still farther the familiar hearthlike glow of the mainland towns. The night struck me as particularly peaceful."

But as he passed a livery stable he suddenly heard a horse bellowing, and then the "thunder of a score of hoofs crashing . . . against the stalls." Like Sergeant Cook, he couldn't understand the reason for such nervous behavior, and the stableman could only say in bewilderment,

"Restless tonight! I don't know why."

Hopper finally arrived home, a room in a hotel on Post Street, and fell exhausted into bed, hoping for a good night's sleep. He wouldn't get it. Later he would say:

> The earthquake started without gradation, with a direct violence that left one breathless. "It's incredible," I said aloud. There was something personal about the attack; it seemed to have a certain vicious intent. My building . . . quivered with a vertical and rotary motion,

and there was a sound as of a snarl . . . My head on the pillow, I watched my stretched and stiffened body dance. It was springing up and down and from side to side like a pancake in the tossing griddle of an experienced French chef.

The bureau at the back of the room came toward me. It danced, approaching not directly, but in a zigzag course, with sudden bold advances and as sudden bashful retreats—with little bows, and becks, and nods, with little mincing steps; it was almost funny. The next second, a piece of plaster falling upon my head made me serious.

The quake gave one of its vicious jerks, and I had a sudden clear vision of the whole building dancing an infernal dance, the loosened bricks separating and clacking . . . like chattering teeth. And the quake continued, with a sort of stubborn violence, an immense concentration of its deadly purpose that left one without fear, without horror, without feeling. 'It's the end,' I thought, and a panorama of cataclysms swept through my mind: Pompeii, Lisbon, Krakatoa, Manila, St. Pierre, Samos, Vesuvius, with San Francisco as a stupendous climax.

But then his news sense subdued his terror. He was a reporter, wasn't he? What a story! He would record the end of the world, even if no one remained to read his account. He struggled out of bed, quickly dressed, and tottered down to the street, where he found "people half-clad, disheveled, but silent, absolutely silent, as if suddenly they had become speechless idiots. . . . And now, when the roar of crumbling buildings was over and only a brick was falling here and there like the trickle of a spent rain, this silence continued, and it was an awful thing. . . . All of them had a singular hurt expression—not one of physical pain, but rather one of injured sensibilities, as if some trusted friend had suddenly wronged them."

Hopper, strangely, felt elated, remaining calm as he absorbed the scene almost like an outsider, as a reporter should, though he could be living his last moments on earth.

"I threw my chest out and looked with amazement upon my dazed co-citizens," he would recall. "And yet, a few days later, when I saw a friend who had met me just at this time, he told me that I had been so excited I couldn't talk, that my arms shook, and that my eyes were an inch out of their sockets."

As Hopper stumbled ahead, he took notes for his story, describing the condition of every building he passed. Never could he have imagined such horrific scenes.

"Good Lord!" he finally burst out. "I'm not going to take a list of all the buildings in the city."

When Hopper saw a man at a window of one building about to climb down a rope of knotted sheets, he shouted to him to wait. The reporter then scrambled up hills of rubble to the third floor, but was immediately diverted to another room after glimpsing "a slim white hand and wrist [reaching] out of the debris" piled on a bed. He pushed aside the debris and found a woman still alive and carried her to a wagon outside. He then returned to the building and saved two other women; he found still another victim, but she was dead.

When Hopper learned that someone lay under the ruins outside, he beckoned two other men and they began digging with their bare hands. The three were soon joined by a fireman, but then another fireman came by and cried:

"Come on, Bill, there's fires."

As the two firemen left, one of Hopper's other companions exclaimed, "What's de use of digging out those that's dead?"

Hopper agreed and ambled on toward the *Call* building, taking notes as he went. He had forgotten about the man who was about to climb out of a window with a rope of sheets.

What a story! The end of the world—or at least the end of San Francisco.

ALMOST FLUNG OUT OF BED, George Emerson, who was to be married that day, also found himself trapped in a world crumbling into chaos as dishes, vases, and other fragile items crashed to the floor in a shower of glass and plaster.

With every jolt, the building seemed to leap higher. And as he hung to the side of the bed, Emerson felt utterly helpless. All he could do was wait, a toy of fate, as the room rotated, dipped, reversed its motion. The thunder he heard was the voice of God; the world was doomed. Couldn't God have waited a few more hours so his soul could first be joined with Josephine's?

Gradually, however, his panic gave way to logic. Perhaps this was just a nightmare and he would awaken to a day of joy after all! But as the room continued to rock in all directions for endless seconds, he realized this was no dream. The world was here to stay, at least for a while. This was an earthquake!

Once the shaking had stopped, Emerson hurriedly dressed and rushed to Josephine's home on nearby Bush Street to make sure she and her family were unharmed.

Finding them safe inside their partially shattered house, he agreed that the wedding would have to be postponed—but only until the next day. He then left to take the ferry to Oakland, where damage was also heavy, to visit his sister.

Don't worry, he told Josephine. He would be back later that day—in time to get ready for the wedding.

AS SERGEANT COOK stood in the doorway across the street from a teetering building, he saw its front wall begin to collapse. At that instant two men dashed out the door, and because a canvas awning stretched across the sidewalk they were unable to see the debris that was plummeting down. Cook screamed a futile warning, but within seconds they were buried under about twenty tons of bricks and mortar speckled with bits of tomato and other produce.

Though there was little chance that the victims could have survived, Cook started off to seek help and barely escaped the same fate. As a great aftershock at 8:14 A.M. rocked the city and another wall collapsed, he was struck in the back and legs, but managed to stagger on.

"The noise and the dust, and the feeling of destruction, all combined to daze a man," Cook would relate. "All about us houses were tumbling, and falling walls and chimneys, and cornices were crushing men and horses in the street. The district at that hour was crowded with produce wagons, and through the uproar of the earthquake you could hear the cries of people and the whinnying of the horses that were hurt or terrified."

Another witness would further describe the scene: "Humanity began to pour out of the buildings like ants. Men cried like children but such a wild howl it was. I had often heard women and children weep but never had I heard such sounds come from men. I saw women in their night robes, and men in pajamas and striped underwear all around me. Many knelt down and prayed while others laughed in an idiotic manner at the outlandish array of wearing apparel."

One woman who didn't laugh lived in a house that jumped four feet off its foundation and then bumped along the ground "like corn in a popper" before coming to a shaky rest.

Sergeant Cook heard the cries of two brothers who had recently opened a little restaurant on Washington Street. They had been trapped in the basement when their building collapsed. Many people desperately dug through the debris, but as one of the diggers would explain:

"We dug like mad for about half an hour, and then [a fire that had broken out nearby] was closing in about us, and the flames were burning us as we worked. We stuck at it as long as we could, but finally were driven off, and we had to leave the two poor men to perish like rats."

Nearby, another man trapped in the wreckage and badly wounded, screamed, "Shoot me! For God's sake, shoot me!"

A merciful policeman obliged, shooting him twice, but not accurately enough to still his frantic cries. A young man then grabbed the officer's pistol and, holding it to the man's head, blew his brains out.

At the same time, one of the whinnying horses, while pulling a dray, had stepped into the fissure running down the middle of the street just as the chasm closed. The trapped animal, however, was later freed when a pick was used to break the ground around its feet. Other horses were not as fortunate. One two-horse team, crushed by a falling wall, sat up dog-fashion unable to move. A policeman took out his pistol and put them out of their misery.

When the walls of one building toppled onto the street, Cook saw a bed that had landed on a pile of rubble. Whoever had been asleep must be dead, he was sure. But when the dust had cleared, Cook saw the covers on the bed move, and there lay a woman!

"What's the trouble?" she asked in bewilderment.

"Don't you realize that we've had an earthquake?" Cook asked, equally incredulous.

The woman stared at him as if aroused from madness.

Despite his injuries, Cook, who would later become police chief, staggered off across the wreckage in search of others he knew must be entombed, perhaps still in bed fast asleep—or dead.

MEANWHILE, Cook's fellow officer H. C. Schmitt, after his chance meeting with the sergeant, entered a produce warehouse on Washington Street to get a glass of water. While drinking, he heard a thunderous noise and, as crates of oranges stacked up high next to him began to fall, he barely dodged them and ran to the door but was waved back by people standing in a doorway in another warehouse across the street.

Just then, unlike the unlucky men Sergeant Cook had tried to warn, Schmitt heard the patter of bricks on the awning over the sidewalk and jumped back into the arch of the doorway just in time, his hands braced on his helmet to help protect his head from what he thought could be a mortal blow.

At that moment, Schmitt would say, "the front fell out from the three top floors, crushed through the awning as if it were paper, piled up on the street and sidewalk, and crashed in through the entrance where I was standing. The dust and debris covered my feet and rained a wall of ruin and rubbish in front of me that reached as high as my neck."

As Schmitt climbed over the ruins, his "hand clutched at one place what I fancied was the hair of a dog that had been carried down from one of the upper floors and crushed in the mess." He jumped to the pavement, and when he had thanked the men across the street for saving his life, they expressed concern about the owner of the warehouse he had just escaped from.

"Have you seen Mr. Puccinelli?" one of them asked.

No, Schmitt replied, admitting that he had been too self-absorbed to notice anybody.

Someone then said he thought he had seen Puccinelli running out the door.

Suddenly, Schmitt turned pale, and he ran back to the heap of debris in front of the door. The hair on the dog's back! It was, Schmitt would discover in horror, the hair on a man's head. Puccinelli had been crushed to death and buried in the debris.

Schmitt looked around him. A crescent of sunlight had begun to filter through the dust, and the sky was turning blue, just as he and Sergeant Cook had anticipated. A beautiful day ahead.

CERTAINLY NOT for Antonio Compania.

This veteran fisherman and some other employees were at work in a ramshackle building in the meat and fish market area north of Market, when suddenly the roof and walls started to crumble. In terror, Compania's companions fell to their knees and, while masonry rained down on them, pleaded with the saints to save them. And the saints responded; all but Compania escaped.

Panic-stricken, the fisherman dashed into an open refrigerator with foot-thick walls and without thinking slammed the door shut behind him, though it couldn't be opened from the inside.

At the same time, other markets in the area also collapsed in a tapestry of horror. A police officer would report:

> The spectacle was pitiable. The fronts of the low buildings on either side of the street between Montgomery and Sansome had fallen out and buried a number of men that were working in the various fish and meat markets at that busy hour. They had also buried and crushed numerous teams and wagons. Roofs and rear walls falling in had crushed others. . . . We helped all we could to dig and drag from the ruins the dead and the injured that were littered all about. Legs and arms were sticking out here and there to guide us.
>
> The crippled horses were pitiful to see. I must have shot a dozen or more. . . . One of [these] was buried up to his head, and it was all bloody; but he was alive and trying to wriggle his neck free when I put him out of his misery.

But there was nothing that could ease the misery of Antonio Compania, who was slowly freezing to death in the silent darkness.

CHAPTER 8

Birth and Death

EVEN BEFORE the earthquake, Rebecca Dulberg lay sweating in her misery, wondering if she would survive. She was pregnant, and shortly before midnight found herself in labor. Her seven-year-old daughter, Etta, had dashed off to find a midwife who lived nearby, and soon returned with her. Rebecca was in great pain, and adding to it was the thought that there would be one more mouth to feed.

She and her family—her husband, Bernard; Etta; and two younger children—lived in an already overcrowded shack south of Market Street, a poor, largely Irish and German workingman's district housing about one-sixth of the city's population. Ironically, Bernard had come from an extremely wealthy Rumanian Jewish family that owned a department store in Bucharest. One day when he was traveling through a little village, he gazed upon a beautiful young girl and soon married her. His family was appalled. A working-class daughter-in-law? They immediately disowned their son.

Penniless, Bernard eventually left for the United States, and his wife followed. But he could find only menial work and remained impoverished. Still, Bernard did not regret his decision to marry out of his class. But why such bad luck now? With Rebecca pregnant again, could the family's situation get much worse?

As dawn approached, the pain grew. The midwife encouraged her to "push"; the baby was coming. Then, suddenly, the house pitched back and forth and started to collapse; like many homes south of Market, this one had been built along a filled-in creek and thus was extremely vulnerable to major quakes. Crockery and lamps tumbled to the floor, and Rebecca was almost thrown out of bed—just as the baby was starting to emerge. At the same time, with gas escaping, the kitchen began belching flames.

After recovering from shock, the terrified midwife suddenly ran out the door of the tottering house, disappearing into the dawn even as Rebecca, with a child half-born, screamed for help.

GIMPY BILL was screaming, too. On Washington Street near Montgomery, a part of a building's brick wall had crashed through the ceiling of a neighboring house and trapped Bill, a legless cripple, in his room. Bill, known only by his nickname, scrambled from his bed and strapped himself to his rolling "car," a small platform fitted with castors. He tried to open the door, but it was blocked by debris. His screams were apparently unheard, with the saloon downstairs closed. The house trembled again and seemed about to cave in. A legless man, it appeared, could only say his last prayers.

But Gimpy Bill had no time for prayer. In desperation, he twisted his blankets into a rope and managed to lower himself from the window to the street, which was still rolling with almost the ferocity of a bucking bronco. Ignoring the storm of falling plaster, he pushed himself along on his "car," maneuvering through the rubble that blocked his way. Where would he go? He didn't know, but he followed the throngs of shocked, silent people heading west. Maybe they knew a safe place.

Though Bill could move hardly faster than a tortoise, none of the refugees passing by would heed his pleas for help. He begged one drayman carrying refugees in his wagon to take him along, but the man refused. How much money would a poor cripple have? But Bill refused to give up. He grabbed a rope dangling from the tailboard and held on while the horse virtually galloped over the rubble-covered cobbles dragging him along on his "car."

What if his tiny, unstable vehicle overturned? He would surely die. But somehow he couldn't let go. He had to prove that even a man without legs wasn't helpless. He would fight, whatever the odds, to survive.

* * *

ON MISSION STREET, south of Market, Patrolman Harry F. Walsh was sipping coffee in a rear machine shop of the Meese & Gottfried Company waiting for the watchman, a friend of his, when the floor began to shake and the windows to crackle and then burst into a geyser of glass. He dropped his coffee and ran for the front entrance as heavy machinery on the floors above thunderously crashed down through the ceiling all around him. But the big iron drop door was shut, and the key was in an office behind a distant wall of swirling dust. A worker helped him to lift a corner of the door, however, and then managed to slither out—only to run for his life, leaving Walsh trapped in the shuddering structure.

With no one to help him, the patrolman made his way through the dust even as machines continued to fall through the ceiling, and finally found the key and crawled into the street.

"Fremont Street was then rolling in waves," Walsh would later say. "First it opened and closed in big cracks. Then I noticed that the street was moving in waves like the sea, and was lifting under me like the sea."

As Walsh ran for the alarm box on the corner, the Meese & Gottfried Building "crumpled up and fell flat." He chilled at the thought that he had escaped so narrowly. He now found himself tramping through a wasteland of lumber, masonry, and twisted steel, tripping over trolley wires, slipping under electric lights and electric lines hanging in festoons. Some people were lifting up the fallen trolley lines so they could pass underneath them—not realizing how fortunate they were that the current had been cut off.

Walsh kept staring at the flattened building, certain he would never again see so incredible a sight. He was wrong. He suddenly saw scores of crazed steers charging down the street—and he was in their way!

SEVERAL BLOCKS NORTH of Market, Jessy Wilson was awake when the earth started shaking, and she listened in dismay to the rumble as it blended with the sound of the cupboard doors flapping in and out like huge wings. A bookcase with a hundred books fell on top of Jessy's cot, which stood at the foot of her mother's bed. Even the bulbs in the chandelier popped out, while pictures, lamps, and other loose objects lay shattered.

"Mama, mama," Jessy cried, "are you all right?"

Because her elderly mother was senile and couldn't take care of herself, Jessy felt she had to sleep in her mother's room. With the house on the verge of collapse, she jumped out of bed and dove for her slippers, which she needed to avoid cutting her feet on broken glass. She rushed to her mother's side to make sure she hadn't been struck by falling plaster. Jessy took her mother in her arms as she would a child and cried out, "Lord have mercy on us!"

She walked her mother to the front door and sat her on the outside steps, out of harm's way. But the old woman thought only of going back upstairs to put the books back in the bookcase. When told of the danger, she simply replied.

"Oh, nonsense, the earthquake happened three years ago."

Jessy could only stare at her with troubled compassion. She would die to protect her mother. And she felt it was perhaps best that this beloved woman was not aware of the danger. But what about herself? How could she face this crumbling world, especially burdened with so great a responsibility? She would later write:

"I longed for someone in their senses to be with. It was so dreadful to feel this terror and be alone with Mama, who was not in her senses."

And the terror had only begun.

PATROLMAN HARRY WALSH was stunned as he found himself facing scores of maddened bulls stampeding toward him on Mission Street. Some *vaqueros* had been driving them toward the stockyards at Potrero when the earthquake frightened the animals into frantic flight. It appeared they might trample him, but suddenly the front wall of a great brick warehouse toppled down and struck them with such force that many crashed through the pavement into the basement.

When Walsh saw two of the steers crippled on the street, crying and moaning, he took out his pistol and shot them. He then saw others running toward him, but he had only six bullets left. At that moment he saw a friend and saloon owner, John Moller, running past and cried that he needed ammunition.

But before Moller could answer, he saw the steers charging toward them, bellowing with pain and fright, and started to run toward his nearby saloon for shelter. As two of the beasts approached the pair, Walsh aimed his revolver and waited, knowing that such a weapon would be effective only at very close range. He couldn't afford to miss.

"As I shot down one of them," Walsh would relate, "I saw the other charging after John Moller, who was then at the door of his saloon and apparently quite safe. But as Moller turned, he became paralyzed with fear. He held out both hands as if beseeching the beast to go back. But it charged on and ripped him before I could get near enough to fire."

Moller was taken to a hospital, where he died. Walsh, borrowing a rifle from someone, helped to shoot fifty to sixty more steers terrorizing the fleeing refugees.

CHAPTER 9

The Miser and the Melting Pot

DEL CRESPI soon realized that the noise he had heard as he lay awake thinking of Lillian was not the tormenting slam of her door. But even as his house "shook from one end to the other," he wasn't sure *what* was happening. In a panic, he jumped out of bed and tried to run to the front door, though "the walls seemed to hedge me in," he would recall, "and the floor kept jumping up and hitting me in the chin."

Finally outside, Del sat on the curb "naked, stunned, and puzzled, while I looked about me in bewilderment and fright, and saw the streets rise up like cream puffs and the house across the street crumble and fall into the street."

Del learned it was an earthquake only when his mother and three elder brothers rushed out from the heavily damaged house and told him. Where was his sister? his mother cried. Del rushed back into the creaking house and found her still asleep. Then, hastily stepping into a pair of shorts, he ran back outside with his sister before the roof could fall in. Now all members of the family were together—except the father. He had gone to San Jose on business. Was he safe? How would he get home? As they feared, the trains had stopped running.

"Me, I got to worrying about Lillian," Del would recall. "That was the only time I was glad that she was in the country."

Later, Del helped put up a makeshift tent in an empty lot across the street from his shattered house on Jones Street, only one block from the bay. And he made forays into the wreckage to bring out blankets, other household items, and a wood-burning stove, which, installed on the curbstone, would serve as a kitchen. But it was a kitchen without food.

Del and his mother thus went off to Tony's store on the next corner, hoping it would be open. Miraculously, it was, and the boy's mother bought spaghetti and a few other items worth $14 and handed Tony a twenty-dollar bill.

"I got no change," Tony said. "Pay me some other time. And for the boy, I have something for him."

And he handed Del a gumdrop.

"I couldn't understand his sudden generosity," Del would say. "The gang used to call him 'Tony the Miser'; he used to cut off the specks on peaches and paint them so he could sell them. I remember once my mother gave me a dollar to buy a ten-cent can of milk, and I gave it to Tony the Miser. He said, 'Bambino, no can change; tell mommy I give a credit for it.' He had a sign on his wall about six feet long reading: ME NO TRUST. The only way I could account for his seeming change of heart was that he thought the world was coming to an end."

If it was, it would end in a way that would surely please God—at least as far as Del's neighbors were concerned. The Crespis would not be eating spaghetti alone, for the neighbors, of varying races and cultures, contributed their traditional foods to joint meals. Into one big pot went kosher salami from the Cohns, potatoes from the Murphys, sauerkraut from the Michaels, tortillas from the Garcias, and rice from the Satos. The earthquake bound together people who had seldom mingled with one another before.

And their bond, which embraced other neighbors as well, did not loosen after dinner—or after the disaster. If Mrs. Cohn was sick, Mrs. Murphy would nurse her while Mrs. Gonzales took care of the children. Mrs. Tenebaum gathered up clothes from the others and washed them at the beach. Everybody's children would go around and gather pieces of leather so Sato could fix everybody's shoes. Italians, Jews, Irishmen, Germans, Mexicans, and Japanese had become simply San Franciscans.

As the disaster escalated, so would their respect and affection for one another. After all, they might have to die together.

CHAPTER 10

The Accordion and the Cops

THE GUESTS in the four-story Valencia Hotel on Valencia Street between Eighteenth and Nineteenth Streets south of Market would never have time to know or help one another, as Police Lieutenant H. N. Powell could testify. He stopped there on his rounds at about 5 A.M. on the morning of the quake and found the night clerk "behind the desk resting but ready for business. It was the time that he had to put through the calls for roomers that had to catch trains or had to get to work early." In the hotel café, newspapermen were playing cards and sipping beer.

Suddenly, as Powell was leaving the hotel, "Valencia Street not only began to dance and rear and roll in waves like a rough sea in a squall, but it sank in places and then vomited up its car tracks and the tunnels that carried the cables. These lifted themselves out of the pavement, and bent and snapped."

Two stories of this second-class hotel sank underground, and the third story was pitched into the street, which, like an accordion, had swelled up in waves. While people living on the third floor climbed from their windows right onto the pavement, scores of people on the first two floors drowned in water flooding in from a broken water main in front of the hotel, many of them apparently after lingering in agony.

"In the first gasp of recovery from the shock," Powell would relate, "it did not occur to one that the tragedy was so complete. . . . The Valencia Hotel looked no worse than the street. Later—a second or so later—one realized that the crumpled four-story building was full of living people."

Of some 120 guests, few appear to have survived. Perhaps as a sign of the city's resiliencies, one of the survivors was an infant who lay smiling, fast asleep in her dead father's arms.

THE EARTHQUAKE did not distinguish between the shack and the château, except for some of the more modern steel-framed buildings that stood up well. The majestically domed City Hall, which took twenty years to complete and was the largest, most spectacular building in California, the pride of San Francisco, was not one of them. The massive pillars that supported the cornices and cupola of the structure cracked and then crashed thunderously, with huge stones and chunks of masonry cascading down and large chandeliers swinging crazily before falling and shattering into a thousand pieces. Part of the great bronze dome, 335 feet in height, roared down and buried homeless people sleeping on the steps, as well as several passersby, under tons of bricks and ground concrete. One gigantic cornice crashed into an apartment house across the street, crushing its whole front wall. In the sudden darkness, dust from the masonry and sooty smoke from fireplaces drifted through the remains of what had been the city's nerve center, its monumental pretense now exposed. A journalist would comment:

"One of the pediments with two Corinthian columns makes a ruin as picturesque in its isolation from the whole as the detached pillars of an ancient temple."

What made this great ornate, steel-girded structure collapse so quickly and completely? For one thing, the high steel towers vibrated too intensely; but more importantly the mortar that had been used to cement the walls and pillars was of inferior quality. Ironically, Mayor Schmitz's office had been destroyed in part because of the mortar purchased in the graft-tainted negotiations that had taken place since construction began in 1871. As with other graft-plagued structures, including the Hall of Justice, the earthquake shook off the masonry enveloping the steel framework like the wind shaking leaves off a tree.

*   *   *

THE ONLY PEOPLE in the City Hall at this early hour were the police guards and those in the Emergency Hospital posted in the basement, who were trapped under the wreckage. Officer Edward J. Plume, sitting at his desk in the City Hall police station, was suddenly thrown out of his chair and choking in a cloud of dust. He and his companion, Officer Jeremiah M. Dwyer, stumbled over chairs and desks to the door and ran across the street through a dark, smothering haze. In their near-blindness, they almost fell victim to a new disaster: The front walls of the Strathmore, an apartment building in the their path, began to fall, and they barely escaped being buried under a mountain of debris.

Amid the scream of half-naked people running in all directions, the two officers suddenly realized they had left three prisoners—one man and two women—locked up in the station. Had they been killed? In desperation, they rushed back to City Hall, both men limping painfully after tripping over fallen wires.

"When we got to the prison door," Plume would later report, "the man inside was shaking his cell door and howling to be let out. There was not a sound from the women. The cells appeared to be unharmed, as far as we could judge. We opened the women's cell and found them both lying on the floor senseless. The unfortunate girls had fainted from terror."

The officers released the man, then the women once they were revived and had recovered from their "hysteria." They were luckier than many of the prisoners held in the Hall of Justice. While some were marched in shackles to Fort Mason, the most dangerous were paraded to the waterfront and sent to the federal prison on Alcatraz Island. A few, however, managed to break away and lose themselves in the crowd of fleeing refugees.

The two liberated women, apparently prostitutes, had been arrested by a highly respected policeman, Officer Max Fenner, who had just been killed when a wall fell on him as he ran out of a café. One observer would report:

"He was buried under the pile of debris, and on top of the pile lay the body of a very lovely girl, stone dead. She had jumped out of a window five stories above, and was killed instantly."

Ironically, while fellow officers carried Fenner's body to the Emergency Hospital—which they did not yet know had been sealed in by debris—other officers were releasing the two women Fenner had arrested from the jail in that shattered building.

Meanwhile, a police officer who had been patrolling in the rubble-insulated hospital would report on the scene of terror:

> My idea was . . . that the whole City Hall had fallen on top of us and we were buried for good. . . . The lights had all gone out. It was black, dark, and smothering. Nobody could see his hand in front of his face, while the scattering bricks and plaster and mortar threw out a suffocating dust that filled wards and corridors and was choking me. . . . Every entrance to the hospital was . . . blocked clean to the top of each doorway, or higher.
>
> Even when the quaking and twisting ceased, the lumps of masonry still kept falling; and above all these noises of crashing and breaking, and the bellowing and thundering of the quake itself and the thuds of the pillars and cornices as they hit the ground, there were the shrieks and yells of the lunatics, and the moans and cries of the other patients. Everybody seemed to be yelling and shrieking at the top of his voice.

People on the outside thought that everyone in the hospital had been killed, but miraculously no one was harmed. No human, that is: One ambulance horse, a nervous animal named Bob, had met a tragic fate. When the earthquake struck, he sprang from his stall, snapping the chain that tethered him, and as he galloped across the street was crushed to death when the cupola of the City Hall fell on him.

With the help of Patrolman John McLean, a powerfully built police-man, hospital aides were finally able to clear away a portion of the bricks and debris that blocked the hospital entrance. McLean fired a shot through the entryway, alerting his comrades that at least some people remained alive, and shortly, the survivors stumbled through an opening to the out-side. Soon afterward, at about 6 A.M., they were transferred to Mechanics Pavilion, about a half block away on Larkin Street.

But what about the lunatics, six men and women, still locked in their cells? When the hospital matron, Rose Kane, was pulled to the street, she suddenly realized they had been left behind. Almost hysterical, she virtually dragged Patrolman McLean back over the mountains of rubble until, guided by their cries, they finally reached the patients. As he tore each cell door open, McLean, holding a revolver in one hand and straitjackets in the other, yelled to the howling inmates:

"Put your arms in this jacket or I'll blow your head off!"

The pair finally brought them outside, where they were tied together and taken to the Presidio to be locked up there. Some reports indicated that several other inmates, perhaps because they were unreachable, were left behind in their cells. Those who were moved would soon be joined by other San Franciscans who had been driven insane by fright or the loss of loved ones or property. More than one had even tried to kill family members with a knife or meat cleaver.

The sane, for their part, would find that rescue from the calamity was by no means a certainty.

CHAPTER 11

The Dishware and the Dragons

IN A SENSE, Hugh Kwong Liang, a fifteen-year-old schoolboy, had always understood the meaning of terror. He was virtually a prisoner within the bounds of Chinatown and entered the white areas of town only at the risk of being beaten, stoned, or even murdered. In fact, Chinatown was almost a separate, self-governing city at the time, an impoverished crazy quilt of narrow, garbage-strewn, incense-smelling alleys with intriguing names like Consort of Heaven and Virtue and Harmony.

Despite the elegant street names, the twenty-five thousand people who were shoehorned into Chinatown's twelve square blocks—many living in filthy, rat-ridden, tightly packed rooms called the Palace Hotel, the Dog Kennel, and other self-mocking designations—experienced little of heaven. No additional space was available, and the municipal government wasn't interested in easing their lot.

Virtue, on the other hand, was not necessarily a prized quality. Indeed, beneath the exotically named alleys, many cellars, often interconnected, served as secret halls of vice. A visitor could lose his shirt (playing games like pie gow, fan-tan, or chuck-a-luck), his mind (smoking opium), his life (resisting thieves), or his health (cavorting with prostitutes smuggled in from China, sometimes in padded crates labeled "freight," and kept as slaves in cells called "cribs").

Probably the last prostitute to operate independently had been Madame Ah Toy, who arrived in 1851 during the gold rush and, in a luxurious "parlor crib" perfumed with incense and adorned with silk hangings and plush cushions, offered miners her charms for a pinch of gold dust. But she was soon driven out of business by customers who mixed gold dust with brass filings. After that, Chinese pimps made sure the gold was pure. And now the only dust the two thousand or so prostitutes could collect was the kind that infested their grimy-walled cells, where these girls, some as young as twelve, lured their customers with cries of "two bittee lookee, fo bittee feelee, six bittee dooee." Sold by their fathers into slavery, many had arrived hidden in padded crates marked "dishware" that were rushed through customs by bribed inspectors.

So indifferent was the municipal government to this slave traffic that the press would routinely refer to it, especially in human interest terms, without stirring it to action. A typical press report read:

"Tom Gubbins, a Chinese interpreter . . . eloped with Fung Chow, an inmate of a house on Baker Alley, . . . and the young woman's owner, she being held as a slave, has since been endeavoring to find the couple, his purpose being to recover his human chattel."

Fighting over the slave-girl trade were rival tongs, which had started out as family groups and small associations for the protection of the Chinese community, but developed into criminal secret societies. They kidnapped or purchased "Daughters of Joy" in China from impoverished families, smuggled in opium, and advanced passage money to coolies arriving from China, who were kept as virtual peons until their debt was paid. With members killing one another off, however, the heyday of tongs had passed in 1897 with the moblike slaying of their most powerful leader, Fong Chong, known as "Little Pete."

A sensitive playwright and avid lover of cricket sounds, his favorite "music," Little Pete was, for an artist, strangely obsessed with his appearance. It was perhaps fitting, therefore, that he was in a barbershop having his forehead shaved the usual inch above the hairline (to give him a "highbrow" look) and his long, shiny queue washed and braided when gunshots suddenly added blood to the oiled hairdressing. His hatchet men had fought a barbarous seven-year war, partly over the ownership of Lily-Foot Wan Len, queen of the slave girls, and he was now its most illustrious victim—murdered even before the barber had a chance to cut enough hair to sell to a toupee maker.

Little Pete's elaborate funeral, reflecting the power of the criminal hold on Chinatown, featured burning joss sticks (incense) in front of an idol, a popular orchestra playing the funeral march, and mourners tossing bits of paper punched with square holes to confuse the devils trying to kidnap the spirit of the departed. An odd procedure in this case, since many believed the devils already owned Little Pete's soul.

With the "slave ships" bringing the prostitutes from China came an even more insidious evil: rats, carrying fleas infected with the bubonic plague. The disease had killed more than a hundred people in recent years—Mayor Schmitz's best-kept secret. How could he let this be known and create panic among the voters, who would force him to shut down these disreputable enterprises and strip him of his share of the profits? The local government, and bribe-taking policemen, thus fostered anti-Chinese sentiment among the whites by encouraging and supporting the vices that sullied Chinatown's reputation.

Similarly, shady Chinese entrepreneurs promoted this reputation to stimulate tourism, paying tourist guides to take their gullible wards on adventurous visits to underground dens of iniquity, complete with the smell of opium, "false walls," and evil-looking, sword-bearing "bandits" lurking in the shadows. The tourists would also hear tales of a mysterious labyrinth of secret passages reaching ten stories into the earth—a description that would prove to be colorfully bogus.

Such theatrics helped to hide from view the harsh, humdrum reality of the everyday life of simple Chinese like Hugh Kwong Liang, virtually all of whom were seen by whites as intriguing, untrustworthy, lewd, and capable of murder.

Paradoxically, in the first years of the gold rush, the Chinese, who came to dig for gold, were welcome in San Francisco and were even offered naturalization. After all, there had been fewer than twenty Chinese living throughout the United States before the magnet of gold enticed them here, and even then they arrived in relatively modest numbers—about fifteen thousand. No real threat.

But the Chinese rejected the offer. They had come to earn money, not citizenship. They wished eventually to return to the land of their ancestors, who, they proudly felt, had evolved their own original formulas for living and had produced a culture far superior to that of westerners, whom they called Barbarians. As Charles Caldwell Dobie would write in *San Francisco's Chinatown:*

"The Americans were intent on building a new empire—the Chinese were intent on nourishing an old empire with sustenance from a virgin country. It was China that received the greater part of their gold gleanings; it was China that sheltered their hearthstones; it was China that would finally receive their bones. A people with faces turned ever toward the land of their origin do not take root."

The Chinese did business with white people but retained their own lifestyle. The men wore skullcaps over hair twisted into pigtail queues; the women, black gowns over black pantaloons, with sandals fitted on tiny bound feet, the "golden lilies" of Chinese literature.

This reluctance to assimilate into American society, to learn local customs, laws, and language, began to irk many westerners, who mistakenly took the silent cultural snobbery of the Chinese for timidity and lack of intelligence. In fact, the newspaper *Alta California,* of June 4, 1853, flatly declared that the Chinese were "mentally inferior to whites." And Governor Leland Standord would tell officials that the Chinese, as a "degraded and distinct people, would exercise a deleterious effect upon the superior race."

By the mid-1850s, however, attitudes began to shift. Many Chinese were resigning themselves to permanent residence in the United States, while the whites demanded that they return to China. During the gold rush, after a man named Wah Lee set up the first Chinese hand laundry in a dark cellar, many Chinese, noting his success, also turned to this business, or else to cooking, shopkeeping, or housecleaning. The whites were delighted with these services. But after the gold rush, when the Chinese started to compete with whites for jobs, and whites, during hard times, were forced to work beside "Pigtails," white fury exploded. All the more intensely in the 1860s when tens of thousands more Chinese poured into the country to build the Central Pacific intercontinental railroad and then settled in large numbers in San Francisco.

Nor was the tension eased when the whites noted that Chinese workers, who arrived in the country alone, earned a family man's salary while driving thousands of unemployed whites into poverty, suicide, or crime (a

charge that dissipated when women, wives as well as prostitutes, began to
arrive from China).

A cry of "Yellow Peril!" went up.

Violence escalated, and thousands of white laborers armed with pikes,
the "pick-handle brigade," assaulted the Chinese, shouting, "The Chinese
must go!"

The politicians heard the cry. Thus, in the 1860s and 1870s, tax collec-
tors, sometimes imposters, in the mining regions, grabbed Chinese unable
to pay taxes, tied their queues together, whipped and occasionally shot or
stabbed them. In 1870 the municipality of San Francisco passed an ordi-
nance forbidding the employment of Chinese on public works. Finally, in
1882, Congress passed an Exclusion Act prohibiting further Chinese
immigration for ten years, except for students, merchants, tourists, and
diplomats. Other municipal efforts to quarantine, raze, and move Chinatown were foiled only when they were found either unconstitutional or
impractical.

It was in this tense, rancorous atmosphere that Hugh Kwong Liang
grew up. His father, Liang Kai Hay, arrived in San Francisco in 1871,
impoverished yet determined to make a good life for himself and his
future family. He was ready to gamble what little money he had to make
this dream a reality. He thus bought a lottery ticket for fifty cents and won
$10. Then he bet the $10 on the same numbers, and he broke the lottery
bank, winning $10,000. With this money he leased a building on Wash-
ington Street in Chinatown and opened a grocery store in the basement,
which flourished—in part, perhaps, because he stood before an altar every
morning and evening and offered incense and three cups of tea in honor of
the God of Prosperity (*choy shen*). He married a young girl from a leading
clan, and in 1871 Hugh was born.

Hugh had gotten to know some white people who occasionally bought
groceries in his father's store—delicacies like eel, octopus, shark's fin, sea
slugs, seaweed, lotus roots, pickled almonds, and twelve-inch-long string
beans. Some customers were arrogant and aloof, seeming to view his people with contempt. He heard them whisper about the Chinese being
unwashed and smelling bad—even while they reveled in a Chinatown that
welcomed them with red lanterns swinging gaily in the wind and brightly
colored strips of paper hanging from the balconies of the rickety China-

town tenements that offered little hint of the darkness, and often despair, within. Another white visitor might recoil on seeing the "nasty-looking things" in the window, or sneer, quite seriously, that rats were the principal Chinese delicacy.

This intolerance of people who were "different" grew from resentment to fear. It stemmed from the initial Chinese rejection of American citizenship and values, and then from the economic threat the Chinese posed. As an Italian worker would tell an inquiring sociology professor:

"We were afraid of them. The long queues and their dress—they looked as though they came from Mars."

Sometimes Hugh and some friends would venture into the white world, but at considerable risk. White boys would catch them and beat them up. And they had little trouble catching Hugh, since they had only to grab him by his queue, which Chinese wore as a sign of their subjugation to the horse-loving Manchu dynasty.

But Hugh considered himself fortunate—at least compared with the Chinese peddler who carried fruit, vegetables, and, on Fridays, fresh crab in a hand wagon or in buckets attached to the two ends of a pole resting on his shoulder. He was often stoned as he shuffled through white neighborhoods selling his produce—even on the Chinese New Year, when he brought lilies for the ladies and litchi nuts for the children.

So appalling had the persecution and discrimination become that in 1900 Hugh's mother decided to return to China with her four younger children, leaving Hugh, then only nine, to look after his father. But five years later, while Hugh was still going to a Chinese elementary school (Chinese children were forbidden to attend the superior white public schools), his father died of pneumonia. A distant cousin took over his store and lived with the boy in a back room.

HUGH WAS FAST ASLEEP on the morning of April 18 when, at 5 A.M., the tower bell of Old St. Mary's Church on California Street pealed five times, promising all who listened a day of heavenly peace and comfort. But Hugh didn't wake up—not even thirteen minutes later with his bed rocking from side to side and debris from the cracked ceiling showering on him. He dreamed he was in a boat about to drown in water that was pouring in. He finally awoke when his cousin stood over him, crying:

"Get up! Get up!" (*Dey loong jun! Dey loong jun!*)

The Earth Dragon! Most dragons were benevolent beasts, bringing rain to the farmers and symbolizing the loyalty of the ancient emperors to their subjects. But the Earth Dragon was a hideous monster, and now it was awake and trembling with anger!

Hugh leaped out of bed, dressed, and ran to the door to peek out. He saw the insides of the building across the street exposed, with the residents still in bed screaming. People were throwing household articles from their roofs, imperiling the lives of the people running along the street. Fearing that his own building might collapse, Hugh hurriedly gathered all his belongings and stuffed them in an old oakwood trunk.

Meanwhile, all the people of Chinatown, it seemed, had rushed into the street, chattering in their sing-song register and gazing at the destruction. Many had gathered in Portsmouth Square and were praying to the gods of their houses when one of the steers careening through the downtown area galloped toward them, fire in its eyes.

A bad omen! A sign that the world was crumbling! Could not this bull be one of the four on whose backs, they believed, the world rested? No wonder there was an earthquake! They stoned the animal and stabbed it with knives and a machete, trying to force it back into place. But a policeman then shot the wounded bull dead, and the people, fearing that the world would now topple over, swarmed into their temples, mainly into that of the revered Kwan Tai, the warrior god. They confessed their sins to the deities and urged them to appease the anger of the Earth Dragon. As Erica Y. Z. Pan would describe the scene:

"Countless red papers, bearing sacred hieroglyphics, were burned and cast heavenward to please the angry gods, which seemed bent upon their destruction. Holes were dug in the ground and flaming papers buried in the hope of mollifying the dragon."

The faithful, through some metaphysical process, felt they heard Kwan Tai assure them that no one would have to flee Chinatown. And wasn't he the most powerful god?

The Fire God would apparently disagree.

CHAPTER 12

The Crackle of Terror

A S THE HOURS PASSED on April 18, Josephine Hoffman grew frantic with fear that the chaos would prevent her fiancé, George Emerson, whom she was to wed the following day, from getting a ferry back from Oakland, where he had gone to see his sister. And her alarm grew when she started to smell smoke from fires caused by the earthquake.

Virtually all of the city's buildings were heated by wood or coal stoves and many had gas lighting fixtures. So fires broke out when the earthquake toppled over stoves and chimneys. Only blocks away on Hayes Street within an area called Hayes Valley, a woman kindled a fire in her lightly damaged two-story frame building between 9 and 10 A.M. to make a ham and eggs breakfast for her family. But with her flue blocked, burning cinders from the stove set the wall afire, and within minutes the cry "Fire!" echoed, as in gold rush days, throughout the neighborhood. Flames, carried by a stiff southeast wind, would ravage building after building in what would become known as the Ham and Eggs Fire.

This fire would cross Franklin to the east, Gough to the west, and Hayes to the south, and fuse with other lesser ones, many of them caused by other people who tried to make coffee without realizing that chimneys were down. That day, flying embers from these fires would spell the dem-

olition of such major buildings as St. Ignatius Church, the St. Nicholas
Hotel, the Mechanics Pavilion, which had been turned into a hospital, and
the already ruined City Hall. Like some ravenous vulture, the fire would
devour the crumbled leavings of the earthquake.

Among this fire's first tragic victims were a mother and her young son
who lived in a hotel on the north side of Geary Street, a short distance
from Josephine's house. When the walls collapsed, the fallen front granite
doorway pinned them as they tried to flee the earthquake. Rescuers furiously tried to save them, but they were working against time. When one of
them cried, "The fire will be here soon!" and it appeared that rescue was
impossible, the mother grabbed a loose stone and beat her son over the
head with it. It was better to kill him with a stone than to let him burn to
death, as was her own fate.

Josephine did not yet realize the extent of the disaster, but her fears
were not eased by the scenes now framed by her window as streams of
refugees stumbled by. When the earthquake had struck, people looked like
frenzied ants whose homes had been stirred up with a stick. They were
bewildered, panicked, and hysterical as the cries of children, the sobs of
women, and the shouts of men mingled in a cacophony of terror.

But after the first moments of desperation, the silence of shock and
despair set in as they gazed at their collapsed and damaged houses, and in
the horrifying quiet they acted rationally, deliberately, like people turned
into lifeless robots.

Some headed east toward the Ferry Building to catch a boat, some
northwest toward the Presidio's open grounds, which also led to docks, others southwest toward the high ground of Twin Peaks or Golden Gate Park,
the San Bruno hills down the peninsula, or simply to some square or vacant
lot. The refugees remained silent, cool, almost fatalistic, it seemed—even
when, shortly after the first tremors, the somber symphony of trunks being
dragged over cobblestones in erratic cadence began competing with the
relentless crackle of flames in the distance. The great fire had begun.

One man would later claim that on the first day of the fire he played the
role of doctor—delivering with a spoon and a string six babies in the door-
ways of smoking buildings on Market Street, the offspring of very pregnant mothers forced to leave their beds and flee for their lives.

Many of the refugees had at first doubted the fire would spread far, especially since the wind in the early hours jostled the flames forward only about a block every two hours. Indeed, many of them had waited too long before deciding to leave and were thus unable to save more than the meager bundles they were now clutching. Though a few joked to relieve their stress, most were too devastated to comprehend fully, even as they fled, the enormity of the tragedy from which they were fleeing. It was easier not to comprehend for people wracked with fright, especially for those guilt-ridden as well as for speeding past neighbors pinioned in the wreckage and crying for help.

The refugees, many of them holding a handkerchief to their faces to keep from getting burned, staggered along under a rain of cinders. Behind them they dragged not only the inevitable trunk stuffed with clothes and other elementary needs, but also all the symbols of their life, however pitifully unnecessary for survival—beds, sofas, tables, sewing machines. Whatever they could pile on homemade carts, toy wagons, wheelbarrows, lawn mowers, baby buggies, or anything else with wheels. Often children and elderly or ailing people rode atop the boxes and bags.

One elderly woman carried a birdcage holding four kittens, with the dispossessed parrot perched on her hand. A maid held a broom in one hand and a hat with ostrich feathers in the other. A man was overdressed, stuffed into three suits, with five derbies stacked on his head, while another man was underdressed, wearing a tailcoat but neglecting to put on his pants. Still another wore nothing at all—until he yanked a coat off a woman's shoulder, wrapped himself in it, and continued running.

This man was apparently more modest than a woman who sported only a hat and gloves until a prudish policeman sent her back to her shattered home to dress "properly," despite the risk. Many walked barefoot, bloodying the street as they stepped on broken window glass. Weeping mourners pulled trash carts carrying dead bodies. One man pushed along a piano until it got caught in a cable car track. He offered to give it away, but he couldn't have paid anyone to take it. A newspaper delivery boy tossed aside his papers when one solicited customer cried:

"What do I need a paper for? It's the end of the world!"

Automobiles and horse-drawn vehicles bulging with goods wove their way through the multitude. Among them were trucks from elite establishments like Shreve's and Gump's, crammed with silver candlesticks, priceless paintings, and other objects of art—each vehicle guarded by two men gripping shotguns. Some wealthy individuals, after burying many of their treasures in their gardens, decided to take the rest with them, and thus hired, at extremely inflated prices, the large but stinking garbage wagons driven by out-of-town hog farmers. These farmers, dressed in hip boots and blue dungarees, were glad to dump the swill they had collected for their hogs to make room for valuable furnishings and their owners, who sat in the filth and tried to ignore their nausea.

The army was supposed to commandeer all vehicles, except those with special permits, for ambulance service and for the hauling of dynamite and other fire-fighting equipment. But many unauthorized drivers continued to operate them—until stopped by soldiers, some of whom would become "reasonable" on hearing the jingle of gold coins.

The procession halted only when the cry "Mad dog!" pierced the air. But a shot was immediately heard, and people, some laughing nervously, continued on past the dead animal lying with saliva oozing from its mouth. Many refugees, utterly exhausted under their burdens, simply lay down in the street to rest, or, if they were lucky, found a few unoccupied square feet of space in the crowded gardens they passed.

In the eerie calm, one refugee would say, "We all talked with each other and even tried to joke a little. But I noticed that the eyes of most of the men and women were roving restlessly, nervously, and the tones of their voices were pitched high. This seemed to get on my nerves, and I wondered, was I, too, talking in a shrill voice?"

Finally, to Josephine's great relief, Emerson emerged at about midnight from the parade of dispossessed, who were among the 100,000 people who lost their homes on this first day of the catastrophe. But however greedy the fire, it still seemed to be at least a day away from the Hoffman home, and it would probably be extinguished before reaching it.

Should they postpone the wedding again?

No, they decided. Nothing further would interfere with that sacred ceremony.

Not even a fire that threatened to consume the whole city.

ONE PERSON was actually saved by the fire, at least temporarily—Antonio Compania, the fisherman. Locked in the refrigerator in the meat and fish market, he was freezing to death when the heat from the flames seared the outside and neutralized the temperature inside.

But fate would deal harshly, and ironically, with Compania. When all the ice in the refrigerator had melted, the water flowed down a drain and the interior became parched and suffocating. The fisherman apparently rapped on the wall, perhaps even when firemen arrived seeking to put out the fire. But no one could hear him. Indeed, for days the refrigerator would stand alone in a wasteland of charred ruins for about a mile in every direction.

Encased in a metal coffin without a drop of water, Compania, possibly against his will, remained alive—barely.

GIMPY BILL, the legless refugee, also remained alive, apparently *because* of his will. As he hung on to the rope attached to the tailboard of a horse-drawn wagon, the animal suddenly lurched to a halt. The axle of the dray had broken and the wagon was unusable—just as the smell of ash began to pollute the air. The city was on fire! How could he now escape? Looking around, he saw a young boy approaching.

A dime, Bill cried, if the boy would pull him up a nearby hill with a rope. The boy agreed and, playing the horse, puffed up the steep grade and left Bill at the top. He rolled into a grocery store and pleaded with the manager for shelter.

The fire, Bill assured the man, could not possibly reach so far.

Okay, the man agreed, he could stay in the barn in back of the store.

So that night Bill slept in the barn, but he awakened when the wind filled the barn with cinders. The hill was aflame. Once more Bill mounted his rolling platform, pushing himself forward with calloused hands, trying to keep ahead of the fire. And again, none of the fleeing people running past would stop to help him; nor did he have a dime left to hire someone.

If only he had legs.

AS THE FIRE EDGED toward the home of Ida McMahon on Sutter Street, north of Market, her husband, John, bag in hand, stared at her with bleary, drunken eyes and snarled that he was leaving. She and their daughter would have to fend for themselves.

Ida froze. She was already frantic with fear of the fire, and now her intoxicated spouse was deserting his family—leaving her and Ruth, their ten-year-old daughter, to their fate.

How, she sobbed, could he leave his pregnant wife and their child at a time like this—after eleven years of marriage? She was shocked by her husband's response: "Marriage?" he scoffed. They were never married! The "minister" and witnesses at the "wedding" were his friends. Their wedding had been a sham.

And McMahon stumbled out the door.

Eleven years! Ida remembered the tall, good-looking sailor who attracted her the moment they met in her hometown of Cairo, Illinois. She was drawn to his glib talk and hearty laugh. Shortly thereafter they were married—or so Ida thought. They left for St. Louis, his hometown, and in the next three years, three children were born, two of whom died shortly after birth.

Meanwhile, McMahon began drinking heavily, lost his job after he was out of the navy, and depended on Ida for the sole family support. For years, she had slaved away as a maid, sometimes as a factory worker, trying to earn enough to keep the family from going hungry while her husband spent much of the money on drink. And the more he drank, the harder he beat her. Eventually, they moved to San Francisco, where another child would soon be born.

With fingers of flame reaching now to within a block of her home, Ida packed a few things and with Ruth dragged herself out into the choking black smoke that rolled through the street. Where was the hospital? She wasn't sure. What would happen to her young daughter and the baby she was carrying? Finally, she fell in the street and was unable to get up, while the fire ate its way toward two more helpless victims.

CHAPTER 13

The Cruel Trap

JESSY WILSON wondered whether she and her senile mother would be victims when her husband, Willie, returned from a trip to his office downtown in the commercial district and told her the city was on fire and that his office building had been burned to the ground. At first Jessy couldn't imagine that the fire would ever reach her home north of Market on Bush Street, which was many blocks away. The danger was the earthquake. There had already been several tremors, and another one might bring down the house. But what if the fire did spread to the neighborhood? Agonizing over this possibility, she sat beside her mother all day, listening to her nonsensical ramblings.

As the fire, crackling over a forty-block front, edged ever closer and a dense smoke pervaded the atmosphere, Jessy realized that her worst fear was being realized. Her home could burn. While she despaired, she didn't want to frighten her mother, remaining silent when asked what happened to the sun, why it looked like a red ball in the haze that fringed the dense cloud of smoke hovering like a pall over a seething wall of flame. A "red ball" that another refugee, Edward Hart, would describe graphically:

"It was broad daylight. No—it was artificial daylight. It was discolored—it was red filtering through a covering of murky black . . . RED. A blazing red . . . a hot red, a consuming red. . . . There was no afternoon, there was no night, there was no morning."

Some San Franciscans were as overwhelmed by the beauty of the "red ball" and the world it inflamed as by the horror. One survivor, Sydney H. Williams, would remark in wonder: "While the colored sky indicated that something terrible was happening, the effect was a rare spectacle on a grand scale. It was an awe-inspiring beauty never seen under ordinary conditions."

A malicious beauty that Jessy could not find words to describe to her mother.

At 9 P.M., as the fire gradually crept toward them, she and Willie decided to join the desperate procession as soon as possible. Willie went to find a carriage and finally acquired one at an exploitive price after two hours of frantic searching. But where would they take Mama, who needed constant care? To Jessy's sister, Lara, they agreed, since she had three daughters who could help look after her. But on arriving, they found with sinking heart that the house had been badly damaged and Lara and her family had fled.

They ordered the driver to head for the home of Lara's son, where Lara had certainly gone. But they were wrong. Lara's son and his wife, however, offered to care for Jessy's mother, though they had their hands full with a four-week-old baby. Deeply relieved, Jessy and her husband rushed back to their own home in their carriage to see what they could save. They arrived at about midnight, though it looked like high noon; the fire was closing in on them, swallowing blocks of buildings at a time.

Jessy ran upstairs and gathered portable family belongings, including those of two young daughters who were staying with a relative in another town. She was especially careful to find the things her mother treasured most, among them some large valuable paintings that she wrapped in blankets. When the disaster was over, she wanted her mother to live as satisfying a life as possible. Since there was already too much to transport even in a cart, she packed few of her own possessions.

Back on the street, she discovered there was no longer even a cart— the driver, impatient to leave, had vanished into the night. In desperation, the couple ran down the street in different directions to find another vehicle, and searched all night. At about 10 A.M. the fire reached their corner, and a militiaman came to Jessy and ordered all occupants to leave the house at once.

She would later lament: "I thought my heart would break to leave the dear house Papa had bought—in which we had lived for thirty-five years, and all the precious things in it. All my books and treasures I loved so. My piano and musical library and the many things that were so dear to us."

Weighted down with baggage, the couple struggled to the home of Cousin Mary, but when they arrived, found that Mary had also been ordered to evacuate her home. The fire, it seemed, was following them like a maniacal stalker. Leaving their baggage on the sidewalk, they walked to the house where they had left Jessy's mother to make sure she was safe, and found, as Jessy had feared, that her mother's temporary guardians couldn't meet their guest's demands without neglecting their infant.

Jessy then thought of her doctor, who had earlier offered to have her mother stay in his house. The couple split up again to look for a carriage, and Jessy finally found one, again at an exploitive price. Since the drayman wouldn't wait for Willie to return, Jessy and her mother left without him for the doctor's house, but it was perched on top of a steep hill and the horse was unable to climb it.

Sorry, the driver said, but he would have to leave his passengers here. They must walk the two blocks to the house.

The two women got out of the wagon, but Jessy's mother, like the horse, could not negotiate such hills. So they simply remained there on the street with nowhere to sit—until a man dragging a trunk dropped dead from the exertion. They then sat on this trunk, which had helped to kill the man but, ironically, would help the two women to survive.

Meanwhile, the fire continued to creep forward, determined, it seemed, to devour them. Only two blocks from salvation, they were trapped by the hill, tormented by the swirling cinders, and almost overcome by the heat, which had become so intense that papers in the street burst spontaneously into flame. Yet Jessy's mother, who couldn't understand why they didn't go home, was too exhausted to walk another step. The fire was winning, but if they had to die, Jessy knew, her dear mother would die in her arms.

CHAPTER 14

Napoleon to the Rescue

O NE REASON the fire seemed to be winning was that San Francisco's top firefighter was not around to fight it. When the earthquake struck, Fire Chief Sullivan was asleep in his apartment above the engine house, his wife in an adjoining room. The cupola of the California Hotel next door suddenly fell about sixty feet onto the roof of the fire station. The heavy masonry crashed through the roof, then through the third and second floors, finally driving the ground floor into the cellar.

Untouched, the fire chief sprang from his bed, snatched the mattress and blankets, and ran into the next room to cover his wife with them. Just then he, the bed with his wife in it, and most of the furniture fell through the gap caused by the plunging masonry, and in a cloud of mortar dust, the couple were buried under the debris in the cellar. Three days later, Sullivan died in the hospital, mainly from injuries caused by steam and scalding water spurting from a radiator on the spot where he landed. His last words reflected his concern for his wife's condition and the welfare of the city and fire department.

His wife would survive—but would San Francisco?

BRIGADIER GENERAL Frederick Funston, deputy commander of the army garrison in the Presidio, thought it would—if he could control its fate. A tough, redheaded soldier, Funston thrived on challenges to his courage and tenacity, perhaps to prove to himself and the world that academic failure in his early life was misleading and irrelevant. Moreover, only five feet tall, he was apparently driven, Napoleon-like, by the need to compensate for this perceived handicap by displaying the riskiest heroics.

The son of a farmer and Civil War Union veteran, Funston, now forty-one, grew up on a Kansas farm on the fringe of the Plains frontier, where he spent more time hunting in nearby creeks and woods than doing his homework. Since he craved risk and the respect it yielded, he tried to enroll in the United States Military Academy at West Point but failed an entrance examination. He then studied at the University of Kansas, but being an indifferent student he never graduated, relying in part on clever fraternity pranks to win the admiration of his peers. He then worked as a journalist, but grew bored of interviewing. Next, seeking adventure in travel, he served as a railway conductor but enjoyed his job only when throwing drunks off the train.

Funston finally found a job that suited him. Having as a farm boy developed a strong interest in botany, he started working for the United States Department of Agriculture, and was soon studying desert plant life in Death Valley. After living for several months in furnacelike conditions, he nearly died. Still, this experience only whetted his appetite for assignments that would test his valor and resourcefulness.

On new missions for the Department of Agriculture, Funston blazed a fresh trail through Alaska and sailed down the Yukon alone in an open boat. Craving further excitement, he then volunteered to fight in the Cuban Army in its war against Spain, surviving capture and a death sentence by the Spaniards while recovering from a bullet wound in the lung. Shortly afterward, he joined the U.S. Army and was sent to help crush Philippine rebels who, like the Cubans, had been revolting against Spanish rule. They would have succeeded if the Spaniards had not surrendered the Philippines to the United States. The frustrated rebels then turned their guns on the Americans, and Funston would now face them with his usual reckless abandon.

While under fire, he crossed the Rio Grande on a raft and set up a rope bridge, allowing U.S. troops to tramp to the opposite bank and pursue the enemy—a feat that earned him a Congressional Medal of Honor. Finally, he all but won the war when he slashed his way through the wilderness of northern Luzon and captured the rebel leader in his stronghold. Funston was heralded in the United States as a national hero—with the full agreement of his troops. They remembered, for example, when he once mistakenly blamed an enlisted man in front of his unit for some misdeed, yet had the courage to apologize to the soldier when he realized his error.

But for all the glory, Funston was still dogged by failure. In early 1906, he returned to Cuba to seek a peace between the warring factions of the new republic, but was accused by Secretary of War William Howard Taft and other American leaders of "misinterpreting" their instructions. As a result, Funston was denied promotion to the rank of major general and sent to the Presidio in San Francisco shortly afterward to command the army's Department of California. He was distraught. Why should his superior, bearded, pince-nezed Major General Adolphus Greely, command the Pacific Division when he, "Freddy," as Funston was fondly called by his men, deserved the job? Was his subordinate, unchallenging position a proper reward for a fighting general who won the Congressional Medal of Honor? Unhappily, he was now in command only when his superior was out of town—as Greely was on April 18, attending his daughter's wedding.

That morning, Funston, shaken from his sleep by the earthquake, dizzily grabbed some civilian clothes, which he could quickly don without concern for a neat military appearance, and staggered to the door of his Nob Hill home at Washington and Jones Streets. How bad was the damage? He had to find out. He joined throngs of other curious people who had run out of their homes, some rushing to the commercial area to save valuable records in their offices or stores, if they were still intact.

At the crest of Nob Hill near the Mark Hopkins mansion, people, some of them homeless, stood gaping at the blazing sheets of flame rising in huge billows that broke into circles and churned through the roiling black clouds, suffocating the district south of Market. Some of the spectators were only half clothed, though many of the men had grabbed their derbies, if not their waistcoats and ties, before dashing outside, and some women were fully dressed in their floor-length skirts, long tight-fitting jackets with puffed sleeves, high-necked blouses, and broad-rimmed, flower-decorated hats—an accoutrement that, whatever else they wore or didn't wear, they would not be seen without, even during an earthquake.

Strangely, awe and fear seemed tinged with a certain cheerful if nervous exhilaration, and the spectators, most of them not yet victims, even joked about the almost comical sartorial styles on embarrassing display. For some, one writer would note, this was "a holiday—a carnival. Leaving their bric-a-brac where it lay, people went to see the sights, to laugh at their neighbors' experiences, and to congratulate each other that it was no worse."

These "sightseers" were relieved that their own well-built homes and the modern, steel-backboned structures in the commercial area below seemed to have suffered relatively little damage from the earthquake or the fire, unlike the smaller, flimsier buildings in less affluent areas, which had easily crumbled. They stared with chilling fascination at the screen of fire and smoke smothering the district south of Market. Well, at least it was the squalid part of town where the drunks and troublemakers lived in flophouses. Thank heaven Nob Hill was safe. The San Francisco fire department, the best in the nation, would surely see to that. What a show!

Some wanted to see the show up close. One observer would report:

"Down the street came a great automobile. It was occupied by two society women who had recovered from the shock, if they had not slept through it. They were out to see the sights—the awful, heartrending sights—and their chauffeur was bowling them along at a fairly rapid rate of speed on the only open street near Market. It was heartless, cruel, inhuman, unnatural, fiendish—for they laughed as they came through the lines of suffering mortals and between the rows of wounded and dying."

Funston hurried down the hill several blocks to the Phelan Building, headquarters of the U.S. Army's Department of California, hoping to direct rescue operations from there, but he found the severely damaged structure deserted.

Running to Sansome Street in the business section of the city, he assessed with despair the damage done to some of the other buildings in the area. Frightened people streamed into the streets from these partially shattered structures and, choking from the bitter fumes and the dust from fallen parapets, watched the gathering clouds of fire with horrified fascination while the ominous bells of the fire department's horse-drawn steam-pumping engines suddenly clanged furiously in every direction.

Even so, at least a third of the city's fire stations had been so shaken by the earthquake that they could not respond with great urgency. At engine number 2 on O'Farrell Street, near Market Street, the doors had barely swung open when some of the horses that were used to pull the engines burst out and stampeded down the street. At engine number 4 on Howard Street, south of Market, Fireman James O'Neill was killed when a wall of the American Hotel collapsed onto the firehouse as he was drawing water for the horses.

Nor could the firefighters who arrived at the smoldering scenes do much, though the black shadows visible through the smoke swirling around roof and tower attested to their desperate struggle. Funston watched as firemen on the ground leaped from their engines and connected hoses to hydrants while people cried, "Open the valves! Water!"

But only a trickle dribbled out. Two of the three main storage reservoirs serving the city straddled the San Andreas fault in the Peninsula south of the city, and the third reservoir skirted it. The reservoirs, the earth-fill dams, and one concrete dam survived, but all of the three thirty-inch conduits from the main reservoirs were cracked where they crossed the fault or nearby marshy areas. Eighty thousand gallons of water were washing away. Within the city, hundreds of ruptured pipes snaked uselessly through the blazing districts, and almost all the cisterns were dry. San Francisco was burning, and one of the nation's finest fire departments in a city almost surrounded by water could only watch the fire in agony, helpless to spray more than a few drops into it.

Ironically, two of the three distributing reservoirs were undamaged and the third still rippled with over one-sixth of its capacity. So while there was enough water to fight the fire, about eighty million gallons, there was no way to immediately pipe it into the distribution system.

In any event, the trickle from the hydrant convinced Funston that "a great conflagration was inevitable, and that the city police force would not be able to maintain the fire lines and protect public and private property over the great area affected."

Only his federal troops, the general decided, could give such protection, even though he remembered that during the Chicago fire thirty-five years earlier, General Sheridan had ordered the army into the city only to have the governor declare the move unconstitutional and demand its withdrawal. And so "Freddy" once more became the intrepid soldier who had crossed the Rio Grande under fire.

As acting commander of the troops in San Francisco, he would do with them as he saw fit without seeking guidance or approval from the politicians in Washington, who he was sure were trying to ruin his career and would certainly try to limit his authority. Yet, Funston could have communicated with Washington, since the postal telegraph office at the corner of Market and Montgomery Streets would stay open until that afternoon. Thus, at 6 o'clock that morning, the chief operator telegraphed his office in New York:

"There was an earthquake at five-fifteen this morning, wrecking several buildings and wrecking our offices. They are carting dead from the fallen buildings. Fire all over town. There is no water, and we have lost our power. I'm going to get out of the office as we have had a little shake every few minutes and it's me for the simple life."

Shortly, the operator contradicted himself: "We are on the job and we are going to try and stick."

In any case, Funston now saw fit to order all available troops into the city; in effect, to institute martial law on his own, though this was illegal. He would contact his two top officers, Colonel Charles Morris, commander of an artillery and cavalry garrison at the Presidio, and Captain M. L. Walker, commander of an engineering corps at Fort Mason, and order them to send their troops into the endangered areas. He would then inform Police Chief Dinan of his decision.

But Funston was loathe to contact Schmitz himself, whom he despised. He was a soldier who, while sometimes undisciplined, was honest, straightforward, blunt, a man inculcated with earthy rural values. The corruption and greed of Schmitz and his associates infuriated him. They would, in his view, place the city at mortal risk simply to grab a few more dollars.

And as Funston watched the fires rise in the distance, his resentment seemed to grow, feeding his rationalization for personally undertaking the rescue of San Francisco at whatever constitutional cost. Had not Fire Chief Sullivan warned the mayor that, in the event of a major fire, the fire department might not have enough water to prevent a catastrophe? And now, as Sullivan had foreseen, the hydrants emitted only a dribble. Funston regretted that he lacked the power to march into City Hall and throw out Schmitz and his fellow "crooks."

Why not resign from the army and run for mayor himself? his wife suggested.

No, he was a man of action. All those papers to read, all those lobbyists clinging to him like leeches. Besides, he hated the small talk at the fancy cocktail parties that rather vulgarly sustained the rich and powerful in San Francisco.

Funston now approached a policeman and asked where he could find a telephone.

Don't waste your time, the policeman replied. The earthquake had damaged the whole telephone network.

Funston asked the officer to find the police chief and tell him of the troop movement. Then, after failing to flag down a vehicle, he ran to the army stable on Pine Street more than a mile away, arriving, he would say, "in so serious a condition that I could scarcely stand."

He immediately ordered his carriage driver to deliver a verbal message to the Fort Mason commander: Tell Captain Walker to bring all available men to the Hall of Justice at once and report to the mayor for duty, as the city was in flames. The general then scribbled a note to Colonel Morris with the same order and sent an aide, Lieutenant Long, to the Presidio to deliver the message.

Captain Walker was shocked when Funston's driver awakened him and told him of the general's order. He had been jolted awake earlier by the earthquake but, too bleary-eyed to recognize its intensity, went back to sleep. And here he opened his eyes to learn he must order all the men under him in Fort Mason to help save the city from catastrophe! He leaped out of bed, dressed, and called out his troops, 5 officers and 150 men, whom he led into the streets of San Francisco at 7:15 A.M.

Lieutenant Long had a more difficult time at the Presidio getting Colonel Morris out of bed. When Morris had read Funston's note, he was furious. Send troops into the city? Was the general crazy? Did he think he was Czar Nicholas, who had just crushed a revolution in Russia? Or

Kaiser Wilhelm, who was rattling the German saber in Europe? An American general took orders from his civilian superiors!

"Go back," he acidly exclaimed, "and tell that newspaperman that he had better look up his army regulations and there he will find that nobody but the president of the United States in person can order regular troops into the city!"

Morris finally got up, but only to show Long out and slam the door in his face.

In desperation, the lieutenant ran to the bugler as he was about to blow reveille and cried that the colonel wanted him to sound a call to arms immediately.

And within minutes, a dismayed and disorganized company of about 350 men stumbled from the Presidio into town, finally led by a reluctant Colonel Morris, who rode in his horse-drawn carriage, perhaps lamenting the refusal of the army, bound by tradition and fearful of innovation, to exchange horses for gasoline-operated automobiles. The army, after all, was made up of common people. It should ride in those "toys of the rich"?

By noon General Funston had more than 1,500 troops in the city, many mounted on horses, who, together with 600 cadets from the University of California, were helping the police to patrol the Market Street area. At the same time, he sent the army tug *Slocum* to Fort McDowell on Angel Island, off the shore of Marin County, to deliver an order to the 22nd Infantry based there: Head for San Francisco immediately! He also sought troops from Alcatraz Island in San Francisco Bay, Fort Baker in Marin County, the Presidio in Monterey, and Vancouver Barracks near Portland, Oregon. And to his nemesis, Secretary of War Taft, he wired a message on Wednesday morning requesting tents and rations for twenty thousand people and boldly adding:

"I shall do everything in my power to render assistance and trust to the War Department to authorize any action I may have to take."

Who would dare argue with him while San Francisco burned? Nobody. But distrust of him continued to fester in Washington. General Bell, the chief of staff, irked that he hadn't been fully informed about what Funston was doing, shot back a telegram commanding him to "wire details as comprehensively as possible." And President Roosevelt himself sent identical telegrams to Mayor Schmitz and Governor Pardee, perhaps really intended to jar General Funston:

"Hear rumors of great disaster through an earthquake at San Francisco, but know nothing of the real facts. Call upon me for any assistance I can send."

But what was Funston doing specifically? Washington wanted to know. He was still vague. What was he up to? Secretary of War Taft would rap out a message:

"I wish that you would report to me at once what you have done, the measures you have taken, and under what authority you are acting. . . . Wire as soon as possible."

Later, Taft, in his frustration, would snap to his aides: "It would take an act of Congress to relieve [Funston] of the responsibility for the violence the army did to the Constitution."

Returning home on the first morning of the catastrophe, Funston sat down with his wife for a cup of coffee. He was exhilarated. He had taken charge of the crisis, as he felt uniquely qualified to do, and would issue the orders while making it appear that the civil authorities approved of all his actions. The general gambled that these authorities would not officially protest. The following day, Funston would reply to the War Department rather testily, using the Southern Pacific wire at the ferry:

"Your . . . dispatches received. Have already filed several for you [which were apparently not received]. Impossible now to inform you as to full extent of disaster. City practically destroyed. Troops have been aiding police and maintaining order. Martial law has not been declared. Working in conjunction with civil authorities. Have not interfered with sending of any dispatches. You cannot send too many tents or rations. About 200,000 people homeless. Food very scarce. Provision houses all destroyed. All government buildings in city gone."

Whether his foes in Washington liked it or not, whether he would be court-martialed or not, General Funston was now the military dictator of a fascist-style San Francisco.

CHAPTER 15

Inoculating the Mayor

FEELING AS IF "a huge dog was tossing a rag doll," Mayor Schmitz was awakened with a start when the earthquake struck, but he found that little damage was done to his home on Fillmore Street, some distance west of the downtown area. He dressed and went outside to assess the wreckage elsewhere, and saw little that worried him. Just another earthquake, he thought, though perhaps a bit stronger than usual. No reason to rush to City Hall any earlier than normal.

At about 6 A.M., however, two of his aides rapped on his door and greeted him with the shocking news, according to one of the aides, John T. Williams. A calamity! City Hall looked like a huge birdcage, with only its steel frame still standing, and many other buildings had collapsed as well. Worse still, fires had begun to erupt all over the city.

"I had no idea it was as bad as that!" Schmitz exclaimed. "Out here there are only a few chimneys down."

He must now save the city. Was this the miracle he had been hoping for, the one that might keep him out of jail?

Schmitz rushed out with his aides and climbed into their automobile. As the car wormed its way through crowds of refugees fleeing in all directions, the mayor glanced out at the undulating blue bay and said:

"What a mockery to see how calm and placid the waters of the bay are when on shore we have such a disaster."

As they turned onto Van Ness Avenue, the car overtook Captain Walker's troops from Fort Mason at the northern end of the street and drew to a halt.

Schmitz asked Walker where they were going.

He had been sent by General Funston to report to the mayor or the chief of police at City Hall, the captain replied.

"I am the mayor," Schmitz exclaimed. "The new City Hall is destroyed. I am now going to the Hall of Justice. Report with your company at the Hall of Justice, where you will receive orders what to do."

Schmitz appeared furious. Funston had had the gall to preempt him . . . sending troops into the city without consulting him! Besides, hadn't the general already enjoyed his share of glory? Now it was the mayor's turn. He could not control the army, but he could present a new face to the public—and make it forget the old one.

"We then proceeded to the City Hall," Williams would say, "and it was very obvious that the mayor was deeply grieved when he beheld the way it had been shaken. . . . Then we set out for the Hall of Justice downtown. As we were turning into Market Street the mayor had a full view of the wreckage that had fallen from buildings, facing that thoroughfare."

"This is terrible!" he exclaimed, "but thank God I am mayor of a brave people."

A people, he hoped, that would be grateful to him for his leadership at so critical a moment. He would rescue the city—and who would throw a hero into jail? After all, some of San Francisco's most respected historical figures were rogues. There was William Ralston, the visionary banker who built the Palace Hotel and financed mining ventures, then drowned himself when charged with overdrafting a few million dollars. And there was Henry Meiggs, who developed North Beach and built Fisherman's Wharf, the world's greatest wharf; he vanished when it was discovered he had fraudulently endorsed city securities to finance his dream and eventually committed suicide. Such men were now honored for their contributions to the city, as Mayor Schmitz would surely be—even if he didn't kill himself.

Schmitz arrived at the Hall of Justice on Kearny Street across from Portsmouth Square at 6:45 A.M. Hardly more than an hour earlier, the

bawdy houses that had prospered within view of the guardians of justice—
no surprise in this criminally run city—were scenes of chaos. One writer
would observe that "hysterical women with painted cheeks vomited forth
from brothels and dance halls." Another would report:

"Ashes were coming down thicker and thicker. Bank notes and burned
pages from municipal records were crunching underfoot. The air grew
hotter and hotter, and suffocating. The wild yells, the clang of the ambu-
lances as they rushed to the emergency, the wounded and dead piled in
heavy wagons, reminded one of Dante's *Inferno,* but Dante had nothing on
this hell."

The mayor, his felt hat shading his haggard, troubled face, stared
through what seemed like a dirty snowstorm at the ornate central tower of
the ministry, which was on the verge of collapse. Was this building any
safer than City Hall? However apprehensive, he entered and was greeted
by a number of aides, including Police Chief Jeremiah Dinan and Acting
Fire Chief Dougherty. Dougherty and not Dennis Sullivan? Schmitz was
deeply shocked on learning of Sullivan's incapacitation, it seems—though
he would no longer be hounded by a man who, he seems to have felt, was
a bit too honest to serve as a public official. He appointed Dougherty as
acting fire chief, replacing Sullivan, who would die three days later.

The mayor would now take charge—theoretically, since martial law
had not been officially declared. But General Funston, finally deigning to
consult with him later that morning, would make it clear that it would be
he who would have the last word and wield the real power—though he
would consult with civil authorities about how the troops would be used.
The mayor needed the army to keep order, didn't he? As Brigadier General
Henry Noyes would state in the *Journal of the Military Institution:*

"At eight o'clock General Funston took charge of the city."

Now about an hour earlier, Schmitz, still believing *he* was in the sad-
dle, went with his aides to the basement of this temporary city hall, sat
down, and in candlelight—the electricity had been cut off—began map-
ping out plans for saving the city. The news was bad, Dougherty reported.
The fire was almost out of control and water was as scarce as whiskey in a
convent.

There was a moment of silence. Schmitz knew why. Dennis Sullivan
had pleaded with him in vain for money to implement his plan for dealing

with a major fire. Why hadn't he listened to the fire chief? Now Dennis wasn't able to lead the struggle, and Schmitz would have to depend on old John Dougherty to extinguish the most menacing fire the city had ever seen.

Dougherty was well aware of his inadequacies as a fire chief and had never aspired to be a great leader—only a good fireman. He had come with his family to San Francisco from Massachusetts when he was only five years old and, self-educated, exhibited a talent for mechanics at an early age. He became a plumber and a gas fitter before joining the fire department as a machinist. Disappointed by the department's neglectful treatment of firemen and their families, he ran for the California senate and was elected in 1882. He achieved his goal; the senate passed a bill he introduced calling for new benefits to the families of crippled and deceased firemen throughout the state.

With the good deed done, it was back to the fire department for Dougherty, who became Sullivan's deputy in 1893. But if his fellows loved this good-hearted, good-humored veteran with the narrow, twinkling eyes as the man responsible for giving them vital new security guarantees, they reserved their awe for Sullivan, whom they viewed as a uniquely imaginative administrator and inspirational leader. Now, suddenly, John Dougherty was the one in charge.

Four separate curtains of flame, Dougherty pointed out to Schmitz, were ravaging the commercial district north of Market and were moving westward toward Van Ness Avenue; more than a dozen fires south of Market were raging southward and devouring the Mission district; and other scattered blazes were wreaking havoc across the city. All were being driven by gale-force wind drafts created by the fires. And with the water mains broken and the hydrants virtually dry, there was little water to fight a runaway conflagration—twenty-three cisterns holding 16,000 to 100,000 gallons, a few thousand gallons of sewer water, and water drawn from the bay with interconnected hoses that could reach only limited distances. And the naval craft needed to supply necessary equipment would not reach San Francisco for many hours.

Dougherty reported that he had already sent a message to the Presidio requesting that all available explosives, with a detail to handle them, be used to create firebreaks that would keep the flames from advancing. He was following the advice of Dennis Sullivan, who had argued that if any-thing happened to the water supply, the only way to save the city would be to dynamite buildings in the path of the fire to create wastelands that the flames could not cross, and set counterfires that would burn their way toward the main conflagration. Thus, Colonel Morris in the Presidio was sending several wagons of powder—dynamite in granular form—while the Engineering Department was delivering three hundred pounds of stick dynamite.

Since little stick dynamite was immediately available, the powder would be used, even though it might set afire buildings that were still unburned and feed, rather than halt, the spreading flames. A risk, yes, but without water, there was little choice. Schmitz agreed, as had General Funston. The mayor himself would dispatch a telegram to Oakland Mayor Frank Mott reading:

"Send fire engines, hose, also dynamite, immediately."

The question was, would the explosives arrive in time? Sullivan's plan had been to dynamite and set fire to several blocks of small buildings in the downtown area almost immediately after the main fire started to spread, when the blaze would still be too weak to jump a large gap between structures. But more than two hours had already passed since the fires broke out, and they might be unstoppable by the time the explosives arrived. Nor was there much inclination to set counterfires, at least at this stage, lest they nourish instead of fight the conflagration.

If Schmitz harbored doubts about Dougherty, he had full confidence in Police Chief Dinan, who headed a six-hundred-man force that the mayor hoped would help him refurbish his tarnished image by keeping order dur-ing this crisis. Funston's army, after all, would be used to glorify the gen-eral's role, not his own. He knew he could rely on Dinan, whom he had appointed police chief about a year earlier. Dinan wisely realized that his interests would best be served by not poking into City Hall "business" that concerned only the mayor and, of course, Ruef.

Nor was Dinan a hypocrite. Why should he deny his policemen their time-honored custom of accepting small gifts in the traditional San Fran-cisco fashion? After all, weren't disreputable enterprises like those in Chi-natown, the Barbary Coast, and Tenderloin areas largely responsible for the booming tourist trade?

Dinan's ability to shut his eyes at appropriate moments was not the police chief's only admirable trait in Schmitz's view. He was also innovative; he had, for example, just added the first patrol car to his teams of horse-drawn buggies, making crime fighting far more efficient. He had also increased the number of police patrols.

Schmitz would need them now. According to Williams, he told Dinan: "The United States troops are on their way down here from the Presidio. As soon as they arrive, send fifty men into the banking district, put ten men on every block on Market Street and a guard for the City Hall. Give these men instructions to be as merciful as possible to the poor, unfortunate refugees, but to *shoot to kill everyone found looting*. We have no time to waste on thieves."

At the same time, Schmitz softened his hard line with an order to Dinan to release all people already in jail for having committed lesser crimes—with a warning that they would be shot if caught breaking the law again.

Schmitz had another concern. Some of the city's wealthiest homes on Nob Hill, Van Ness Avenue, and elsewhere were in danger. And drunken workers from poor areas like south of Market, the Barbary Coast, and Chinatown might go on a rampage in these neighborhoods, looting the homes and even killing their owners. He headed a labor party, true, but some of his best friends—and benefactors—were among the city's richest citizens. He ordered Police Chief Dinan:

"Close up every saloon at once!"

Schmitz then met with a small group of leading citizens, most notably the distinguished lawyer Garret W. McEnerney and millionaire businessman J. Downey Harvey, who helped him choose a cabinetlike Committee of Fifty (which would gradually expand to about a hundred), excluding both Ruef and the equally corrupt board of supervisors. The mayor decided to dissociate himself from his unprincipled cohorts, at least temporarily, in an effort to inoculate himself against a jail sentence later.

Schmitz hoped his friend and mentor, Ruef, would understand; after the crisis, he would bring Ruef back into the ruling circle, though in a role with minimal influence, to appease his enemies. During the city's agony, Ruef worked with firemen trying to save his own home on Lombard Street from going up in flames, but in vain. Homeless, he met the brother of a leading businessman, J. B. Levison, who had been fighting vigorously to have him thrown into jail, and the man took pity on him.

"Well, come home with me," he said. "You can have a bed in my brother's house."

And Ruef was soon asleep on a mattress in Levison's bedroom— alone, since Levison wasn't home. The businessman would later say, in a modern rendition of Little Red Riding Hood and the wolf:

"I came in, and I saw that big nose sticking up out of my bed, and there was Abe Ruef, the man I was fighting tooth and nail, sleeping in my bed."

The "wolf" was permitted to stay the night.

Ruef would claim that he engaged in relief work, and he was reported to have spent some of the time with his family aboard a yacht anchored in the bay, where he could reflect on the irony of his downfall. He had survived every political storm with guile and glibness, only to be done in by Mother Nature—who couldn't be bribed—while his protégé ruled without him.

In the selection of the Committee of Fifty, Schmitz would claim, "I considered neither nationality, creed, nor political affiliations, but picked out the men of the community that I thought were best fitted for the task that then confronted them, and seemed by their abilities best equipped to solve the problems and carry into effect the propositions that would come before them."

Although Schmitz, never himself a worker, headed a labor political party, he apparently did not think anyone from the working community was "best fitted for the task." Whom, then, did Schmitz embrace? Some of San Francisco's wealthiest and most professionally prestigious men, among them his worst enemies, including James Phelan (whom he named chairman), Rudolph Spreckels, and the attorney who was to prosecute him!

With bitter irony, they would find themselves taking orders at this desperate moment from a man whom they could barely wait to lock behind bars. It was partly, and precisely, because of their impatience that he appointed them. Would they really send to jail the man who was leading the struggle to save the city?

When by midafternoon about half of the select committee had maneuvered their way through the burning streets to the Hall of Justice, Schmitz silently greeted them in the shadows cast by candlelight, savoring this moment of dark triumph that could mean his salvation. He suddenly felt a breath of freedom he had apparently not enjoyed since he stood on the stage of the Columbia Theater and led his orchestra with a wave of his baton. He felt, he would claim, as if he were starting a new life.

Schmitz was no longer, at least in his eyes, a prisoner of greed who buried his self-contempt in the pernicious logic that it was the politician's privilege to partake of spoils.

CHAPTER 16

The Lord, the King, and the Executioners

IN THEIR CYNICISM, those tending to think the worst of Mayor Schmitz might even have sympathized to some degree with the religious zealots who claimed that the city's corruption and sinful practices had provoked God into unleashing this disaster. There were signs to "prove" this. Look how swiftly the flames spread! And why did fire break out in the tall buildings mainly on the top floors before eating its way down? Not, as experts said, because broken gas mains on the ground floor had sent gas rushing upward to ignite at the top, but because this was a signal coming from Heaven: This is your punishment!

Only a few days earlier, Prince Benjamin, patriarch of the Flying Rollers of the House of David in Benton Harbor, Michigan, had sent a missionary, Mary McDermitt, to warn the people of San Francisco and their leaders that they must give up their sinful ways immediately or God would bring down upon them an earthquake, fire, and pestilence within a month—a foretaste of what would happen at 3:10 A.M. on Christmas Eve, 1916, when the world was to end. Did they wish to be among the 144,000 Americans who, like Noah, would survive in an ark? (Immigrants with less than a year's residency were ineligible.) The ark would be built with money that doomed sinners should turn over to the Rollers before they were thrust into hell. Maybe the devil would go easier on them.

Anyway, with Mary McDermitt's threat fulfilled, the Flying Rollers celebrated with a brass band. God and Mary had given the sinners of San Francisco what they deserved.

Meanwhile, across the bay in Oakland, the Reverend Clifton Macon would thunder to his flock: "I am convinced in my own mind that this disaster, with all its horrors, is a visitation from Almighty God. We must not be ashamed to recognize the fact that the conditions which brought about the destruction of Sodom and Gomorrah, of Jerusalem, and, perhaps, also Pompeii and Herculaneum, existed in [San Francisco]. . . . Like the great king of Babylon, who glanced over the city, and as his bosom swelled with pride, exclaimed, 'Is not this great Babylon which I have builded?' And, as the Scripture tells us, that night was the city overthrown and the king slain."

GOD MIGHT be behind this violent "overthrow" of San Francisco, but the king was still alive. Indeed, to the frustration of many in the Committee of Fifty, Mayor Schmitz was, ironically, emerging with more power than ever—power that they were investing in him! With the quiet authority of the orchestra conductor he had been, Mayor Schmitz took charge of this critical meeting of some of the city's most powerful and aggressive citizens. One observer would say:

"It was a revelation to see men who were masters of business and captains of industry utterly at a loss and incapable of any initiative in such a terrible emergency. [Schmitz] ran the Committee of Fifty as he would a hurry rehearsal. . . . He swung his baton and played his new band with as much aplomb as if he had been conducting it for years."

"The conflagration," Schmitz would later recall, "was raging all around; there was the roar of the dynamite explosions, and there was a fresh earthquake shock while the committee was in session. Then the news was brought in that the building was unsafe, and then a dynamite explosion nearby shattered every window of the room where we were meeting. These incidents, however, did not deter anybody present from continuing the business in hand."

Schmitz had prepared a proclamation announcing how soldiers and policemen should deal with looters, whom he himself had seen in action while en route to the Hall of Justice. He solemnly read the proclamation to the committee:

The Federal Troops, the members of the Regular Police Force and all Special Police Officers have been authorized by me to KILL all persons found engaged in Looting or in the Commission of Any Other Crime.

I have directed all the Gas and Electric Lighting Co.'s not to turn on Gas or Electricity until I order them to do so. You may therefore expect the city to remain in darkness for an indefinite time.

I request all citizens to remain at home from darkness until daylight until order is restored.

I WARN all Citizens of the danger of fire from Damaged or Destroyed Chimneys, Broken or Leaking Gas Pipes or Fixtures, or any like cause.

E. E. Schmitz, Mayor

The request that all citizens remain at home might have drawn laughter if the situation had been less desperate. After all, how many citizens still had a home? Nor was the order for soldiers to kill civilians applauded. For everyone knew it was patently illegal to issue such an order—and the word *kill* was emphasized in capital letters, suggesting that no questions need be asked. Anyone could be killed on the least suspicion. The proclamation, in effect, decriminalized murder. But no one spoke out—not even the lawyers. And Police Chief Dinan had apparently approved the order in advance.

One person, however, openly opposed the order. It was Colonel Morris, who had refused at first to send his troops into the city without presidential approval.

Would the mayor be responsible for this mandate? he demanded.

Schmitz would later say: "I told him yes; that I would be responsible for that order. We could not take prisoners; we must stop looting, and therefore shoot anyone caught looting. . . . I told Colonel Morris and also [Captain Walker] to let the news be widely spread that anyone caught looting should not be arrested but should be shot."

The colonel, Schmitz further ordered, would place a special guard around City Hall to carefully keep watch over the vaults of the treasurer's office there, which held about six million dollars. And he ordered the arrest of profiteers—draymen and others—an order interpreted by some soldiers as a license to kill them like looters.

There was no time to argue; fire was the friend of the poor, offering them the opportunity to grow rich. Looters must be killed before they could indulge in another "gold rush," even if they plucked almost worthless trinkets and cheap silverware from the ashes or a few coins from a broken vault. With righteous fury, Schmitz, who was facing jail for massive thievery, would summarily execute all alleged petty thieves—those shabbily dressed, culturally ignorant mortals who could hardly tell the difference between a diamond ring and a cigar band. Within hours, he would boast to his colleagues that his policy was working:

"Let it be given out that three men have already been shot down without mercy for looting."

And to help enforce the antilooting order, as well as the alcohol restrictions, Schmitz would ask Governor George Pardee to rush in the National Guard. The mayor didn't wish to depend entirely on the federal troops under General Funston, whom he resented for "usurping" his authority while exercising full control over those troops. So why not use the militia, which the mayor could control to some degree, as a counterpoise to the general's power?

But Schmitz realized soon after the militiamen arrived that to maintain order he needed more, not fewer, federal troops. The militia were often undisciplined, and even many of his policemen were unreliable, running off to save their own families. He thus wired the naval station on Mare Island:

"Earthquake, town on fire, send marines and tugs."

But was such a force sufficient? However reluctantly, Schmitz sent word to Funston that more of his troops were needed in the city as well. And Funston would oblige, dispatching men from Alcatraz Island, Angel Island, Vancouver, and Monterey.

Even as the Committee of Fifty was meeting for the first time, civilians were dragged from the street by policemen and ordered to run off by hand five thousand copies of the mayor's proclamation on presses that could not operate with electricity, since all power was shut off. The meeting did not last much longer, for the Committee, spurred by a shift in the wind that propelled the fire toward the Hall of Justice—as if in contempt of the city's leaders—moved to the Fairmont Hotel, which was still under construction atop Nob Hill.

"It did not seem possible," Schmitz would say, "that the fire could reach it, or that it could do any damage to it if it did extend so far."

But by the next morning, April 19, "The flames came sweeping up from all sides. . . . The Fairmont had . . . caught fire, and we had to move our quarters from there to the North End Police Station . . . eleven blocks away." After a few hours, there was yet another close escape and the committee moved on to Franklin Hall at the corner of Fillmore and Bush Streets, away from the downtown area, where it would meet every morning and afternoon.

CHAPTER 17

Succumbing to Catastrophe

WHILE the Committee of Fifty debated myriad issues—relief for the tens of thousands of refugees, the need to dynamite buildings to halt the spread of the fire, punishment for vehicle drivers who extorted excessive fares for carrying people and their belongings—John Dougherty rushed in his buggy from one fire line to another. His fire department, though crippled, had managed to check many of the initial fires, mainly roof and chimney blazes. But there were simply too many to put out, and eventually they would merge into one overwhelming conflagration. The fires were eating their way toward one another, stretching their tentacles in every direction.

As the hours rolled by, the downtown area continued to drown in the fire and a pall of smoke, with almost every window belching flames like blast furnaces. The temperature, often as high as 2,000 to 2,200 degrees Fahrenheit, was so great that buildings were set on fire by heat emitted by flames raging more than 125 feet away. Glass softened and ran in a molten state, and sometimes iron articles fused together. Only the best system of fireproofing, rare here indeed, could stand the test.

The blaze seemed to move in concentric circles, enveloping the most impregnable buildings in flanking movements, as if some demonic supergeneral were masterminding the attack. The flames destroyed even such

cherished buildings as libraries holding over a million books and muse-
ums housing priceless art treasures. In the downtown commercial area, a
cluster of only about a dozen buildings survived, dominated by the vener-
able fifty-two-year-old Montgomery Block, a huge structure with iron
shutters, thick walls, and home to Poppa Coppa's Italian restaurant, a
mecca for artists and writers.

So powerful was the wind draft caused by the fire that within an hour
Rincon Hill south of Market off the waterfront became a burning mountain in one of the most deadly forays of the conflagration. At the time, the
destroyer USS *Preble,* commanded by Navy Lieutenant Frederick Newton
Freeman, arrived in San Francisco from Mare Island, across the bay near
Vallejo. With the help of a fireboat and a tug, the ship pumped water
toward the hill, using interconnected hoses—but to little effect. Freeman
sent two of his officers to warn the impoverished people living there to
flee. One of them, Commander John E. Pond, would later report:

> The fire was sweeping up the hill at such a rate that it seemed
> impossible that anyone on the hill could escape its path. The scene
> was heartrending. Those who heeded the warning escaped to the
> waterfront, but many who delayed to gather personal belongings
> became panic-stricken when they found escape in one direction cut
> off by flames and smoke, and ran screaming in all directions like a
> hive of ants whose hill had been disturbed.
>
> The old and crippled, taken out of their houses on mattresses,
> were carried a little way and dropped, then picked up by someone
> else, carried a little further and dropped again. The whole section
> was swept clean in less than an hour, and many must have perished.

By 2:20 P.M. the situation in the city was partially summed up with
staccato urgency by the chief operator at the postal telegraph office near
the corner of Market and Montgomery, the only direct link with the outside world:

> The city practically ruined by fire. It's within half block of us. The
> *Call* building is burned out entirely, the *Examiner* building just fell
> in a heap. Fire all around in every direction and way out in resi-

dence district. Destruction by earthquake something frightful. The City Hall Dome stripped and only the framework standing. The St. Ignatius Church and College are burned to the ground. The Emporium is gone, entire building, also the Old Flood Building. Lots of new buildings just recently finished are completely destroyed. They are blowing up standing buildings that are in the path of flames with dynamite. No water. It's awful. There is no communications anywhere and entire phone system is busted. I want to get out of here or be blown up.

A little later came the message: "I'm packing up the instruments."

And some minutes still later: "Instruments all packed up and I'm ready to run."

A final message was stark: "Good-bye."

San Francisco, it seemed, was now isolated from the world.

In desperation, Dougherty ordered his men to supplement what little water they had with everything from barrels of wine to wet blankets. They couldn't even use sewer water any longer since coal oil dumped into the sewers by grocery stores only fueled the conflagration. If all else failed, dynamite might work. Crates of the explosive were on the way from the Presidio, the Judson Powder Works at Pinole, and the Southern Pacific Company. General Funston had informed Mayor Schmitz and the Committee of Fifty that only the widespread use of dynamite to create firebreaks could save what remained of the city.

But Dougherty was despondent, doubting his men could save more than a few structures. The struggle seemed hopeless and he was almost helpless, especially with the alarm system and communications dead. The alarm system, powered by wet cells in the alarm station in Chinatown, was destroyed when the earthquake knocked over the glass jars where the cells were kept. All the fire stations were isolated islands, hunting for scattered fires, unable to coordinate operations with one another. Meanwhile, eight fire engines were stalled in a semicircle around the Ferry Building, immobile because the entire west side of East Street had burned, and the wreckage blocked traffic.

As a result of this chaos, Dougherty could not carry out Dennis Sullivan's plan to move all fire engines into the business district. With three fires in the outer districts of the city tying up nearly a third of the available engines, the business district, with few firefighters around, quickly succumbed to the raging storm as Sullivan had feared. Furthermore, the firefighters were in grave danger. One at the Third and Howard station had already been killed when part of a plunging cornice struck him as he poked his head out of a window.

Literally adding fuel to the flames were arsonists who feared their homes, already damaged by the earthquake, wouldn't burn down and make them eligible to collect fire insurance. To become eligible, they set their houses on fire themselves.

With the firefighters steeped in pessimism and almost subdued by fatigue, few paid attention to John Dougherty when his buggy careened into sight. If only Dennis Sullivan were still around!

Block by block, San Francisco succumbed to catastrophe. First it had been battered by an earthquake that rocked even some of the sturdiest structures, ripping and cracking their foundations and sending tons of brick and plaster plummeting to the ground in a rain of death. And now the ruins had melted into furnaces, ejecting huge clouds of smoke that were transforming the blue heaven into a churning black shroud.

Adding to the terror was the great roar of escaping steam from a powerhouse on Stevenson Street, between the *Call* Building and St. Patrick's Church. The tall chimney stack atop the powerhouse fell and broke its steam pipes with a cacophonous boom at about the same time that the chimneys on the other two structures toppled.

"A tidal wave!" went the cry of many who mistook the roar for the sound of rushing water. The city would sink into the sea and everybody would die!

And even as some eastern newspapers reported this sensational rumor as fact, the rumor in San Francisco was that Chicago had "also" been engulfed by a tidal wave, that New York suffered worse than San Francisco, that Salt Lake City had disappeared, and that it was impossible to locate Seattle.

Only after the initial scare was it clear to San Franciscans that these rumors were false. Still, a catastrophe was demolishing a good part of San

Francisco, including such prominent structures as City Hall and the Hearst, *Chronicle,* Phelan, Crocker, Mutual Bank, Union Trust, Oberon, and Shreve Buildings. Even the new Flood Building, the largest office structure in the West and a shining symbol of the city's development, lay in ruins, as did Temple Emanu-El, an architectural marvel, and the Emporium, the city's biggest department store.

CHAPTER 18

The Puny Millionaires

WHERE COULD the fire be stopped as it worked its way to the north and the west? Mayor Schmitz and his men decided that a stand must be made at Powell Street, which stretched from Market northward up to Nob Hill, then swooped down to North Beach. Powell was edged by the expansive Union Square several blocks from Market and also by several large vacant lots beyond it, which could serve as firebreaks.

The structures along Powell were among the most prized and elegant in San Francisco, belonging to or catering to the superrich—not like the cheap housing south of Market where the poor workers lived. There was the huge Flood Building at Market, the St. Francis Hotel across from Union Square, and the still-unfinished Fairmont Hotel on Nob Hill.

Also gracing Nob Hill were some of the city's most magnificent mansions, including those of the "Big Four"—millionaires who had built the intercontinental railroad and accumulated enormous wealth through, many people felt, vast corruption and bribery: Leland Stanford, Collis P. Huntington, Charles Crocker, and Mark Hopkins. None of these men were alive, but their empires still cast a giant shadow over the economic and cultural life of the city. Prodded by social-climbing wives, these men each tried to erect a palace more splendid than those of others as an everlasting monument to himself and his huge bank account.

Where would they build these monuments? One barren hill had remained virtually unoccupied in the mid-1800s because it was too steep for a team of horses to negotiate. Once someone invented a cable system that could pull a coach up the grade, however, this seemed an ideal place to build a castle. From the top of the hill the Big Four could gaze down with kingly dignity upon the common people, people who were much like they had once been, but who were not clever enough to invest in the right mines and railroads.

The dignity of Leland Stanford, a vain former grocer who wanted to be loved, helped to gain him the presidency of the Central Pacific Railroad and the governorship of California. So dignified was he that he often pondered a question for a frozen minute, even one about how he was feeling, making the startled inquirer wonder if the man was actually alive. He seemed to come to life only when reading the laudatory editorials he paid an editor to write about him, and especially when his wife gave birth to a child in 1868. He pompously told guests, "I wish to introduce my son"— then had a liveried waiter uncover a silver platter on which lay the child in a bed of flowers!

The guests had more to admire than a plateful of his squirming offspring. The mansion he built atop Nob Hill, fashionably named after the nabob rulers of India, was more like a museum than a home. It boasted a Chinese amber glass skylight, a room furnished by the Chinese government, a mosaic-tiled Pompeian room, an East Indian reception room, an art gallery decorated with shrubbery that tinkled with mechanical singing birds, and a music room with a music box that sent classical notes thunderously reverberating throughout the house.

To Collis Huntington, who had once run a hardware store in Sacramento, the notes seemed flat. Stanford's role in building the intercontinental railroad, he would smirk, had been limited to turning over the first shovelful of dirt and driving the golden spike. Whatever Stanford's role, Huntington's was no less curious. The ruthless, sometimes vindictive purchasing agent of the Central Pacific, the giant among the Big Four, had a bribery payroll that included virtually the entire U.S. Congress. His power was so great that he rerouted the railroad when the town of Paradise, California, refused to shell out the money he demanded for laying tracks through it.

At the same time, Huntington, bald and burly, saved considerable money in obtaining the land on Nob Hill where he would build his home. When his business agent, who owned a house there, died, Huntington sent his condolences to the widow—together with a polite postscript informing her that her late husband had been bilking the company of a large sum of money. Shortly, the courts turned over the agent's estate to the railroad as compensation for the irregularities, and Huntington built a dream palace of his own. Did he have any principles? Yes, one observer would insist: "He was scrupulously dishonest."

Charles Crocker, on the other hand, retained some of the common man virtues of his earlier days. A huge man, he dug irrigation ditches in the San Joaquin Valley to shed some of his 265 pounds, supervising others in true blue-collar fashion as he roared "up and down like a mad bull." His wife, Mary Ann, however, wanted not a ditch but a dwelling—a palatial one. And Crocker agreed.

But when he tried to buy an especially desirable piece of land on Nob Hill, the owner refused to sell it. Crocker, however, had the last laugh, for he bought land surrounding the coveted acreage and built on it what one observer described as "a cross between a Moorish palace and a railroad depot," complete with wooden balustrades, scrolls, spires, gables, and a seventy-eight-foot observation tower. The stubborn neighbor found himself cut off from all sunlight, and Mary Ann finally had her palace, for the neighbor decided he preferred cash to claustrophobia and sold his land to Crocker.

Mark Hopkins, like Crocker, was essentially an unpretentious man driven by a socially ambitious wife, Mary. He didn't dig ditches, but, as a very frugal man, he rented a small cottage in San Francisco and spent much of his time puttering in his vegetable garden, even selling some of the produce to neighbors. Mary was humiliated. But let her husband earn a few dollars selling tomatoes; she would spend millions building a three-story Gothic-style mansion—called an "architectural monstrosity" by some—at the summit of Nob Hill. It would feature a turreted entrance, a seventy-five-foot-long oak-paneled dining room, a ballroom, a music room, and a library. Mary's bedroom would have a velvet-padded door, a ceiling aswarm with angels, and ebony-paneled walls inlaid with ivory and semiprecious stones.

But Hopkins would never have to give up his beloved garden for a world in which the only tomatoes he could savor would be served to him on a solid silver dish; he died before the mansion was completed.

All these stunning shrines to hyperinflated pretension were about to be challenged by a deadly reality.

With a small stream of water from an old cistern, firemen tried to fight the fire as it made its way up the hill, but after two hours they gave up when flying embers attacked the wooden spire of a church near Bush Street west of Powell. The fire line had been broken and the exhausted defenders fell back.

The people atop Nob Hill—who had earlier been captivated by the sight of the less affluent areas in the distance vanishing in an ocean of flame—suddenly had a change of heart. The mindless monster, unable to distinguish between the rich and the rabble, the patrician and the plebeian, was now threatening to devour *them*! Their magnificent San Francisco, built by their ancestors on a foundation of gold, was now to go the way of the shanties.

Especially critical to many of these people was the threat to the Hopkins mansion, which had become the Hopkins Institute of Art. Students and teachers, many sent from the University of California, as well as passersby forced to assist with a naval officer's gun in their ribs, frantically carted out hundreds of art treasures.

Urged on by Mayor Schmitz, who personally appeared on Nob Hill to oversee the struggle there, the rescuers deposited items on the lawn of the nearby forty-two-room brownstone home of James Flood, which strongly challenged the Big Four abodes in the competition for ostentatious splendor. This mansion, however, lay on a foundation of silver rather than gold. In his youth, Flood, wearing a tall silk hat and a business suit, had run a lunchroom next to the San Francisco Stock Exchange. While slicing roast beef he listened to the brokers boast of their stock picks. He invested accordingly and "naively" sank the profits into a speculative silver mining venture in Nevada. One morning he awoke to learn the mine, the Comstock Lode, had yielded silver worth $300 million, making him one of the world's richest men! He continued to sport his silk hat, but he no longer sliced his own roast beef.

It seemed appropriate that Flood's gambling spirit should watch over and perhaps save some of the country's most precious art in this time of desperation. The fire, it was hoped, would not damage the enormous spread of lawn, but it did. Most of the artwork was burned when the Flood mansion caught fire, though some paintings were saved by a professor who cut the canvases from their frames and rolled them up so they could be carried away.

By dawn Thursday, April 19, the gabled, castlelike home so meticulously built by Mary Hopkins, with all its turrets, stacks, and dormers, had also been reduced to a charred ruin. And on Friday, the mansions of the other three railroad tycoons suffered the same fate. Indeed, only a few chimneys and skeletal buildings, among them the Flood mansion and the Fairmont Hotel, which had been scheduled to open less than a month later, remained standing—giant hollowed-out tombstones against the scarlet sky.

Even the Fairmont barely avoided being turned to dust. On the first night of the fire, soldiers had stored fifty cases of giant powder in the hotel, and then, in the chaos that followed, forgot that the powder was there. But when the flames began chewing on a corner of the hotel, Police Chief Dinan suddenly remembered the explosives within and, in desperation, sent men to remove the boxes even if they had to die in the attempt. Braving the flying sparks and what seemed like the breath from a furnace, the men carried the boxes out of the hotel minutes before a great explosion would have scattered fragments of the building all across the city.

The fire was destructive enough, turning snobbish Nob Hill into another wasteland—a desolate plateau as bare and black as the impoverished area down below, south of Market. As one observer would say:

"The flames took all there was to take, after the earthquake had given it a mighty shake, as if to remind millionaires of their puniness."

CHAPTER 19

Not Even the Dead Were Safe

SOUTH OF MARKET, where Dennis Sullivan, under his plan, would have made an all-out stand and perhaps stopped the fire, had become a sea of flame by noon of April 18 from the waterfront west to Sixth Street. Many cheap hotels and lodging houses, together with rows of flimsy frame houses tilting against one another like broken toys—including the Dulberg family's shanty—tottered on their foundations, many sinking into the soft, filled-in land as the fire devoured them.

Despite the carnage, some of the tenants in these overjammed death traps, remnants of another age that smelled of rotten food and filth, were drunk and refused to leave their rooms until the last minute. One man even threatened officers with a gun before they threw him into the street. Another saved himself by jumping out of a window into a bedspread, which broke his fall even though he plummeted through it.

And still another, who had gone to bed drunk and thought the near destruction of his room was a nightmare, suddenly realized the nightmare was real when a child's foot poked through a crack in the ceiling, which closed immediately, severing the tiny foot. Driven almost mad, he leaped through a window but also managed to survive.

There were others who could not save themselves. One survivor, Edward Graff, would record in his diary:

We learn of the collapse of a lodging house on Seventh and Howard Streets with about seventy-five occupants. A number of us hasten thither to help rescue the unfortunates. One dead man is already stretched out on the sidewalk and his wife is bending over him greatly distressed. So complete is the wreck, so inextricable the mass, that an attempt to be of assistance is useless. As though this is not horror enough, fire breaks out among the wreckage to roast the poor wretches who are still alive. Leaving there we meet a poor mother piteously imploring for the rescue of her two babies who are among the entombed.

A doctor, Margaret Mahoney, would report: "One woman [who fled a burning building] tried to go back; her husband was there; she wished to die with him. God only knows how many perished. There must have been several hundred incinerated; many of them poor girls, outcasts for whom none will ever make inquiry."

Two men found themselves trapped atop the tall Shot Tower rising over the docks at First and Howard Streets as fire raged through the lower floors. They desperately pulled up buckets of water and spilled them on the flames, but despite their efforts the tower crumbled and they plummeted into the inferno. Tragically, tons of falling bricks buried many of the people who had been watching the drama from the street. One woman climbed out of the window of a house nearby and jumped to the street a second after the structure collapsed and began to burn. Of the forty people in the house, she was the only survivor.

Not even the dead were safe. A team of horses pulling a wagon loaded with bodies was trapped by the fire, and as the driver ran for his life, the corpses and the horses were incinerated in seconds.

But amid the horror, an old woman living in the area who had someone carry her furniture to the street refused to leave until she could find a wagon team that would transport these precious possessions elsewhere. Policemen finally stamped on the chairs and tables, wrecking them irreparably, and the woman tearfully agreed to leave just as the flames swept in.

In Brunswick House, one of many seedy hotels on Sixth Street, the hotel's owner, Thomas Bowes, and his fiancée, Edna Ketring, who were to be married later that day, slept soundly. When the building began to crack and echo with screams, Bowes stumbled out of his room and headed toward Edna's down the hall, crying out her name. He pushed open the door and was within four feet of her, his arm reaching for her, when the hotel collapsed and broke into three parts, two of them pitching into the street. The couple were buried under debris as the two stories above them fell in.

Somehow, Edna managed to extricate herself, but where was her fiancé? Was he alive, perhaps trapped under a beam? The young woman screamed his name and cried for help, her shrieks mingling with those of other victims in the hotel. But time had run out; dry, fractured lumber fed fires that had been ignited by electric wires, overturned stoves, and cracked gas pipes and were now already devouring the shattered hotel, a five-story-high wooden relic from the middle 1870s.

Even as smoke began to choke her, Edna desperately dug into the ruins with her bare hands. But finally, almost overcome by the fumes, with the crackle of fire and the rattle of death in her ears, she was forced to scratch her way out of the smothering dungeon of debris to the street, together with about fifty other survivors. Left behind were more than a hundred people, including Thomas Bowes, who would be incinerated dead or alive. The hotel literally fell to pieces.

Edna was inconsolable. Only four feet away . . .

AT THE NEVADA HOUSE, two buildings away on Sixth Street, William F. Stehr stood by the window watching in horror as the world disintegrated around him. Though he rented a room on the third floor, he pondered whether to jump to the roof of another smaller hotel next door. But as he wallowed in indecision, that hotel suddenly collapsed with a deafening roar and "spilled down in a cloud of dust from which I could plainly hear the agonizing screams of the inmates."

Hardly had Stehr put on his trousers and shoes when he heard another thunderous crash; Brunswick House had also flattened and was tumbling into a heap of ruins. Half-dressed, Stehr ran to the door and tried to open it, but it had jammed. Stehr would relate:

As I was tugging at it, I felt the floor tilting and sinking under me,
and I knew the house was going down like the others. So I hung on

instinctively to the door handle while the whole floor dropped. As it sank, I felt three distinct bumps as the lower floor collapsed in turn under the weight of the roof and the top story. With each bump came a frightful crash and cracking of timbers and glass and the cries of other people in the house who were being destroyed.

The cries of these people who were being killed, especially the women, were dreadful to hear. . . . Then came another bump, very sudden and very severe. The place fell in on top of me, the breath seemed to be knocked out of my body and I went unconscious.

CHAPTER 20

The Vengeful Demons

T HE FIRE that consumed many of these shattered hotels and lodging houses was sparked in a Chinese laundry on Howard Street near Third Street, not far from the waterfront. The earthquake had upset a stove, and the burning coals that spilled out set the frame building on fire. Soon this fire, joining with others, burned down the Grand Opera House where Caruso had sung some hours earlier, and finally reached its most auspicious quarry—the Palace Hotel.

The magnificent seven-story Palace more than lived up to its name. Built in 1873 to 1875, it was perhaps the leading symbol of San Francisco's leap from wild, isolated frontier town to sophisticated metropolis. One writer would claim that it "surpassed in size and grandeur all the hotels of America and Europe." Designed as an enormous quadrangle surrounding a glass-covered courtyard, it covered almost two and a half acres of land and achieved its splendor with the artful mingling of thirty-two million bricks and thirteen million square feet of marble.

The Palace was, in fact, the sturdiest, most earthquake-proof and fireproof building in San Francisco, thanks to the iron resolve of its builder, William C. Ralston, who spent $5 million to seduce the world's elite with the biggest and most elegant hotel anywhere. It was the final proof that

San Francisco had come a long way since those violent, lawless days when the city, riddled with bandits and vigilantes, was burned down regularly.

Personally, Ralston had come a long way since he served as a clerk on a Mississippi steamboat. He saved his pennies, invested in the Central Pacific Railroad and several other enterprises, started a Bank of California, then, like James Flood, grew fabulously wealthy when his investment in the Nevada silver mines paid off. His bank would soon resemble an ornate Roman temple, and the home he would build in a San Francisco suburb was even more lavish than those of the Big Four and Flood, with doorknobs and balustrades made of pure silver. So why not build the most luxurious hotel in the world?

Ralston expended so much money on the Palace and his own home that his bank was drained of most of its capital—in part, ironically, because Flood withdrew his own silver fortune from the vaults in order to start a bank of his own. Ralston shut the doors of his failed institution and, in despair, disappeared—into the soothing depths of the bay. But the Palace would remain his monument.

Built on massive, twelve-feet-deep pillar foundations, with two-feet-thick outer brick walls, the hotel was said to be strong enough to defy the blows of a wrecking ball. It had eight water tanks—one in the basement and seven on the roof—and five miles of piping connected to 350 outlets from which snaked about twenty thousand feet of fire hose. Three high-pressure pumps in the basement could maintain water pressure at a hundred pounds per square inch. And for extra safety, guards pressed electric buttons indicating all was well as they made their rounds every half hour.

Surely, it seemed, this monstrous home-away-from-home for princes, presidents, and other world dignitaries would escape the fate of the old, rundown hotels. Was it not built to withstand even the worst catastrophe?

Its most distinguished guest now was Enrico Caruso, who had gone to bed lighthearted, with the cheers of his audience still ringing in his ears. But he awakened terror-stricken, now hearing the crash of buildings blasting in them. According to his own account:

When I was awakened by the shock, I opened my eyes and said: "What is it?" I thought it was my valet, Martino, coming into the room to wake me. I thought he was shaking me. The next moment I thought differently. I sat up in the bed, which was rocking like a ship at sea. Everything in the room was going round and round. The chandelier was trying to touch the ceiling, and the chairs were all chasing each other. Crash—crash—crash! I jumped out of bed and ran to the window. I threw it open and looked out.

It was a terrible scene. Everywhere the walls were falling and clouds of yellow dust were rising. The earth was still quaking. My God! I thought it would never stop. I put my hand to my forehead and waited. It seemed like eternity.

Meanwhile, Alfred Hertz, Caruso's conductor, rushed into the suite to see if the singer had been injured. According to Hertz, Caruso "embraced me hysterically and, crying like a child, repeatedly insisted that we were both doomed."

Hertz tried to calm him, worrying that the shock might have ruined his vocal cords. Would Caruso ever sing again?

"Try to sing," Hertz urged him. "Sing, Enrico, sing!"

And Hertz joined him at the open window overlooking Market Street. Terror reigned. Women leaning out of windows in other buildings from which bricks and masonry streamed down were crying that everybody inside had been killed; teams of horses were breaking away from their drivers and stampeding down the street, some of them tripping over live electric wires and falling electrocuted; twisted trolley car rails were poking into the air like huge, bent paper clips; tugboats on the bay were wailing a shrill clamor, punctuating a "low grumbling [that sounded] like the roar of ten thousand lions," as one observer would say; a policeman running down the street as someone tried to stop him was yelling:

"Let me loose! The end of the world has come and I must report for duty."

Show the world, Hertz urged amid the pandemonium, that nothing could frighten Enrico Caruso.

The singer considered the challenge, his heart racing with fear, then reluctantly burst into song, emitting a few faultless notes, and it immediately became apparent that his voice was as rich and melodious as ever. But he remained in shock, explaining:

I ran to the door and out into the corridor. Such screaming I never heard in my life before. Everywhere women, men, children, running about in their nightclothes. I put on my trousers. Oh, first I put on my shirt. I did not take time to look for anything except my jewelry. I snatched up my watch, my diamond pin, and my rings. Then I did what you call—skiddoo. I was on the third floor, so I had to run downstairs to the lobby. I ran out into the street. By this time all the guests were running out of the hotel. I can never—no never—forget the scene.

We all huddled together for an hour, waiting for another shock. But it did not come then. No, it waited until we ventured back into the hotel—then it came. Again I ran out into the street. Oh, my poor heart—it was going now tum-tum-tum, very quick—like that!

After a while my valet, Martino, he got my trunk from my room. I would not go up, but Martino, he was the brave fellow. He put my clothes, my pajamas, into the trunk, but he forgot lots of things. Yes, he forgot my soap, my brush and comb, and other little things. But they do not matter. Ah, yes, I forgot, my opera costumes—they were all destroyed, my beautiful costumes.

Caruso had learned about this disaster when he started for the Opera House to salvage the costumes, only to be told that the building had burned down with the opera company's eight carloads of wardrobes and stage settings within. The first tremor had caused the world's largest chandelier to snap from its moorings and crash to the floor, where only a few hours earlier white-tailed and bejeweled operagoers had been seated. Caruso stared at the bearer of bad news, his face pallid and sweaty, and muttered, "Vesuvius!" The curse of Naples was pursuing him for refusing to sing in his homeland. The demons were out to get him!

And they seemed to catch up with him when he began to inhale the bitter scent of smoke. Other guests smirked at his flightiness as they anxiously milled about in the lobby, most of them dressed in nightclothes, some with bare feet bloody from stepping on broken glass. As one would later say of him:

"One incident struck me as funny and almost without knowing it I started laughing. It was Caruso, the famous tenor, who . . . was running about in the scantiest of attire, shouting excitedly and twirling at his mustache with unconscious nervousness, jostling everybody and not knowing where to go." (According to another witness, he was actually wearing "picturesque" pajamas, contradicting the singer's claim that he had put on his shirt and trousers.)

Josephine Jacoby, an opera singer who had performed with Caruso the night before, would say that the tenor "tore about in a frantic state, rejecting all attempts at consolation."

Yes, his voice was still sublime, Caruso concluded. But with the end near, would only the angels ever hear it again?

WHEN WILLIAM STEHR RECOVERED consciousness in the wreckage of the Nevada House, he thought he could hear the *angels* singing. Was he alive? Or was this some kind of dark heaven? He felt himself all over. Yes he was alive—though barely. All his bones were intact, but his whole body was bruised, and when he tried to raise himself he could not lift the debris locking him in place; his feet were pinned fast.

"While I was gasping for more breath for a second struggle," Stehr would say, "I heard somebody running over the debris over me, so I shouted for help as loudly as I could. No attention was paid to my calls; so I began to struggle again, and presently managed to release my feet. But I lost my left shoe. . . . Then I began to hear other agonizing screams for help, and screams of 'Fire!' And soon after I began to smell smoke, and I fancied I could hear flames crackling sharply. This made me struggle desperately, and soon I got my arms out over my head, and could feel an opening that led upwards on a slope."

Managing to squeeze through the opening, Stehr crawled along until he saw a glimmer of light and, spitting out the dust and plaster that bemired his mouth, ecstatically inhaled a breath of fresh air. But to move toward that light, he had to pull away the laths and plaster blocking the passage. Scratching away with his last strength, he managed to dig a hole that he could worm his way through. But his troubles were not over.

Stehr would continue:

I had to turn on my back and crawl upward through a sort of chimney that was bristling with nails and splinters of laths and plaster that tore my sides and my clothes. But eventually, I squeezed through and found myself sitting amid the ruins nearly on a level with the street, and all around me was ruin and debris.

I was too exhausted to mind much, and I was bleeding badly from a cut over the scalp. As the blood was running into my eyes, the first thing I did was to sit on the debris and tie my handkerchief around the cut on my head to stanch it. . . . As I was sitting there, trembling and trying to collect my scattered senses, a man . . . climbed up beside me with a bottle of whiskey and told me to take a drink. I took it and thanked him. It made me feel much better. Then he went off with the bottle to give a drink to somebody else.

I began to hear again the cries and shrieks that I had ceased for a time to notice. It was very dreadful when someone gave a long agonized scream when the fire caught him, and then ceased. . . . Somewhere near and behind me there was a cry. A woman had struggled through the ruins somehow, as I had done, and had got an arm through the debris and was begging for help. I ran over with some other men and began to pull away the boards behind which she was struggling. Soon we got her out and took her across the debris to the street.

Meanwhile, other men desperately chopped away with axes at the ruins to free a little girl, who was dragged to safety just before the flames reached her—thanks to people who held up a wet blanket between the diggers and the fire. They were too late, however, to save anyone else. One man who, like Stehr, managed to escape, told of two others caught in the ruins as the fire edged toward them.

"I'm not at all hurt," one of them said, "but there's a big beam across my back and I can't get out. I guess they'll have us soon, though."

"I could get out all right myself," the other man replied, "only my wrist is held tight in the timbers."

Within minutes, they were blackened corpses.

Somehow Stehr—bleeding, bruised, and utterly spent—defied the fire and managed to reach his telescoped room, hoping to save some of his possessions. He poked his arm inside but was able to pull out of a bureau drawer only two shirts and a suit of underwear. Yet, somehow these items seemed like cherished luxuries to a man returning from the dead—in a dirty shirt.

CHAPTER 21

The Tongue of a
Poisonous Snake

I N THE MECHANICS PAVILION, where patients escaping from
the Emergency Hospital in the shattered City Hall had been taken, it
was difficult to tell the wounded from the dead. Suddenly turned
into a makeshift hospital, this square barnlike structure sprawling between
Larkin and Polk Streets west of City Hall was a mecca for sporting events,
balls, fairs, revival meetings, and the first flickering silent films. The previous evening, beneath its high-vaulted ceiling, thousands had screamed
for their favorites at a roller-skating derby; a few nights earlier, boxing
fans had roared as Philadelphia Jack O'Brien knocked out Bob Fitzsimmons in the thirteenth round.

Now patients, doctors, nurses, and other hospital staff were docile and
silent, steeped in shock.

But calm soon turned into chaos as burned, maimed, mangled people
from all over the city arrived in every kind of vehicle and were carried in
on shutters, doors, or anything else that could serve as a stretcher, and laid
on the floor. Among them were survivors and dead brought over from St.
Luke's Hospital, which had collapsed, burying patients and medical personnel under tons of debris. The dead were hauled in and placed in a corner while doctors, Red Cross workers, Salvation Army volunteers, and
navy nurses from Mare Island rushed in to treat the injured.

Meanwhile, other volunteers seized cots, mattresses, and bedding from doomed department stores, hotels, and rooming houses, and a police patrol cleared a drugstore of bandages, splints, and other essential supplies. The splints would replace those made from packing cases. One young woman, a Salvation Army volunteer, seized a chair when she found a drugstore locked, and smashed in the glass doors.

Inside the Pavilion, a nurse assured a young, seriously injured husband and wife, lying next to each other, "Don't worry, you'll both recover soon."

"I hope so," the man replied, "but if we both don't live, we both want to die."

The assistant surgeon, Dr. Tilton Tillman, frantically dressed wounds, wishing only that he had enough instruments and equipment to perform operations on the most serious cases. How many more would join the dead before the day was over?

Chief Surgeon Dr. Charles Miller, his face gray and gaunt, took Dr. Tillman aside. Fires were threatening the Pavilion from three sides, he reported.

"It will burn like matchwood when it catches."

Driven by a furious wind, the Ham and Eggs Fire had caught the spires of St. Ignatius Church, perhaps the world's most beautiful Jesuit church, and soon the whole structure with its stunning murals and other works of art had become a flaming torch. Sparks from the fire were already dropping on the huge, dry roof of the Mechanics Pavilion and some shingles were smoking.

At about 10 A.M. someone yelled, "The roof is on fire!" even as wagons and cars were lurching up to the Pavilion with more wounded. Dr. Miller frantically ordered Dr. Tillman:

"Get all the patients on the Polk Street side of the building, and have them in double rows as close to the exits as possible. I'll give you express wagons there. Get the patients into them as quickly as you can."

They would be sent to the Presidio Hospital and other hospitals around the city and to Golden Gate Park, where an outdoor emergency hospital had been set up, with patients laid out on the grass.

The exodus began at about 11 A.M. Volunteers from the street carried patients in steady streams to impressed wagons, trucks, and automobiles,

some choking on the smoke and ash drifting in as the flames approached. Soldiers stopped one truck loaded with pianos and unceremoniously dumped them into the street to make room for patients. Orderlies, sweating profusely in the intense heat, desperately ran back and forth carrying the helpless.

"Hurry! Hurry!" people were pleading.

In the distance, they could see a tongue of flame suddenly strike at someone like the tongue of a poisonous snake, turning its victim into a ball of fire.

Finally the heat from the blaze became unbearable, and the driver in the last carriage pulled away from the Pavilion. But did the carriage transport the last patient? Many doctors and other medical personnel would insist that all wounded and dead had been evacuated. But others did not agree. One of the doctors helping in the evacuation would report: "We managed to get all the living patients safely out before the fire got too hot, but about twenty dead in one corner of the building could not be removed and were cremated."

And a Red Cross worker, O. K. Carr, would state:

I was with the Red Cross and still have my badge. We were in the Mechanics Pavilion after the quake, and when the fire came so close that we saw the building must go, all the injured that it was thought would recover were first taken away. Those with mangled bodies and broken or burned limbs begged to be shot to escape being burned alive. Three hundred and fifty in the Pavilion were chloroformed by doctors and nurses and shot by soldiers. It was done as an act of humanity.

I was among the very last to leave the building, and we did not leave a single person to be burned alive. I did not administer chloroform to anyone, nor did I put anyone to death. Only the doctors and regular nurses handled the drug, and the soldiers did the shooting. When official lists of the dead (in the city) are published and show only a few hundred dead, it is either from ignorance or willful suppression of facts. There were 350 who died in the Mechanics Pavilion alone.

Minutes after the exodus ended, the Ham and Eggs Fire devoured the Pavilion and roared on to swallow the ruins of City Hall with its public library of eighty-five thousand books and most of the city's records.

Whatever the truth, there were reports of other mercy killings during the disaster. An observer in another hospital would write that when the hospital seemed doomed, "there remained six patients who could not be removed" and "were given strong injections of morphine by the doctors and left to their fate." Moreover, soldiers shot two men in a mercy killing when the pair found themselves trapped on the top story of the Windsor Hotel on Market Street and were about to be burned alive.

THE MORGUE was soon packed with bodies, and the overflow had to be placed in the basement of the adjacent Hall of Justice. One observer would say:

"The abundance of death and disaster throughout the entire city was so terrible that the police officers who would ordinarily have taken pains to count and identify all the dead and injured persons in whose discovery or rescue they were concerned had no time to make records, notes, or inquiries. All they could do was help to dig out the killed and injured from debris that had overwhelmed them, and then commandeer whatever vehicles were available to take the dead to the morgue, and the injured to some hospital."

A police officer would report: "I was detailed to remain at the morgue and assist in removing the dead from the wagons . . . driving in by this time in an endless cavalcade. I was also to prevent the bodies being rifled of valuables by the ghouls and thieves that came along pretending to be anxious to identify their own dead. . . . The saddest thing I saw was a case where three bodies were brought in all clinging together. It was a young man, his wife, and their baby, all crushed and stone dead. We drew together two of the morgue slabs and laid them out all together, with the baby between the mother and the father."

And there would be more arriving from the various emergency hospitals, including those set up aboard steamers and other craft afloat in the bay.

But even death did not bring peace to the victims. The fire followed them, and Mayor Schmitz ordered that the bodies be removed to Portsmouth Square, where more than fifty would soon lie wrapped in winding sheets, to the horror of fleeing refugees who feared this could be their fate, too. Shortly, the corpses would be buried in shallow graves dug by prisoners from the jail in the Hall of Justice.

CHAPTER 22

The Angel and the Newborn

O UT OF THE SMOKE and dust, a man suddenly appeared with the providential alacrity of the angel who saved Isaac from Abraham's knife. He lifted the pregnant and abandoned Ida "McMahon" from the street and carried her to the Hearst Hall Maternity Hospital, her ten-year-old daughter following along. The next day Ida's baby was born, its first moments of life set against the backdrop of the firestorm raging only blocks away.

For the next few days Ida's rescuer, George Harrington, would not leave her side, day or night. He calmed her, assuring her that her daughter was being well cared for, that the wind was carrying the fire away from the hospital. She told him of the hard life she had lived with her "husband," and of his final betrayal. Ida and the stranger grew so close that when mother and daughter left the hospital, they took the ferry to Berkeley and moved in with their rescuer since their own home in San Francisco had turned to ash.

Days later the couple stood before Reverend C. K. Jenness in Berkeley's Trinity Methodist Episcopal Church and were married. At last the past had evaporated in the joy of a new life. But then Ida saw John McMahon sitting in the church audience. Why had the beast come?

The joy suddenly dissolved in a horrifying realization: Her phony husband had kidnapped their daughter, her bridesmaid, and disappeared into the wreckage-strewn street.

AS THE FIRE ROARED into the ramshackle district south of Market, an area built on "made" ground that would suffer more casualties than any other, refugees jammed the streets and ran westward. Many stormed into the car barn of a United Railroads plant hoping to find safety. But they were only reluctantly welcomed by a company official—a member of Mayor Schmitz's Committee of Fifty—who regarded the lower classes with disdain.

"One fellow," he would later say, "came along with a weeping jag and accosted me outside the plant.

" 'Well,' said he, 'I've lost a wife and five children; wouldn't that worry you?'

"I told him to go inside and go to sleep. You could scarcely keep these poor refugees out of the place. They seemed to permeate it like rats."

In a vain effort to stop the fire from spreading in this district, the military forced refugees at gunpoint to tear apart the outer walls of the tenements so that the roofs and floors would collapse inward. Other refugees were driven to an open area at the Third Street bridge by soldiers advancing with bayonets poised. A report in the *Oakland Tribune,* reflecting the sharp class divisions of the time, read:

> When the disaster occurred, Captain Dwight E. Aultman, with a squad of only ten men, fought his way from Folsom and Second Streets to South Park, driving an army of the rabble, men, women, and children, before him. Many of these people herded together were entirely or partially under the influence of liquor, and a little later, when the butts of the casks and barrels of a winery nearby were smashed and the liquor let loose, these people got down in the streets and drank their fill of the flowing streams.
>
> Captain Aultman . . . controlled that drunken mob with the handful of soldiers, although most of those held in check were led to believe that a much larger force was in charge of them.

According to the report, "the poorest of the poor, in fact the riffraff and scum of the city," had been "brought together in an effort . . . to ameliorate their condition," but while several doctors were available, proper facilities and supplies were not. One man had been shot in the finger—accidentally, the soldiers claimed—and had to have it amputated, though no anesthetics were available. He was plied with whiskey, then was held down by several people while the operation took place.

HOWEVER BAD the "condition" of the "drunken mob," no residents of this district south of Market felt more entrapped than the Dulberg family. After the midwife had fled their house in fear while the mother lay there with the infant, a girl, only partially born, seven-year-old Etta and her father were forced to complete the delivery—with the jolting help of another violent tremor—as smoke from the burning kitchen filled the room. The family was desperate. How could they escape with a newborn? Yet they must get away before the house collapsed or burned down. They tried the door but it wouldn't open, since the house had sunk into the ground. As Etta would describe the situation years later:

"Here we have Mother crying. The baby is crying. My father doesn't know what to do as he walked back and forth with his two youngest children in his arms. And we kids are crying. The kitchen is on fire. Everything is falling down and we can't open up the door."

Just when the family's fate appeared sealed, two teenage boys who lived next door peeked in the window at the behest of their mother, who was worried about her neighbors, knowing Rebecca was pregnant. The two boys broke the window and crawled inside, and, with great difficulty, battered down the door. They carried Rebecca and the infant outside on the mattress, and laid the mattress on the sidewalk, though streams of refugees were stumbling by.

"It's surprising that people didn't step on them," Etta would later say.

Bernard then went off and returned with a horse and wagon he had somehow found. When the mattress with mother and baby were placed in the wagon, Bernard drove to Mount Zion Hospital nearby and left Rebecca and the infant there. With his three other children, he returned to the house to gather their belongings—only to find it a mass of charred wood and all their possessions gone. The children, who wore only shirts, were crying for food, but there was none. Where should they go now? What should he do? A sympathetic passerby offered an answer: Go to Van

Ness Avenue—food was being distributed there. Bernard snapped his whip and the horse galloped off.

Though Van Ness Avenue, still untouched by fire, was lined with many mansions, there was plenty of room to set up at least temporary refugee camps on empty lots. As Bernard stopped in front of a camp and jumped to the ground, a militiaman approached him with rifle and bayonet poised. Pointing to some women making coffee, he brusquely ordered:

"Leave your three children with these ladies and come with me."

Bernard could not speak. He had lost everything he owned in the fire. Would he now lose his children, too?

CHAPTER 23

Criminals in Uniform

HERE WAS REASON to fear a military order in this city aflame, though many uniformed arrivals—federal troops, militiamen, marines, and University of California cadets—treated people with great sympathy and understanding. Officially, they were ordered to guard the mint and post office, assist the police in keeping the crowds away from dangerous buildings, patrol the streets to keep order and prevent looting, and help firemen fight the fire. At bayonet point, they prodded exhausted people forward, often up steep hills strewn with abandoned trunks in a desperate race with the flames.

And many did more. To stop the sale of food at exploitive prices, they forced grocers to give away their goods for free, sometimes throwing items into the air to be caught by those leaping highest. Some owners tried to find ways to save at least part of their stock. One terrified dealer nailed boards across his blown-out windows at four-inch intervals and permitted people to take only what they could reach through the slats.

From its own stores the army distributed food and other vital items like tents, cots, and bedding to the thousands of stricken refugees crowding the parks, squares, and military reservations. Some soldiers even gave up their own tents to the refugees and slept on the ground. Others dug latrines, banked up the earth around each tent to keep rainwater from running in, and leveled streets between the rows of tents so that refugees could more easily be found by relatives and friends.

But despite such efforts to help and protect the people, some men in uniform went wild and claimed privileges granted only under martial law, which was never proclaimed, though most people thought it had been. In fact, these soldiers, especially many young, frightened, undisciplined militiamen, often went beyond the bounds of what even martial law would permit, resorting to unlawful, often criminal activity.

Such activity was fostered by the lack of a command structure to oversee all the military forces that were deployed. Brigadier General Henry E. Noyes, a senior army staff officer, would later say that he deplored the "curious spectacle of a city patrolled and guarded by federal troops, state troops, municipal police, and amateur safety committees. As a result, there was continued friction and many clashes of authority."

Nor did the eventual division of the city into federal and state "occupation" zones prevent such clashes. The army was responsible for the less damaged area west of Van Ness Avenue, including Golden Gate Park and the army posts, where most of the refugees had fled. The militia, police, and "amateur" forces controlled the severely fire-torn eastern zone. But these lines blurred as forces "infiltrated" each other's areas to help keep order and—ostensibly—to prevent crimes.

Armed with orders to destroy all liquor stocks, many soldiers, mainly the militia and the irregulars, saw no reason to pour good liquor down the sewer when it could spill down their throats. The less desirable brands went to friends. When Supervisor Gus Hartmann, an acquaintance of one militiaman, asked him where he could get a drink, the guardsman replied:

"Why, that's easy."

And he backed toward the show window of a locked saloon, breaking the glass with the butt of his rifle.

"Here!" the militiaman said after pulling out three flasks and handing them to his thirsty friend.

Quickly realizing that someone might be watching, he continued with mock rage, "What are you trying to do, anyway? Get away from here! Clear out!"

And with a wink he roughly pushed Hartmann away.

Three full flasks! Hartmann was overjoyed. As a city official, he knew he shouldn't have encouraged his uniformed friend to disobey the order to destroy all bottles of alcohol. Still, this was San Francisco, where lawlessness was a kind of tradition. Now he could survive the fire in style.

As Hartmann walked jauntily down the rubble-paved street, he met a Red Cross nurse he knew.

"Oh, dear," she greeted him, "do you know where I could get a little whiskey? It's for my patients, you know."

Hartmann couldn't deprive the wounded of his magic potion. With a finger on his lips, he slipped the nurse a flask.

Farther on, another woman he knew stopped him and said she needed some whiskey for an injured husband. One more flask was sacrificed.

Hartmann now encountered a male friend, and he did not claim to have a needy relative. He needed, he said quite frankly, a drink to brace himself. Just a swallow.

Reluctantly, Hartmann drew him into a dark doorway and handed him his last flask. The man raised it to his lips and took a long, gurgling swallow.

"Wow! Ugh! Ur-rgh!" he cried, and he violently spat out what he had imbibed.

It was pure vinegar. The flasks in the window were dummies!

Many people, it seems, would have drunk the vinegar if that were the only available stimulant. Especially along the waterfront, where uncontrolled crowds rushed from saloon to saloon gulping down whatever they could get their hands on. Many would be injured or lose their lives when they became too drunk to get out of the way of the fire or of falling walls. Some even risked instant execution by refusing to help the firemen fight the fire or demanding to be paid for such work. Fire or no fire, how dare the government deprive them of their daily dose of spirits: Wasn't this San Francisco, the city of the hard-drinking forty-niners? A poem composed by an artistic alcoholic soon made the rounds, expressing the frustration of the city's barflies:

> *I haven't any money,*
> *And my credit, too, is gone;*
> *I didn't save the tickets*
> *For the things I had in pawn.*
> *I didn't mind the earthquake,*

Though it shook me out of bed,
And I didn't cuss the fire,
Though it made me beg for bread.
But I called myself a Spartan,
And prepared to face the worst
Till I found myself afflicted
With a cultivated thirst.
Then the awful conflagration
And the horror of the crash
Made an idol of the beer check
That I had and couldn't cash.

Soldiers, especially the militia and irregulars, got even drunker once they took control of the liquor supplies. Some even turned to looting, which they had been called in to guard against, and didn't even bother to hide their crimes. After all, who would shoot, or even arrest, a soldier?

At the corner of Leavenworth and Francisco Streets in the downtown area, several militiamen barged into a house and ordered the residents to leave immediately, claiming that the building was to be dynamited in order to stop the fire. The terrorized occupants rushed out but returned several hours later to find the house still standing and a soldier throwing loot out of their window. When they complained, the soldier replied:

"This house is abandoned!"

Typically, other soldiers in the area refused to arrest the military thieves.

SOME MEMBERS of the United States Army were as zealous as the militia in scrambling for loot. Regulars carried away about half of the supply of cigars from the store of Reynolds & Company, a tobacco firm. According to the owner's lawyers, the store "was entered unauthorizedly by soldiers of the U.S. Army, and looted of the goods contained therein. . . . This betrayal of trust by these renegade soldiers is an added aggravation to the crimes of pillage and loot."

One witness would state: "Upon many occasions, day and night, I saw United States regular soldiers jumping in and out of the ground floor windows of Renaldo's carrying goods away. . . . [And I] heard the soldiers [outside] give warning to their fellows inside [the] storerooms that their officers were coming and to beware."

Other witnesses saw regulars loot a clothing store, George & Company, swearing: "A company of United States regular soldiers were on duty in and around [the store]. . . . [I saw] many of said . . . troops going into and coming out of said L. George's. . . . Soldiers (and civilians, who were not challenged) were laden with bundles and boxes of clothing, underwear, overalls, shirts, etc., etc."

The situation grew worse when, on the first day, Mayor Schmitz issued "something like two thousand special officers' stars" to form "safety committees" reminiscent of the vigilante committees of the mid-1850s. These amateur law enforcers, apparently intended as another counterforce against Funston's units, were even more undisciplined than the state militia. On one occasion, when firemen and sailors were forced to retreat before the fire, a mob tried to loot food and clothing from stores in its path. Helping to lead the way, according to Navy Commander Pond, who attempted to preserve order, were the "special officers" of the safety committees.

"Many men, wearing special police badges . . . had already been passed inside our fire lines; but finding some of them bent more on looting stores than on helping us fight fire or preserve order, we had to cease recognizing that authority and to keep them out with the rest."

Though many civilian looters—denied the privileges of their uniformed counterparts—were shot on sight, looting had become so common that at least in one case, the table—or the couch, to be exact—was turned; a civilian looted a policeman's property while the policeman watched unfazed.

Soon after Patrolman Schmitt returned home following his close call with death in the produce district, the fire threatened to devour his own house. With the help of several soldiers, he managed to carry some of his furniture down the stairs to the street. But before they could complete the job, the roof caught fire, and in desperation the men threw a new couch out of the window. Schmitt would later say:

You talk about people doing strange things during that fire. There is no doubt that nearly everybody became half queer over it. I stood across the street watching my own couch drop to the ground. A man I did not know from Adam quietly walked over, picked up that couch—*my* couch—hoisted it on his shoulder and walked away with it.

Did I call out to him, or try to stop him, or run after him—I, a policeman, looking at a fellow walk off with one of my best pieces of furniture? Not a bit of it. I just kept looking at him. It did not occur to me that there was anything unusual, anything for me to worry about, in the man making off with my couch. But very often afterward, I wondered what had come over me, and was sorry for losing that couch when it was too late.

Nor was Schmitt alone in quietly watching the looter flee with the couch. His soldier friends also stood by and did nothing. After all, hadn't they also done what seemed quite normal?

Surprisingly, some military looters were generous, even trusting, with their victims. One such militiaman ordered a young man named Charles Drummond McArrow to help him search for firearms, which civilians were not supposed to own. The two broke into a glove factory, and the militiaman took a fine leather pair for himself. He offered McArrow a pair, but the man refused to take it. When they later pushed their way through a crowd of hungry people trying to storm an abandoned bakery, the soldier handed McArrow his rifle.

"Hold back the crowd while I take a nap," he ordered. "If they give you any trouble, stick the bayonet into them."

When the soldier awoke, he retrieved his rifle, handed McArrow two loaves of bread as a "gift," and released him.

LOOTING WAS NOT the worst crime committed by some military men. Taking seriously Mayor Schmitz's order that they were "not to arrest, but shoot down anyone caught stealing" (as he would state after issuing his written proclamation), some soldiers, often under the influence of alcohol, went on terrifying shooting sprees. According to one study, at least five hundred people were shot or bayoneted to death on the streets not only for looting but also for the slightest infraction of an order. The bodies of some were hurled into the fire or left for the rats. Often, many suspected looters were lined up and shot one at a time.

One survivor, Halvor H. Berg, would write to his family after the disaster: "One night in the park [the soldiers] shot forty men that was [*sic*] trying to rob."

Another observer, Frank Kester, would report: "A number of looters whose bodies I saw paid the penalty for their thievery."

A militiaman, according to a drayman named Charles Lawson, saw a looter who had "stolen some wine [and forced him to] dig his own grave before he shot him."

Still another soldier, seeing a man bending over what appeared to be a dead body, shot him, then threw the suspected looter into the burning ruins.

A glassblower named Clifford Bales would report: "I saw five men chained together by a stone wall and a soldier guarding them. I asked this soldier why. He said they were caught robbing the dead and had to be shot at sundown. My brother and I decided to see that, but we were about half a block from there when we heard the rifles crack. Oh, well, I guess you can't see everything."

But no one could miss the body of a man swaying in the wind from a telephone pole, left to be devoured by the fire. According to an observer, Tom Tyron, he had been caught robbing a corpse.

Military men shot or bayoneted almost any civilian who refused or was physically unable to clear streets of debris, or who was rummaging through ruins, not bothering to check whether the victims were trying to salvage their own property. Nor did some check whether store owners, realizing they would lose their merchandise anyway, had invited people to help themselves. And they killed anyone found carrying jewelry in his pocket, assuming the person was a looter.

Dr. Alfred Spalding, a survivor of the Mechanics Pavilion fire, would recall what happened to a drayman who demanded an excessive fee from a family whose baggage he had hauled:

"The drayman refused to give up the stuff. Soldiers told him to take the five dollars (he demanded twenty-five dollars) and unload. He again refused. Then they gave him three minutes to 'get busy,' and one held a watch. At the end of the time, the man still refused, and they ran him through with bayonets."

Spalding observed other killings as well: "All along the streets I saw dead bodies placarded 'shot for stealing.' Ten men were shot while trying to get into Shreve's. One man was shot for refusing to carry a hose."

Soldiers shot a deaf fireman who disobeyed an order he couldn't hear. They killed a woman who, claiming she was too weak to wait her turn, went to the head of a breadline and grabbed a bit of food off the commissary wagon. They shot to death a Red Cross official as his car passed a guard post, though a flag flew from his fender and witnesses said he wasn't ordered to stop. They killed a homeless woman in Golden Gate Park when she tried to take some supplies from a nearby tent in which, it turned out, family friends were caring for her three children.

Sometimes they spread terror by either firing into windows or knocking on doors and aiming their weapons at people, threatening to shoot, or actually shooting, if they thought they saw a glimmer of light in someone's house. The experience of Helen Huntington Perrin, a member of a well-known San Francisco family, was typical:

"Mother sent me downstairs to get a couple of brushes from a drawer in the pantry," Perrin would recall. Holding a candle, the young girl "found the brushes and turned to enter the front hall. The front door had been left open, and there in the center stood a man pointing two revolvers at me, saying something I couldn't decipher because of my terror.

"I screamed, 'Mama, mama,' and mother came rushing down the stairs with a lighted candle in one hand.

"The man said: 'Put out that light.'

"Mother replied: 'I have to have it to see.'

"Out went the light."

In another oft-repeated incident, it was not a light but a life that was extinguished. A soldier shot an old woman dead because she was reluctant to snuff out her lamplight—even as other soldiers themselves kindled a flame to brew coffee in Delmonico's Restaurant on O'Farrell Street. That fire roared out of control, fused with another fire, and left the retail district bounding Union Square in smoking ruins.

So common was the military violence that the civilians began to take it for granted. One woman who was watching the fire from a downtown street would report:

"A rough fellow, who had been standing by my side, tried to dart through the line. He looked like a beachcomber. A young lieutenant caught him by the coat.

" 'Here!' he called to his men. 'Shoot this man!'

"I hurried on, without looking back. I don't remember whether I heard a shot fired. But at the time it seemed so trivial a matter that I did not pay much attention."

It became so unsafe on the streets, not only for civilian looters but for all citizens, that even policemen refused to go into districts patrolled by the militia or irregulars, fearing they would be killed. Some, even though in full uniform, were stopped by these uniformed hoodlums and humiliatingly relieved of their revolvers and handcuffs. They considered themselves fortunate.

Teenagers, however, were usually shown mercy. If caught looting, they were simply forced to wear signs around their necks proclaiming I AM A JUNK THIEF. Women were sometimes luckier than men; they were beaten but remained alive. After risking his own life to help his elderly landlady escape the fire, professional nurse Henry Fichtner would report:

"Some of the soldiers acted like irresponsible wild beasts. I saw one soldier . . . beat with the butt of his gun a woman—apparently a servant girl—who wanted to get a bundle of clothing that she had left on the sidewalk in that block. This soldier was worse than a brute, and beat the woman fearfully."

Nor was the city safe for dogs, especially because of a rabies scare. Isabel Evans, a Red Cross nurse, would sob that "a United States soldier shot my pet dog for no reason whatever, so far as I was able to see."

Hers was perhaps the pet dog shot by a militiaman, who claimed he saw a fleeting shadow and fired at it without knowing whether it was a man or an animal. When questioned by his superior about this random shooting, he did not seem perturbed. Didn't his target turn out to be a dog?

Some canines fared better. In a guarded enclosure set off for lost and orphaned children in Golden Gate Park, where thousands of people took refuge, a dog ran under the ropes and scrambled around until it leaped into the lap of a little boy, apparently its master. But an unmerciful soldier seized the animal and kicked it over the ropes.

Shortly, however, the dog came back, but was thrown out again. When it returned once more, the soldier beat the animal and held him up for a comrade to run it through with a bayonet. An officer stepped in just in time to save the dog, and soon the boy, shaken by the near tragedy, was asleep with his head pillowed on the frail body of his beloved pet.

Another boy risked his life with even greater abandon to save a dog from certain death. Charles Nicholas Dray, known as Nick, had escaped from a Sonoma County poor farm and begged a well-known sportsman and munitions agent named Phil B. Bekeart for a job. Pitying the boy, who was hungry, dirty, and raggedly dressed, Bekeart agreed. Some days later, while the agent was away, the earthquake ravaged the city and the fire threatened Bekeart's place of business. The boy, who did not have a key, tried to enter the locked office so he could save his boss's papers, but to no avail.

Noting a big crack in the sidewalk caused by the earthquake, he jumped into the chasm, followed by Bekeart's retriever, Brownie, and managed to reach the office through the basement. He grabbed the records, climbed to safety, and hid the papers. But Brownie was nowhere to be seen. Nick rushed back to the building, and as he approached the crack again, a bullet whizzed by. A soldier was shooting, believing he was a looter.

But Nick would not stop. He jumped again into the crack and grabbed the dog, which had gone to bed in his usual place in his master's office. When the boy tried to climb out, however, he found himself staring into the barrel of a pistol.

He was only trying to save the dog, he cried.

The soldier gasped. Was he to believe that someone would risk his life simply to save a dog?

But he was a very good dog, explained the terrified boy.

And with the fire crackling around them, the soldier shrugged and guided Nick and Brownie through the smoke and flames, which minutes later would demolish the building.

"That's what I call a hero," Bekeart would later comment. "Nick can stay with me as long as I have a cent."

Brownie is thought to have barked, "Amen."

In some cases, civilians, caught up in the violence and terror of the moment, approved of the murder and mayhem. A mob strung up one man to a telegraph pole for cutting off a dead woman's hand so he could steal her bracelet. And no one complained when a soldier shot another man who threw himself on a corpse, feigning grief at the loss of his "mother" while he was actually chewing the diamond earrings off the woman's ear; the loot was found in his mouth.

R. F. Lund, a sales agent for a manufacturing company, would describe why he suddenly developed a killer instinct while walking down the street:

A rough fellow, evidently a south-of-Market street thug, was bending over the unconscious form of a woman. She was clothed in a kimono and lay upon the sidewalk near the curb. His back was toward me. He was trying to wrench a ring from her finger, and he held her right wrist in his left hand. A soldier quietly approached. He held his rifle thrust forward and his eyes were on the wretch.

Involuntarily, I stopped, and . . . my hand went to my hip pocket. I remember only this, that it seemed in that moment a good thing to me to take a life. The soldier's rifle came to his shoulder. There was a sharp report and I saw the smoke spurt from the muzzle. The thug straightened up with a wrench; he shot his right arm about his head and pitched forward across the body of the woman. He died with her wrist in his hand. It may sound murderous, but the feeling I experienced was one of disappointment. I wanted to kill him myself.

ONE ESPECIALLY gruesome incident followed the release of thousands of chickens from a freight car standing on a siding near the waterfront. Why not let the people help themselves before the birds were devoured by the approaching fire? But a drunken marine ordered one man who had grabbed two of the chickens to drop them. After hesitating at first, the man finally obeyed, and the marine, pointing his rifle at him, ordered:

"Come here, sir!"

The man walked several paces toward the marine, then hesitated again and turned back. In fury, the marine ran after him and pricked him in the back with his bayonet. Wheeling around, the man jerked the gun from the marine's hands and began running away with it. An army officer, Captain Ernest Denicke, who witnessed the incident, drew his pistol and ordered the man to stop. When the panicky fugitive continued to flee, Denicke fired and gravely wounded him. For hours, the victim lay on the street unattended and unconscious, until he finally died.

People nearby who might have helped him fled the scene when soldiers began firing at them. The following morning, about fifteen hours after the man was shot, a sergeant weighted the body with irons and threw it into the bay.

The unfortunate man's family would never learn what happened to him. Surely not from military officials, who desperately sought to cover up the crimes committed by the city's protectors. Major Carroll A. Devol, a quartermaster who wrote of the army's role in the disaster, would claim that no regular soldier had killed anyone and that irregulars had killed only three people!

And General Funston himself would agree. Obviously wishing history to record only the fine job many soldiers did easing the misery of the people, he would say:

"San Francisco had its class of people, no doubt, who would have taken advantage of any opportunity to plunder the banks and rich jewelry and other stores of the city. But the presence of the square-jawed, silent men with magazine rifles, fixed bayonets, and with belts of cartridges restrained them."

Some of these men were silent indeed, but only to conceal their irresponsibility and often their crimes.

CHAPTER 24

Bringing Out the Best

ONE REASON for the rampant civilian crime lay in the absence of policemen on the fire-baked streets. The San Francisco force was relatively disciplined despite joining the political leaders in bribe taking. With the army and other military forces on patrol, many policemen raced home, not only to avoid being shot by irresponsible military men—as some of them were—but to be with their families. Navy Commander Pond, whose tug helped fight the fire, would write:

"For four days and nights following the quake, I did not see a single uniformed policeman anywhere in the entire waterfront district of San Francisco."

Navy men, Pond reported, "had not only to fight the fire but to police and patrol the districts in which we worked."

Yet some policemen courageously remained on the job throughout the crisis. One ran to his station after the earthquake even though his two children were dying from injuries, and another told a reporter:

"I saw my house burning a few moments ago. God help the wife and kiddies; I can't. [I'm] on duty."

Some police reports reflected the odd behavior of people—and animals—suddenly thrust into a momentous life-threatening calamity. Thus Officer George R. Grunwald would report:

"I secured a buggy and went to the corner of Fifth and Market Streets, where I found a man tearing out his hair by the roots. I placed him in the buggy and took him to the City Hall where I left him.

"Leaving the north side of [Pacific Street] five cats crawled with pantherlike steps to a house that was blazing on the south side. They went under the steps of this house and were consumed in the flames."

ONE SENTIMENTAL POLICEMAN won the everlasting gratitude of countless children when he helped them realize an impossible dream. A police line stopped all people from approaching the corner of Polk and Sutter Streets, which was about to be dynamited. Many children had come, as if to a funeral, to watch the demise of the famous Blum's Candy Store on one of the corners.

Noting the expressions of sorrow on their faces, the policeman paused for a moment, as if about to render a momentous decision, then said gleefully:

"Go ahead, kids. Help yourselves to the candy. And be quick! We're going to dynamite the place."

One of the children, Sol Lesser, would recall years later: "This was a real dream come true. All that good candy! The whole bunch of us kids went in and helped ourselves to the candy in boxes, which we piled out on the sidewalk. We had been told to take all we wanted and we did just that. We got hold of a Sutter Street cable car caboose from the car barn across the street, pushed it in front of Blum's and loaded it with candy—marshmallows, jelly beans, jujubes, chocolate chips, and all-day suckers. All the things that kids went for."

Hardly had the last jelly bean been tossed into the caboose when the dynamite went off. The boys congratulated one another. What a haul! Sol Lesser would relate:

"We loaded the car with as much candy as we could get into it and decided to take it to our neighborhood to distribute. We had to push the caboose uphill three blocks to the top. . . . Each of us went around to the various neighbors and offered them free candy. Some took the candy doubtfully. Others didn't quite understand and didn't take any, so we got stuck with a lot of it. We stashed away what was left in cellars and other remote places for some possible future use."

Even the luster of a dream fulfilled could sometimes grow dim—
especially after a bellyache. But the memory of that kindhearted policeman would never dim in the minds of those young dreamers. Indeed,
almost eighty years later, Lesser would muse:

"I wonder if that candy which we hid . . . might still be there."

WHILE THESE STORIES suggested a certain human concern about the
condition, fate, and even mood of living beings, some policemen even
risked their lives to help civilians in trouble. Police Sergeant William M.
Ross was one such officer. On the morning of the earthquake, his wife's
uncle, an elderly man who lived with them, had failed to come downstairs
from his room. Ross ran up and found the uncle barely alive, caught in
his folding bed, which had jackknifed when the tremor struck. Ross rescued him, then rushed off to ease the plight of others on this terrible
morning.

On Market Street near the Ferry Building, he joined several other
policemen who were trying to keep people from entering the blazing
financial quarter to recover money, important documents, and other valuables from the safes in their offices. But Ross became leery of this attempt
to stop them.

"This I thought was wrong," Ross would explain, "save in cases where
the danger was so grave as to make the adventure altogether perilous.
Therefore I gave orders that all such men whose bona fides seemed clear
should be assisted in, and not prevented from, undertaking such attempts
at salvage."

It didn't seem fair to him that people should lose all their assets, perhaps everything they had ever worked for, if their lives were not in grave
peril. And he was especially sympathetic to their pleas because he was so
proud of them.

"The nonchalant way in which everybody was apparently oblivious to
great losses and afflictions," Ross would say, "and withal was grateful for
the smallest courtesies, was one of the queer things about the whole disaster, and I don't think it could have happened in any other community."

So when one well-dressed businessman accosted him, pleading that he
had to get through to retrieve vital papers, Ross agreed.

Where were these papers?

In a safe in an office building on Sansome Street, just two blocks away, the man said.

"Go ahead and get them," Ross replied.

But the man now looked down Sansome Street, where many buildings were on fire, and seemed to hesitate.

"Come along," the sergeant prodded him, "I'll go with you."

And the two men started down the west side of Sansome Street. As they passed a fiercely burning building on the east side, Ross said:

"I don't like the looks of it. We had better run by here."

Hardly had they started running when an explosion roared inside the building and the whole front bulged out and toppled into the street, just as Ross pulled his companion into the doorway of an office building on the opposite side.

"The smoking bricks and mortar came pelting in after us and rolling onto our feet," Ross would relate.

Two officers standing farther down the street saw what happened and despaired of seeing their comrade again.

"That's the last of Ross," one of them said sadly.

But it wasn't. Ross and the businessman continued on to the man's office building. Seeing that it was not on fire but that the adjoining structure was, Ross told the man he should hurry and get his papers.

"I'll watch out," he assured him, "and shout up a warning to you if I think there is any danger."

The man looked at the flames crackling all around.

"I don't think I want any papers now," he moaned.

And he rushed back toward Market Street.

Ross was dispirited, wondering what those papers were really worth. But he was a policeman, wasn't he? He was supposed to help people, even if it meant the last of Ross.

As Sergeant Ross demonstrated, while the horrors of the catastrophe sometimes brought out the worst in people, it also brought out the best. And E. E. Bowles, a writer for the *Chronicle,* would report on other examples of the best:

"The thing that impressed me most was the leveling effects of the two disasters on the human family. I have seen sworn enemies for years meet in the street and in the presence of all clasp hands while their eyes filled with tears. I have seen women and babies in tattered calico, and I have seen those same richly dressed women nursing the babies while the tired mothers rested. I have heard rich restaurateurs, noted for their parsimony, call out while standing in their places of business, 'Help yourselves, your money ain't worth a damn today.' "

CHAPTER 25

The Case for the Fire

WHATEVER the worth of money, Amadeo Peter Giannini was determined not to lose a single dollar. As the head of the Bank of Italy, he could not allow his depositors to accuse him of abandoning the assets they had entrusted to him—fire or no fire. Especially since his institution was a "people's bank," and he had personally persuaded many of his clients that their money would be safe with him.

If on the night before the quake Giannini had gone to bed confident of the future, he awoke the next morning wondering if he still had a bank at all. He rushed out of his home in San Mateo to the train that would take him the seventeen miles to San Francisco. When he found that it was not running, he started to walk, then hitched rides in several horse-drawn wagons, which were barely able to move forward since the roads, cracked open and blanketed with debris, were clogged with refugees fleeing in the opposite direction.

He grew more pessimistic as these refugees hysterically shouted tales of catastrophe. People had been crushed under collapsed houses or burned alive; looters were being shot on sight; children were running around looking for their mothers. And as he inched ahead, their stories seemed confirmed by the sight of flames licking a blackening sky over the south-of-Market area. What if his bank with all its invaluable contents had vanished in the disaster? His depositors, the little people, not to mention Amadeo Giannini, might lose everything and perhaps would not be covered by insurance. . . . If only the wagon would move faster!

Finally, after five hours, at noon, Giannini reached his bank, which he was relieved to find still standing and with little damage. That morning, his assistant cashier and a clerk had arrived shortly after the earthquake, and, as on every morning, took a horse and buggy to the Crocker National Bank to pick up the Bank of Italy's cash—about $80,000 on this day—which was kept in the Crocker vaults for lack of safe facilities in Giannini's bank.

On arriving at Crocker, they found the bank in chaos as distraught customers rushed in to deposit valuables in the vaults, believing the fire could not penetrate such armor. At the same time, bank officials were moving out records, securities, and gold—to be put on a boat that would remain in the middle of the bay. Other big banks stuffed records and cash in fireproof vaults.

Giannini was dismayed when he saw the bags of valuables back in his own bank. Why hadn't his assistant and clerk left the bags in the Crocker vaults? Where would they be safe now? He decided on a daring move. The valuables and other portable items—except a $375 adding machine, which Giannini deemed an unnecessary luxury—must be carted to his home in San Mateo. He would be taking a huge gamble, since all this wealth and other belongings could end up in the hands of thieves, military or civilian.

Giannini found a second horse and wagon team with a driver, and even as the pungent smell of smoke began to irritate his nostrils, the heavy canvas bags bulging with the bank's cash and gold were thrust into the wagons and hidden under orange crates, with sacks of records and other items piled on top. Then, with Giannini holding the reins in the first wagon and his two employees crowded into the second one, the two teams of horses jerked ahead on the perilous journey.

It was a journey that could end Giannini's career, and perhaps his life. But it might also provide the seed for an even more illustrious future for his bank and the poor people it served, elevating their economic status and, with the fire already helping to level the classes, their social standing as well.

BRINGING TOGETHER people who had been traditional class enemies was not the fire's only positive effect. It had an especially salutary effect on the health of some individuals.

Police Sergeant Edward Ward, a victim of tuberculosis, expected to die soon and was hoping to live a tranquil life in his last months on earth. But suddenly the earthquake and fire had turned his life into a nightmare. The nightmare grew unbearable when a friend rushed to Ward and blurted that the sergeant's mother had been a victim. While fleeing from her home during the firestorm, she had collapsed in the street and, though in good health, had died of shock.

Ward ran to her home and found that some soldiers had placed the body in a trench nearby and were about to cover it with earth. Breathlessly, he stopped them. Then he lifted his beloved mother out of her grave and carried her to a house seemingly out of range of the fire and pleaded with the occupants to let him remain there with the corpse until the fire no longer threatened and he could bury his mother in the family vault.

But hardly had they agreed when the fire inched closer, and he was on the move again, pursued from house to house. Finally, drained of all strength, he asked some soldiers to help him bury his mother. They placed her body once more in a trench, where it would remain until the fire was conquered.

Wracked by tension, fatigue, and grief, Ward felt he would soon be buried beside her. After all, the doctor had told him that he must not tire himself or suffer stress if he wished to stay alive very long. After this terrible physical and emotional experience, how many days could he have left? The fire would surely exacerbate his already critical condition.

But then, to his utter amazement, he suddenly developed a hearty appetite and stopped coughing. He found he could tramp the street with the same vigor that had energized him when he was a patrolman.

When he returned to police headquarters, the police chief offered him time off despite the fire, and said that perhaps he should retire.

Retire? But he never felt stronger, Ward replied. He was cured! The shock and exercise, it seemed, had produced a miracle. And Ward returned to work, helping to keep order during the disaster. He continued to grieve for his mother, of course; but wouldn't she be happy knowing that her death had, strangely enough, revitalized her son?

JACK BROWN, who was paralyzed from the neck down, had an equally extraordinary experience. When the fire sizzled its way toward his house, friends placed him on a mattress and carried him and two suitcases packed with things he valued to a nearby park. They left him there, with his grips beside him, and promised to return in a few hours to take him to a shelter beyond the fire zone.

After about half an hour, a stranger approached and eyed the baggage, then turned to Brown and asked, "Your bags?"

The invalid nodded affirmatively.

"Paralyzed?" the stranger asked with a smile.

Another nod.

"They *were* your bags," said the man. "They are mine now."

And he picked them up and started to leave.

"I was so mad," Brown would later say, "that I forgot all about the paralysis. For the first time in years I felt the blood surging through my veins. I jumped up, seized a billet of wood, and smashed it on the fellow's head."

When Brown's friends returned, they were dumbfounded to find him waiting for them standing up, with a suitcase in each hand. He was no longer paralyzed and showed no signs of any disorder other than a peculiar twitching of his lips when he told them he wouldn't need the mattress anymore.

ANOTHER handicapped refugee, Gimpy Bill, would never recover from his disability. He couldn't get back his two legs and could depend only on his little "car" to keep him in front of the fire. As the heat of the flames wrapped him in sweat, he paddled on, his heart pounding, his ravaged body numb, his mind aswirl in a blur of chaos.

Suddenly, an automobile chugged to a halt beside him and a soldier stepped out. "Better come with me," he said as he lifted Gimpy Bill into his car.

Shortly, Bill found himself a refugee in Golden Gate Park. Without legs, he had traveled over fourteen miles to safety.

The fire had made it clear: All he needed was a heart to survive.

SOME PEOPLE showed heart in more joyful ways—at least those who took refuge in the Woodland Burial Park. Their joy, to be sure, was tainted by an underlying terror, but it was precisely to suppress their anxiety that they affected normality. One refugee dragged a piano into the cemetery and joined up with a musical team from a dime vaudeville house to stage impromptu concerts for their fellow refugees. Thus, while San Francisco burned, the strains of a guitar, mandolin, banjo, and triangle strumming out popular ballads like *Wait Till the Sun Shines, Nellie* echoed irreverently over the graves, drowning out the crackle and thunder of the flames.

These musicians were not alone in their morbid revelry. A few blocks away a grizzly old man sat on a curb passionately playing his violin in the shimmering shadow of the fire, a modern-day Nero fiddling while his city burned. At the same time, an equally audacious woman on a nearby street madly rapped out the tune *It's a Hot Time in the Old Town Tonight* on a tinny old piano.

In the cemetery, more disturbing than the fire, it seemed, was a fussy old lady who arrived with a parrot and a sofa someone rolled in. The parrot refused to stop talking during the concerts, and its owner, in horror, moved to a more distant tombstone after someone threatened to throw the bird into the meager dinner stew. And the band played on.

Many San Franciscans would join the merrymakers in the cemetery, but they wouldn't be able to hear the music. They were corpses. Victims who perhaps suffered the least were those—often entire families—who suffocated to death in their homes. Some stray dogs, mad with hunger and fright, chewed at the remains of people they had found half-buried in the wreckage.

For some San Franciscans, survival was not their only major concern. There were, for example, those who could not stop counting their material losses. George Chase, an auctioneer, had a special reason for his sorrow. In his rush to gather the family valuables before fleeing the fire, he tossed a diamond sunburst, a diamond pin, a gold watch, several gold rings, and considerable cash into a box that closely resembled another one containing candy. His wife mistakenly packed the box of candy and left the box with the jewelry to vanish in the firestorm.

It was the last the family would see of their treasures, but there was plenty of bitter candy to eat.

CHAPTER 26

A Proud Ending

I N THE PALACE HOTEL meanwhile, Enrico Caruso was determined to save his own treasures—several trunks full of American
and Italian finery, innumerable photographs of himself, and other
invaluable possessions. With none of the five hydraulic elevators working,
he, his valet, and other opera company figures had dragged the trunks
through the wide, red-carpeted hall and down the stairway to the sidewalk,
where they hoped a wagon driver could be flagged down and persuaded to
take the group and their baggage to safety.

Meanwhile, with the dining room closed down, Caruso shambled over
to the St. Francis Hotel nearby, muttering.

" 'Ell of a place! 'Ell of a place!"

Though ravenously hungry, he had to settle for a simple breakfast of
bacon and eggs. Unfortunately, the earth had quaked before he could
enjoy the Palace's famous luxury breakfast: a three-egg omelette, twelve
Olympia oysters with cream sauce, a half jigger of sherry, and a teaspoon
of grated cheese—a meal fit for the world's greatest tenor. After gulping
down the last bit of bacon, he tipped the waiter and the cook a generous
$2.50 each—the meal itself was free—and returned to the Palace just in
time to see four Chinese men making off with one of his trunks.

His shirts! His striped trousers! Even a photograph with President

Roosevelt! Thank God he had a gun and had learned to use it. He drew the revolver, aimed it at the culprits, apparently not realizing that he had neglected to load it, and cried.

"Give me my trunk or I will shoot you!"

The four men merely smirked at this strangely comic figure shakily waving a gun. Then, just as a soldier approached, Caruso's valet, Martino, appeared, according to one account, and explained that he had hired the four men to carry the trunks downstairs to the street so they could be placed in a vehicle. In any case, the soldier took the weapon from the overwrought singer, and the "thieves" dropped the trunk.

Caruso would not admit he had erred. He had saved his trunk, hadn't he? That would teach them to fool with Enrico Caruso! Now he had only to escape the spreading fire.

A fellow singer, Antonio Scotti, found a wagon driver whom he paid $300 to drive Caruso, several colleagues, and their baggage through the wreckage-strewn streets to a friend's house in the suburbs. Once there, Caruso refused to sleep indoors. The house had been shaken by the earthquake—what if the roof caved in?

"Vesuvius!" he kept repeating.

And he lay all night under a tree in the backyard.

Next morning, the group set out for the bay, where they met with other members of the Metropolitan Opera Company. While Scotti was arranging for a launch to take them all to Oakland, Caruso disappeared for some unknown reason. With everybody aboard and the launch owner insisting they leave, a search party went out for him. Oh, God! Would they find him buried under a pile of bricks?

Finally, they spotted his stocky figure at the dock gate, where he was shouting English-Italian gibberish to officials while wildly waving the portrait of himself and President Roosevelt. One official, utterly bewildered, eventually relented and let him pass. And so Caruso reached the safety he craved at last.

The fiery tenor would never return to San Francisco after this experience, which, he would say, gave him a premonition of violent death. Nor would he travel in the future without his own down pillows, linen sheets, and a special double mattress. Perhaps greater comfort would help him forget that another disaster could befall him at any moment.

* * *

LESS FORTUNATE than Caruso—who escaped from San Francisco having lost only peace of mind and the costumes that identified him as a swashbuckling hero—were some other guests of the Palace and its annex, the Grand Hotel. When the earthquake struck, one man in the Grand Hotel, Guion H. Dewey, suffered a broken jaw when a chimney collapsed into his room in an avalanche of bricks and mortar. Managing to drag himself from the debris and escape to the street despite his terrible pain, he went in search of a doctor. Later, in a letter to his mother, he described the nightmarish odyssey, albeit tempered with dashes of compassion, that he witnessed that day:

> I saw innocent men shot down by the irresponsible militia. I walked four miles to have my jaw set. A stranger tried to make me accept a $10 gold piece, I was threatened with death for trying to help a small girl drag a trunk from a burning house, where her mother and father had been killed. A strange man gave me raw eggs and milk, and offered me his own bed in his house, which had not been wrecked (this is the first food I had had for twenty-two hours). I saw a soldier shoot a horse because its driver allowed it to drink at a fire hose which had burst.
>
> I had a Catholic priest kneel by me in the park as I lay on a bed of alfalfa hay, covered with a piece of carpet, and prayed to the Holy Father for relief for my pain and ease to my body. I saw a poor woman, barefoot, told to "Go to Hell and be glad for it," for asking for a glass of milk at a dairyman's wagon; she had in her arms a baby with its legs broken. I gave her a dollar and walked with her to the hospital. I saw hundreds of men with bottles of whiskey tied up in the remnants of bed clothes, begging for food, and I saw men with the Red Cross on their arms looting stores.

When Dewey had found a doctor and been treated, he tried to return to the Palace annex to retrieve his baggage, but the building had become a roaring furnace. Though it had state-of-the-art fire-fighting equipment, the hotel's water supply had been usurped. Firemen had stretched hose from the hotel supply to blazing Market and Sutter Streets, some distance away. And so the Palace Hotel, its reservoir of water exhausted, was left to burn on this first afternoon of the fire. As one observer would sadly, if nostalgically, recall:

> With its flag flying as proudly as ever, the famous pile awaited the inevitable. Soon flames fastened themselves upon it; gradually they spread from room to room and from floor to floor, working their way slowly downward from the roof. The interior, with its rich furnishings, became a seething furnace that burned till late in the afternoon; finally there remained only the massive brick walls, standing as staunch as ever, undamaged by either the earthquake or the fire. Ablaze it was magnificent; burned, it became a majestic ruin, with a dignity and beauty all its own.

With almost the whole of old San Francisco south of Market now a smoldering prairie, the fire rapaciously spread north of Market to fuse with others that had erupted there. The merged flames then ate their way, slowly but certainly, through the more resistant brick, steel, and stone jungle of modern buildings in two directions, one toward Telegraph Hill and the other toward Chinatown.

CHAPTER 27

Ravagement, Racism, and Rats

A S THE FIRE neared Chinatown, only nine blocks south of North Beach, the concern of Del Crespi's family approached alarm. His mother kept talking about her husband. What had happened to him?

"The more she talked about my father," Del would say, "the more I kept thinking about Lillian and about how she was going to get home."

He walked four blocks south to Filbert Street, as he had so many times, "to see if by chance Lillian and her folks had come home." They hadn't returned, and "when I saw that door again the same sickening feeling crept over me, and that sound came back to me." Then he looked across the street to the newly built Hancock Grammar School, which they had attended together, and dreamed of the moment when they would meet there again—if God would only make the wind shift. For the fire was heading north toward Chinatown, and Chinatown was only five blocks south of Filbert Street.

Del walked back the same way he had come, his "Bridge of Sighs," as he would call the stretch. And then it struck him—Chinatown was within view of his own house. His family had better prepare to flee. And they couldn't wait for his father.

* * *

"DURING THE EARLY HOURS, Chinatown seemed fairly safe," Hugh
Kwong Liang would say in describing his reaction after he saw smoke and
flame rising in the distance. "There was that big playground [Portsmouth
Square] at Brenham Place above Kearny Street, with Washington Street and
Clay Street on each side. There were no buildings, only trees. It seemed
unlikely that the flames could leap over the big playground to Chinatown."

After all, hadn't Kwan Tai, the warrior god, promised that no one
would have to leave?

But Kwan Tai was wrong. Since little water was available to fight the
fire outside of Chinatown, General Funston, hoping to create a firebreak,
had ordered his men to blow up buildings bordering on the area. Apparently unknown to him at the time, the officer supervising the detonation,
John Bermingham, was intoxicated; the man would later admit to having
inadvertently started sixty other fires by using explosives. Now, at the
southeast corner of Clay and Kearny, the officer ordered his soldiers to
destroy a drugstore with a rooming house upstairs, using black powder.

Shredded, blazing bedding from a window of one of the rooms flew
across Kearny to another lodging house on the west side of the street at the
edge of Chinatown. This house was ignited, and soon Chinatown was
ablaze, with a strong wind carrying the flames across the "big playground."
The Fire Dragon had taken over and begun to ravage the community.

To the tortured disillusionment of the people, the temple of Kwan Tai
was one of the victims, ironically blown up by soldiers to keep the fire
from spreading—though the temple keeper managed to save the statue of
the now discredited god. What was more terrible, many asked—betrayal
by one's favorite god or destruction of all of one's earthly possessions and
what appeared to be the end of the world?

Hugh and his cousin quickly threw as many belongings as they could
into their trunks and dragged them out to the cracked cobblestone street.
The area was now teeming with partially clad people escaping shattered
houses and desperately running with bundles swung on poles across their
shoulders, the women hopping on shrunken bound feet with children
clasped to their bosoms.

As they ran, flames began to engulf familiar places such as the Restaurant of the Ten Thousand Flowers, the central police station across from

Portsmouth Square, where Robert Louis Stevenson used to sun himself surrounded by Chinese children, the queue-trimming and ear-scraping shops, the headquarters of the tongs on the Street of the Temple of the Empress Mother of Heaven, the fan-tan gambling houses on Fire Escape Alley, and the incense-perfumed bordellos along the Lane of the Golden Chrysanthemum. Only the red-bricked St. Mary's Church, its bell tolling wildly in weird disharmony with temple gongs, as if proclaiming Judgment Day, appeared to shake off the flames, the inscription under its tower clock reading with brutal irony:

"Son, observe the time and fly from evil."

Some Chinese rushed to a nearby white area still untouched by the fire and knocked on doors to ask for temporary shelter. But most were turned away. One mother's request for milk for her baby was met "with either unopened doors, angry looks, or howling epithets," a member of the family would report.

"Chinks," she was pointedly informed, "should take care of themselves!"

To the embarrassment of the bigoted whites, some Chinese took care of *them*. Theater critic Ashton Stevens, John Barrymore's friend, had fled barefoot from his hotel to nearby Portsmouth Square, which seethed with Chinese refugees. One of them noted Stevens's bare feet and said, "A pair of socks will warm your feet. Come with me. I own the drugstore next door to the Chinese doctor."

Soon Stevens was wiggling into the socks. He offered the Chinese man a dollar in payment.

"If you helped me when I was barefoot," the man replied, "what would you say if I offered you money?"

Later, Stevens would write of his "sneaking regret that any part of my boyhood had been given over to stoning Pigtails."

Not all of the Chinese streamed out of Chinatown in this pitiful parade. Many lay dead on the narrow streets, struck by falling debris, burned alive, or buried in the wreckage of their homes. Some enslaved prostitutes were trapped in their locked cells. Five or six bodies were seen thrown about fifty feet into the air by dynamite meant to destroy nearby buildings.

Yet, despite the threat of incineration, many wealthy businessmen were reluctant to leave. They were members of a powerful merchants' organiza-

tion called the Six Companies who owned bazaars bulging with art treasures in silver, ivory, bronze, porcelain, and jade. They would finally escape
with what they could but left enough of their splendid wares behind to
entice a whole army of looters, civilian and military, who, even before the
ashes cooled, would rummage through the ruins for precious items.

Some soldiers would betray a trust. When one Chinese jeweler opened
his safe after the fire, he found that his gold and silver coins had melted.
He asked a soldier to guard the small treasure while he went for a container, and found on his return there was nothing to contain; the soldier—
and the molten metal—were gone.

Erica Y. Z. Pan would observe:

> The looting of Chinatown started almost as soon as the fires
> stopped burning and it went on with some official knowledge. The
> Chinese Consul-General in San Francisco, Chung Pao-hsi, made a
> series of formal protests, including one to Governor Pardee as
> early as April 21, that 'the National Guard was stripping every-
> thing of value in Chinatown.' The Guardsmen were there suppos-
> edly assisting the army to keep order and sanitation; instead, they
> found a treasure to ransack. The complaints were ignored, the fact
> of which shows that the city fathers were not truly concerned with
> the property rights of the Chinese. The looting coninued for days,
> with about 150 militiamen taking part, according to the *Chronicle*.

In some cases, when residents heard the dreaded knock on the door
and were ordered to leave immediately with no time to pack their possessions, they simply refused to go. A member of a police squad would
report:

> When we got upstairs to chase out the roomers, we found that
> every man in that particular gang had packed his trunk and lashed
> himself to it with ropes, so that Chinaman and trunk were in each
> case one complete and apparently indivisible parcel. Few of them
> could talk even 'pidgin' English. But all were bleating vocifer-
> ously, and those that could make themselves understood were yelp-
> ing: 'You takee me, you takee him too!' 'Him' was the trunk.

Eventually, we had to cut the ropes that bound these poor creatures to their trunks, and drive them out, howling, to save them from being destroyed by the fire.

One observer, Myrtle Robertson, would state after the catastrophe: "Of all the suffering from the fire, I think the despised Chinese fared the worst, for they were the poorest and no American homes were open to them. It was from Chinatown that most of the dead bodies were taken, and no doubt untold numbers are still lying under the debris. Probably many of them were opium fiends, who were too stupefied to make their escape from the underground death traps."

Realizing that all of Chinatown was becoming a death trap, Hugh and his cousin, dragging their trunks, stopped a horse-drawn wagon threading its way through the multitude, and the cousin bargained with the owner, who normally charged a fare of one dollar but now demanded fifty dollars.

Very well, the cousin finally agreed—fifty dollars.

Then he gave Hugh the bad news.

Sorry, but he had no more money and couldn't take him along. But Hugh shouldn't worry. He could survive the ordeal, as he was young and spoke the language. He shouldn't fear the future.

The cousin then climbed aboard the wagon with his trunk and waved a cheery good-bye.

Hugh was thunderstruck.

"That was surely cruel and heartless," he would lament. "I was sure he had money, as he took every cent from father's store when we left. As the truck pulled away . . . it was the first time I broke down and cried. . . . What was to become of me, now that I was left penniless and all alone in this mess?"

IF THE THOUSANDS of rats in Chinatown could have talked, they probably would have asked what was to become of them. Smoked out of cellars, warehouses, granaries, restaurants, and sewer pipes, they joined the people in a panicky flight to safety, scurrying to all parts of the city. Where they went, they carried fleas that would infect them with the bubonic plague—the dread disease, known as the Black Death, that ravaged Europe in the Middle Ages.

The rats, many of them fresh from China, where they had stowed away on craft choked with female slaves and other smuggled items, had grown fat on the offal clogging the dark passageways of Chinatown and on the grain in the burlap bags stacked in warehouses along the waterfront. But in the unburned residential districts where the rats had fled, the garbage cans contained few treasures, and they were growing as lean as their human hosts. Yet they did not give up. As one journalist would report:

"Housewives are daily being scared into fits by the flash of a long, gaunt body with gleaming eyes."

These housewives had good reason to be scared; few realized that many of the rodents were riddled with the plague's tiny rod-shaped bacilli. As many as five thousand bacilli resided in the gizzard of some fleas, and eighty to ninety fleas constantly attacked a single sick rat—eight or so a healthy one. Since the bacillus *Pasteurella pestis* aids in the decomposition of living matter, the blood would begin to putrefy, and the victim, man or rat, would literally rot to death.

The bubonic plague was not unknown to San Francisco. In June 1899, a Japanese ship, the *Nippon Maru,* arrived from China after three passengers infected with the bacillus had died aboard. Two other passengers who were deathly ill jumped overboard and drowned as the craft was landing. At the time, San Francisco's record was still clean; no case of the bubonic plague had ever been recorded within the city. However, a few months later, in March 1900, a messenger from a Chinese undertaker rushed into the office of the San Francisco Board of Health and informed a clerk:

"Boss wants you come look at dead man."

Shortly, the city assistant physician examined the body of Wing Chit Kang, a Chinese laborer, and in shock reported to members of the board:

"You know what? I think I've just seen a case of bubonic plague. Purple blotches, swollen lymph glands in the groin. All the right symptoms."

A series of tests confirmed his suspicion and after several other "mysterious" deaths occurred in Chinatown, the Board of Health decided to warn the public of the danger—knowing that throughout history bubonic plague had begun quietly but ultimately had destroyed whole populations. In A.D. 262, for example, the disease killed five thousand people a day in Rome. Between 1347 and 1349, after the Crusaders brought the bacillus back from the Middle East, one-third of the population of Europe died.

And in 1665, almost seventy-five thousand Europeans succumbed to the plague. As one historian would report:

"All business, all commerce, all government, in fact, almost all life ended. Thoroughfares were deserted. Grass grew in the side paths and steps of the dwellings. Homes where the plague had erupted had a big red cross painted on the door, together with a supplication for mercy from the deity written above it. Entire families died."

The most recent serious outbreak of the disease occurred in 1894 in Hong Kong, later spreading to India. Over the next several years, a million people were struck down. It was not unthinkable, therefore, that the bacillus would eventually make its way to San Francisco via rat-infested ships, particularly the filthy smuggling vessels that docked regularly in the bay.

Nor was it surprising that Mayor Schmitz, despite medical disclosures to the contrary, would deny that the "mysterious" deaths reported in Chinatown were caused by bubonic plague—for these reports, if true, could seriously cut into his portion of the ill-gotten profits enriching Chinese racketeers. Besides, how could he afford to offend even legitimate businessmen, who were also his benefactors? Admitting the plague's existence in San Francisco would mean ruining business there and elsewhere in the state. Thus, the business community supported Schmitz's and California governor Lyman Gage's efforts to ban plague research altogether. It was supposedly less ruinous economically, if not morally, to convince oneself that, whatever the evidence, this biblical curse could never reach the New World.

In addition, racial and class prejudice played a role in the controversy, even among some of those who reluctantly accepted the reality of the Black Death. For example, *Scientific American* would report on June 16, 1900: "All of these [cases] were among the Chinese of the lowest class, just those among whom the disease, on account of their filthy habits and the squalid surroundings under which they live, was certain to appear. The Chinaman, unable to work at his usual avocations, spends his time at the opium pipe, or in gambling away the hours. At least ten thousand Chinamen are in danger of destitution."

As soon as Schmitz took office, he declared: "The way to get rid of the plague is to fire the Board of Health."

And as one of his first actions as mayor, Schmitz did so. He thus reversed the policy of his predecessor, James Phelan, who had accepted the doctors' reports and quarantined Chinatown in 1901 when the malady began killing at least one Chinese every week. It was not lost on Schmitz that Phelan had to lift the quarantine after three days under pressure from newspapers, politicians, and business interests. When the president of the Board of Health filed an injunction against Schmitz, barring him from firing its members, the mayor cut off funds for publication of its health reports.

Even the toughest skeptics finally had to surrender when George Pardee was elected governor in 1903 and announced: "The medical authorities have emphatically declared that the plague has existed and does exist in San Francisco, and that settles it as far as I am concerned."

By 1905, many of the buildings around the city were being made rat-proof, but with Schmitz offering little cooperation, Chinatown remained aswarm with the rodents, though the Chinese and the politicians claimed, true or not, that the outbreak had finally ended. According to the record, 118 of the 121 people contracting the plague died of the disease, but no one could be sure how many other deaths were never officially documented, especially since the Chinese seldom cooperated with their white "oppressors" on any official matter. And like these "oppressors," they often concealed news that could frighten away business.

In any event, the earthquake and fire revealed that thousands of the rats that were supposed to have been destroyed were still alive, with many presumably carrying the diseased fleas. Even as the rodents invaded the white areas, sometimes competing with wild dogs for choice morsels of unburied bodies, the government ignored the danger. At a Thursday meeting of the Committee of Fifty, one member, Dr. Marcus Herstein, warned that the city might have to be quarantined, forcing it to delay reconstruction.

But Schmitz was as adamant as ever: There was no plague!

The mayor, however, finally backed down. After all, was there a Chinatown left to profit from? He now ordered the public to kill not only looters, but also rats wherever they were found. In the following months, about 150,000 were found and killed.

Housewives who still had a house poisoned them; houseowners cleaned up garbage dumps and let light into the dark cellars; soldiers bayoneted them; and some civilians fired at them from their windows as they scurried down the street, finding this sport a partial antidote for their terrible tension. But even as the rodents fled the fire into white areas, one politician would assure the public:

"Plague cannot hurt white people. Black Death is strictly an Oriental and Hindu disease, and only rice eaters get it."

Actually, in the three years after the fire, 77 people of the 160 reported to have contracted the plague were officially said to have died from the disease, though the number was surely much higher, especially since no "rice eater" was counted. Ironically, all the "official" victims were whites scattered in the white districts—people who may have found themselves staring with shock into the gleaming eyes of a famished visitor in their pantry.

CHAPTER 28

The Persian Cat

AS CHINATOWN BURNED, the fire also fed on another squalid quarter—the Barbary Coast at the foot of Telegraph Hill. This sin-loving district, with its tawdry activities supported in part by the municipal government, was at the heart of the claim by religious zealots that San Francisco deserved to burn. As a columnist for the religious journal *Sign of the Times* would write immediately after the disaster, referring in particular to the Barbary Coast, San Francisco's "open, flaunting, God-defying wickedness invited" its fiery fate.

One Barbary Coast figure, Jerome Bassity, scoffed at this charge with a special disdain. He was "God-defying"? Impossible. For he himself *was* God—at least of the criminal world, which included many descendants of the Sydney Ducks and other gold-rush hoodlums. Ever since Mayor Schmitz took office, Bassity was at least king, owning more brothels and saloons than anyone else, including one establishment that was unique: The prostitutes were men who entertained women, most of whom wore masks to hide their identity while they were being erotically serviced.

Bassity was looser with his money than were most pimps, especially when his small, shifty eyes focused on a prized catch. He lured some of the youngest and prettiest young women into his stable of about two hundred prostitutes (the young men were said to be charming, too), sometimes after first testing them out personally in the brothels of his competitors. Still, there were some he had to write off, especially those who preferred to go into business for themselves and would not deal with pimps.

There was, for example, Iodoform Kate, a prostitute who now ran a highly successful bawdy house of her own that specialized in young women who were regarded by many clients as the most passionate of all—redheaded Jewish girls.

There was also Rotary Rosie, probably the most intellectual prostitute on the Barbary Coast. Shortly before the fire, Rosie, an avid reader, spent hours in bed discussing literature with a student at the University of California. She fell in love with the young man and, to please him, entertained his fraternity brothers—asking only that they read poetry to her for half an hour. She planned to abandon her occupation and go to college, hoping her new life would one day lead to marriage with her student lover. But though she survived the fire, she could not survive heartbreak when the young man suddenly vanished. In despair, Rosie committed suicide.

Bassity did not always succeed in employing such notable women, who he felt would give his upscale brothels "class"; in fact, his cheaper bordellos barely attracted the diseased streetwalkers. But he did quite well with his human merchandise—even though in his drunken state he would sometimes terrorize the girls by pulling out his pistol and shooting the lights out or firing at their toes to make them dance.

Actually, he was kinder to his harlots than were some pimps. He didn't, for example, force them to drink alcohol—rather than disguised fruit juice—with their customers. But he did refuse to let them leave the table to visit the bathroom. Left with no alternative, these women had to suffer through the evening wearing wet diapers.

Bassity's brothels, dives, and tamale grotto, run with a gang of murderous hoodlums, earned him from $6,000 to $10,000 a month, a huge criminal income at that time. But he didn't keep all of it. Some of the money is believed to have gone to Schmitz, Ruef, and the police for "protection." The rest went to finance an almost obscenely opulent lifestyle.

The "king" was a rather comic figure as he waddled into the most expensive restaurants, his sensual lips curled around a cigar, his beady eyes glancing with contempt at the other guests with their arrogant demeanors, and stuffed himself with sumptuous delicacies. Inevitably, his tubby figure would be draped in a fancy, flowered waistcoat, his middle finger sparkling with a broad gold ring inlaid with two large diamonds, and his fat neck wrapped in a silk scarf held fast by a "headlight" diamond.

"I like the best of everything," he told a reporter. "The best wine, the best food, the best clothing. It takes money to get them."

Bassity had learned early what life was like without money. An orphan at eight, he found himself on the street selling newspapers, then working as an usher in a cheap theater and as a milkman in the red-light district. One of his customers, a madam attracted by his animal-like personality, set him up in a profitable business—a saloon with convenient upstairs bedrooms—and he was on the way to his criminal lifestyle.

With his jewels and silken finery, Bassity stood out like a Persian cat in a garbage-strewn alley when he visited either his own establishments or competitive brothels with such names as The Living Flea, The Sign of the Red Rooster, and Ye Ole Whore Shoppe. Few people who haunted these places wore derbies or diamonds as they mixed pleasure with business—principally running blackmail, extortion, and protection rackets. Sometimes victims, mainly sailors drunk on crude, often drug-riddled alcohol served by amorous drinking partners, were shanghaied and forced into the smuggling trade.

BILL COFFMAN, a young alcoholic sailor and saloon entertainer, was such a victim. One evening, as he stood drinking in a saloon, he passed out—and two days later groggily awoke in a pitch-dark room. Where was he? he asked. The lights went on and a creepy-looking man answered: In a boardinghouse—and he owed the owner twelve dollars for two days' rent. If he wanted a drink he had better sign a paper handed him.

The unfortunate sailor thus learned he was being shanghaied—in the conventional way. In earlier days, he might have been seated over a trap door, doped or beaten over the head, then dropped through the opening into a waiting boat. Or he might be invited, together with other potential victims, to help celebrate someone's birthday with free drinks and food aboard a holiday craft. The happy, drunken passengers would then be transferred to a ship on which, en route to distant ports, they would have plenty of time to work off their hangovers.

Coffman would have more than enough time for that when he was dragged aboard a ship flying the Union Jack and heading for Ireland. Six months later, half-starved, enfeebled by overwork, and blistered from beatings for trying to jump ship, he finally returned to San Francisco with only a thirty-dollar paycheck in his pocket after expenses.

Back in a lice-infested boardinghouse (this one of his own choosing), Coffman soon ran into debt. The owner wanted to have him shanghaied again, but he disappeared into the hellish depths of degradation unique to the Barbary Coast. Ironically, he was saved by the catastrophe of 1906. The disaster would wipe out his past as it would the city that shaped it. Coffman started life anew and became a business leader and a sports figure who founded the annual East-West Shrine charity football game.

THE BARBARY COAST of Jerome Bassity and Bill Coffman stretched north of Market from East Street (later called the Embarcadero) with its rundown sailors' hotels, used-clothing stores, and rat-infested restaurants, to the gates of Chinatown. It had not changed much since the gold rush. Side by side with the other commercial establishments were the numerous gambling houses and brothels that had filled the recreational vacuum in a crude metropolis flourishing virtually without women. In 1869, the *San Francisco Call* succinctly described the district, named by seafarers for the pirate-infested shores of North Africa:

"The Barbary Coast! That mysterious region so much talked of; so seldom visited! Of which so much is heard, but little seen! That sink of moral pollution, whose reefs are strewn with human wrecks, and into whose vortex is constantly drifting barks of moral life, while swiftly down the whirlpool of death go the sinking hulks of the murdered and the suicide!"

And in 1876, a local historian wrote with equal repugnance:

The Barbary Coast is the haunt of the low and the vile of every kind. The petty thief, the house burglar, the tramp, the whoremonger, lewd women, cutthroats, murderers, all are found here. Dance-halls and concert-saloons, where bleary-eyed men and faded women drink vile liquor, smoke offensive tobacco, engage in vulgar conduct, sing obscene songs and say and do everything to heap upon themselves more degradation, are numerous. . . . Licentiousness, debauchery, pollution, loathsome disease, insanity from dissipation, misery, poverty, wealth, profanity, blasphemy, and death, are there. And Hell, yawning to receive the putrid mass, is there also.

Years later, on April 18, 1906, Jerome Bassity would himself learn there could be hell even in his kind of heaven. With the earth rocking under him, he rolled out of bed and, finally convinced this wasn't a murderous plot against him, managed to keep his balance as he swathed himself in his usual attire—waistcoat, diamonds, derby. Earthquake or no earthquake, he would not let the world see him without the symbols of success, the proof that he was no longer a poor milkman. He did make one exception; unable to find a clean silk shirt, he settled for one of cheap black sateen.

Bassity then shuffled outside and watched with horror as flames ripped through Dead Man's Alley—their crackly hiss replacing the usual all-night sounds of raucous music and laughter—and spread across the rest of the Barbary Coast. According to one report, soldiers driving residents from the area shot dozens who, in their drunkenness, were reluctant to leave.

Buried in the debris were the remnants of his many pleasure palaces. No longer could a man even stroll down a two-block stretch of paradise called Morton Street, later incongruously changed to Maiden Lane, and fondle the breasts of women leaning out of windows—ten cents for one breast, a bargain nickel for the other. Bassity's biggest loss would be the profits from a full-body press, based on a racist rate schedule. A Mexican girl cost twenty-five cents; a black, Chinese, or Japanese girl fifty cents; a French girl seventy-five cents; and a white American girl one dollar.

The prostitutes of the Barbary Coast and the somewhat less notorious Tenderloin district nearby survived by fleeing to Union Square—and would resume their careers after the fire, some of them, paradoxically, with a moral standing that rivaled even that of the primmest virgin. One madam would take in a young boy who had lost his parents, his brothers, and his sister in the fire, and raise him with a strict hand, even making him say his prayers at night—while she negotiated with her customers. The boy, William Bon Barton, who would become a wealthy businessman, commented many years after the fire:

"Where else but in San Francisco could you grow up an orphan in a whorehouse and end up in real estate and horses?"

Some San Franciscans, however, saw nothing but evil in even the most kindhearted whore. Hadn't they prophesied that God—the real one— would avenge the sins of reprobates like Jerome Bassity? But Bassity, in a sense, viewed *himself* as a prophet. A new Babylon and Tyre would rise from the ashes, he vowed, and upon the purged earth he would build the world's largest and classiest whorehouse—a stupendous monument to the god of the Barbary Coast.

CHAPTER 29

Black News and White Tails

ON ARRIVING in San Jose late on April 17, George Horton stayed with friends and retired early, content in the knowledge that he would be back with his bride, Amelia, the next day. And Amelia, back in San Francisco, shared his contentment. She knew that George was making an important business deal, and with a little money in the bank they could buy a home and focus on their future.

But when the earthquake struck at dawn, their future seemed to vanish. The boardinghouse in San Francisco was almost destroyed by the quake and then consumed by fire, and the house in San Jose was almost demolished as well. George survived and desperately rushed back to San Francisco to be with Amelia, but was distraught to find their boardinghouse in ruins.

Where was his wife? When the neighbors told him she had been killed in the earthquake, he didn't believe them. He visited every refugee camp, every morgue, every hospital, moving from cot to cot looking for her, but without success. Nevertheless, he still couldn't believe she was dead.

In fact, Amelia *was* alive and had moved to another boardinghouse in a safer area. She immediately sent her brother to San Jose to find her husband, and he reported back that the house where George had been staying was destroyed, and that neighbors had assured him everyone in the house had died.

For her part, Amelia couldn't believe *he* was dead. She sought him everywhere in San Jose and in San Francisco, reading and leaving scribbled notices tacked on note boards in every refugee camp, as he also did. But somehow they missed each other's messages amid the thousands of sad pleas posted everywhere, among them:

Estelle: Come to your mother on main drive of the Park.

Lost. Paul E. Hoffes, nine years old, light complexioned, blue eyes. Please notify his mother. Panhandle, opposite Lyon Street entrance.

Dan McIntyre: your family is looking for you. At the South Drive, back of children's playground, you will find a board reading "McIntyre and Olsen Camp." Your sister May.

One man's notes were especially poignant. He had lost consciousness when his house caught fire and awoke in a hospital where someone had carried him, only to discover his wife missing. After searching everywhere, leaving notes pinned to every note board, he finally found her in another hospital. But where were their three little girls? They searched together and came upon one of them in a refugee camp. Then, after a futile search for the other two, they finally gathered the strength to look in the one place they had dared not inspect until now—the ruins of their own home. To their almost maddening grief, they discovered the charred bones of their two missing children.

Also tragic was the search by children for their missing parents. One young girl, Hazel Mathews, wrote to Mayor Schmitz:

"Dear Sir: Will you please try to find my papa? He worked at the Pleasanton, Sutter and Jones Streets and lived at 654-Post street. I am so worried about him that I cannot study. My papa's name is Joseph."

The Hortons' failure to find each other left them broken-hearted, but they both vowed never to stop their search.

JOHN BARRYMORE was conducting a search, too—for a way to remain in the United States and pursue the "good life." Why, he asked himself, had he ever agreed to perform in the wilds of Australia? Perhaps if he was lucky he would oversleep and miss the ship that was to take him there. But hardly had he stretched out on the bed in the home of his friend when the earthquake almost sent him reeling to the floor.

What the hell was happening? Had he drunk too much?

Finally, Barrymore, gazing at a pile of broken Chinese glass, realized that nature was responsible for this rude awakening. Well, maybe now he would miss that ship after all. He stumbled into the next room and shocked his host awake with the sad news, crying:

"Come and see what has happened to the Ming Dynasty."

Barrymore then calmly put on his white tails, walked out, and tottered over blocks of wreckage toward the St. Francis Hotel, where he had been booked.

Shambling down stylish Van Ness Avenue, Barrymore had to move to the middle of the street to avoid stepping on people who lay on the rubble-strewn sidewalk in their furs and opera cloaks, some asleep, others in a drunken stupor. On seedier streets, people on the dole lay covered with patchwork blankets against the morning chill. Finally, he reached Union Square across the street from the hotel. It was swarming with people. As Adolf Sinsheimer, a survivor, would write in a letter to a friend:

"White people and Negroes and Chinese and Japanese all mixed without prejudice—one bench in the park might harbor all the chief races and no one seemed to be aware of it. One feeling seemed to possess all of them, and the expression was the same in everyone's face—a dull staring look of resigned despair—a waiting for the end—fear—hopelessness. I never before saw people so cling to one another with a complete surrender of individuality."

Among these people were opera singers and other guests at the damaged St. Francis. Barrymore suddenly spotted William Collier, the head of his theatrical troupe, who cried to him:

"Go West, young man, and blow up with the country."

According to Collier, who was wearing only a flowered dressing gown and slippers, the actor was "quite chipper. Seemed not at all upset by the now-raging fire or the dynamiting of the buildings [to stop the fire from spreading]." He was, his friends would taunt him later, perfectly dressed for an earthquake.

Abraham Ruef was the Svengali behind San Francisco's Mayor Schmitz. (San Francisco History Center, San Francisco Public Library)

San Francisco mayor Eugene Schmitz at the time of the disaster. (San Francisco History Center, San Francisco Public Library)

All photographs courtesy of Ron Ross, Founder, San Francisco History Association, unless otherwise noted.

ABOVE LEFT: *Dennis Sullivan was San Francisco's fire chief. He died in the earthquake.* (San Francisco History Center, San Francisco Public Library)

ABOVE RIGHT: *Amadeo Peter Giannini, a banker who kept deposits in his home during the catastrophe.* (Bank of America Corporate Archives, San Francisco)

Enrico Caruso, the world-acclaimed tenor. He performed in San Francisco's Grand Opera House on the eve of the disaster. (San Francisco History Center, San Francisco Public Library)

Abraham Ruef was the Svengali behind San Francisco's Mayor Schmitz. (San Francisco History Center, San Francisco Public Library)

San Francisco mayor Eugene Schmitz at the time of the disaster. (San Francisco History Center, San Francisco Public Library)

All photographs courtesy of Ron Ross, Founder, San Francisco History Association, unless otherwise noted.

ABOVE LEFT: *Dennis Sullivan was San Francisco's fire chief. He died in the earthquake.* (San Francisco History Center, San Francisco Public Library)

ABOVE RIGHT: *Amadeo Peter Giannini, a banker who kept deposits in his home during the catastrophe.* (Bank of America Corporate Archives, San Francisco)

Enrico Caruso, the world-acclaimed tenor. He performed in San Francisco's Grand Opera House on the eve of the disaster. (San Francisco History Center, San Francisco Public Library)

A brick street is split open during the earthquake.

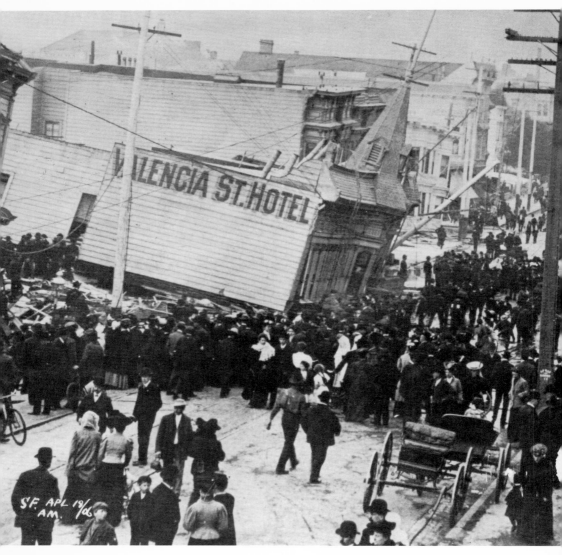

A hotel breaks up, killing scores of guests, including many who drowned in the flooded basement.

One of thousands of disaster victims is carried to an ambulance.

The ruins of City Hall, one of San Francisco's architectural treasures that crumbled in the earthquake.

A horse is killed by falling timbers.

Residents in a park watch San Francisco burn.

The fire as seen from afar.

ABOVE: *Survivors who fled their homes gather in the street with what belongings they could salvage.*

RIGHT: *General Frederick Funston became the "dictator" of San Francisco during the fire.* (San Francisco History Center, San Francisco Public Library)

OPPOSITE: *Firemen try to fight the fire, but, with water mains broken, the struggle is hopeless.*

Soldiers patrol the streets with orders to kill suspected looters.

The ruins of the magnificent Temple Emanu-El.

Soldiers forced passersby to clear away rubble from the earthquake.

OPPOSITE TOP: *A family driven from their home by the disaster finds refuge in a tent.*

OPPOSITE BOTTOM:
Del Crespi with classmates. Only ten years old at the time of the disaster, he searched everywhere for his beloved Lillian. (Courtesy of Sylvia Allen)

LEFT: *Rebecca, Etta, and Bernard Dulberg about three years before the disaster.* (Courtesy of Rita Perada)

BELOW: *Rebecca Dulberg and her four children, including Etta at far left. The baby was born during the earthquake.* (Courtesy of Rita Perada)

Citizens gather for a clean-up effort almost a year after the disaster.

"What's up, Willie?" Barrymore asked.

"Nothing's up at all," was the reply. "In fact, everything is down. Half the town is burning, and the other half is being blown to pieces; but otherwise nothing is up."

Incidentally, said Collier, the ship that was to take them to Australia had apparently disappeared, maybe sunk with all their trunks and wardrobes.

Barrymore feigned sorrow, then spied an attractive woman sitting on a trunk and shivering in the morning cold. He walked over to her, unaware that she was a well-known operatic soprano, and suggested he knew just the tonic for her.

"Though lightly clad," the actor would later say, "she was charmingly unperturbed. I was much the best-dressed person on the square, and she seemed greatly amused by my solicitude."

"Certainly," she said, "if it isn't too much trouble."

It wasn't. Barrymore walked up Post Street to the exclusive Bohemian Club, which was in the line of fire, and gulped down a brandy at the bar. Then, while some members dragged the club's valuable paintings outside and loaded them in two waiting wagons, he poured another glass and carried it back to the singer, spilling much of it. She warmly thanked the actor, and he beamed. Too bad that he would be leaving for Australia that day—if they could find the ship.

Barrymore perhaps didn't realize it, but all was not brandy and romance in Union Square. Another opera singer taking refuge there, Madame Goerlitz, found herself in an agonizing position as a woman begged her to help revive the baby in her arms. The singer could only remain silent. How could she tell the mother that her child was dead?

Meanwhile, Barrymore, frustrated by his travel schedule, walked across the street to the St. Francis to get some sleep and asked the clerk if it would be safe to go up to his room. The front of the hotel was split, the clerk replied, but "there isn't the slightest chance in the world of it ever happening again."

Just then, the hotel shook violently from another tremor and the clerk leaped across the desk and dived out the door. At the same time, a man jumped from the top story of the building next door seconds before that floor collapsed and fell into the street, though he was saved when he landed in a large awning that stretched above the doorway. Barrymore, ignoring the chaos, calmly walked up to his room and went to sleep. Only when he awoke in the afternoon smelling smoke did he get up, discard his opera tails for tweeds, and leave the hotel—just before flames burst from every window and turned the structure into a great torch.

Barrymore drowsily strode to Van Ness Avenue, where the buildings would be blown up later that day in an effort to keep the fire from spreading westward toward the ocean. Here he met an old friend who was trying to get into his home while there was still time to save his possessions, including some valuable paintings. But the man couldn't find his key. To enter, Barrymore threw a rock through the window, and as the two men were picking out glass from the frame, "a man dashed around the corner with the biggest-looking gun" the actor ever saw.

And looters were to be shot on sight!

CHAPTER 30

The Home Bank and
the Burned Home

THE THREAT of being shot for "looting" was a frightening reality very much on Amadeo Giannini's mind as he whipped his horses forward on the evening of April 18. He was headed toward the Peninsula and his home in San Mateo with his two horse-drawn carriages, loaded with gold, silver, securities, and other valuable items. What if militiamen stopped him and charged that he was carrying stolen property—perhaps so they could steal it for themselves?

Adding to his stress were the growing crowds of refugees who blocked the rutted road, dragging along their belongings in any container with or without wheels. Unscrupulous men thrived in a chaotic setting like this. Were there enough policemen to protect him? His career, perhaps his life, depended on the answer.

With the worst-case scenario threatening, Giannini, to his relief, found a parallel side road leading up the Peninsula, and here traffic was relatively light, though the road in places was almost impassable, especially after dark, due to the earthquake upheaval. It seemed almost unimaginable that he should be carrying $80,000 in gold and silver, the whole Bank of Italy, over this primitive country road in the dead of night without any security at all. Never had he looked back more fondly on those days when his greatest concern was the price of grapefruit.

Finally, at about dawn, the horses stamped to a halt before Giannini's home in San Mateo. Exhausted from the trip, his nerves raw, he now faced a banker's nightmare. Where could he safely keep the bags of precious coins? He had no safe at home, and they wouldn't fit under the mattress, where many of his customers had hidden their money before they were persuaded that a bank was more profitable. Ultimately, he dumped the bags in the fireplace. There, in the ash pit, the Bank of Italy was resurrected.

Despite his exhaustion, Giannini could not waste time sleeping. He returned immediately to San Francisco to survey the damage to the former Bank of Italy. The building didn't exist; it had been burned to the ground. Somehow, the tragic sight ignited in him a vision of an almost prophetic nature. He would spark the reconstruction of San Francisco.

AS THE FIRE closed in on Chinatown, Hugh Kwong Liang took courage and joined the crowd of refugees struggling up the steep grades toward the crest of Nob Hill, dragging his trunk behind him with a rope.

The trunk was bursting with his belongings, and he could not afford to have it stolen. He did not have the protection of one wealthy Chinese man who drove past in a horse-drawn wagon with four guards flanking it, each carrying a drawn sword.

To Hugh Kwong Liang, death would almost be welcome.

"As I looked down the hill and saw all of Chinatown burning, including the building on Washington Street where I was born and spent my childhood, a feeling of true madness and awe came over me. To think, even the sacred Kwong Chow Temple with the revered Kwan Tai was burned to ashes. . . . So I turned away from my dear old Chinatown for the last time and joined the slow march with the other refugees."

AT ABOUT 4 A.M., Friday, April 20, Del Crespi lay awake on the ground covered by a blanket and gazed into the sky. Where was Lillian? Was she safe? Was she coming back? He would spend his whole life looking for her. Suddenly, he heard a shuffling noise coming from the south, and he got up and looked down the road. Hundreds, perhaps thousands, of shadowy figures were approaching, silently, unobtrusively, like a procession of ghosts in the night. They were Chinese, "sad and dazed, . . . marching in droves with bundles on their backs."

All of Chinatown, it seemed. And that meant the area was on fire—and that the flames had almost reached Lillian's house on Filbert Street.

"Certainly by this time," Del would later say, "Lillian and her folks would be back, and with the fire so close to her home they would at least try to save some of their belongings."

He walked four blocks down Jones Street to Filbert Street and saw that the fire was only a block away—so close that the militia wouldn't let anyone turn the corner. Del waited there, praying that Lillian would show up in time. But within an hour the fire had reached Filbert.

His school and Rotten Jimmie's clothing shop soon turned to ash, and then, at exactly 11:10 A.M., Del would note, the fire reached Lillian's house. It was too late to save anything, but maybe she had arrived late and was in the crowd of horrified spectators who had gathered at the corner to watch the grotesque spectacle of destruction.

"I looked them all over carefully," Del would relate, "but the one person I was looking for wasn't there."

In tears, he started back toward home.

"Talk about the 'Bridge of Sighs'!" he would lament. "To me the world came to an end."

Not only had he seen Lillian's house vanish, but his new school was gone as well, and so was the new suit he was going to buy in Rotten Jimmie's so that he could impress Lillian when school reopened. Adding to the horror, his boss's house had burned down—before the man could pay him the three dollars he had earned on his paper route. His only satisfaction was that he had seen Lillian's door burn to a crisp. Perhaps the sound of that slam would finally be muted.

But when Del arrived home, his pain suddenly evaporated. Was he seeing things? He called his mother, and she cried:

"Yes, that's Pa!"

Del's father had walked fifty miles, all the way from San Jose. But the family's joy was short-lived, for the fire was rapidly raging toward them, and the militia gave them fifteen minutes to gather what they could from their battered house. Del and the others dashed into the shaky structure, and "grabbed everything we could think of."

Finally, at about 4 P.M., Del watched as the flames embraced the house—the last one in the district to crumble into dust.

"Yes, I cried," he would admit, "but not because the house had burned"—it belonged, after all, to the brother-in-law of A. P. Giannini, and he was rich enough to build another one—"I cried because I had forgotten to get my honorary card out of the house before it burned. I remembered Lillian saying, 'Don't lose your card,' the last time I saw her."

Del bitterly reproached himself. He had saved his tops, marbles, skates, sling shots, and other "junk," but had forgotten his honorary card. How proud Lillian had been when he skipped a grade—not like those guys in his gang. How could he prove that he was smart without the card?

"I thought of the teacher's last words when Lillian and I left school," Del would reminisce. " 'I hope you both enjoy your vacation.' It sure was some vacation!"

CHAPTER 31

A Vow to Love and
a Vow to Die

THE DAY had finally come—Thursday, April 19. George Emerson would wed Josephine Hoffman in defiance of all logic and common sense. They would seal their bond even as their world, black with smoke, was collapsing. George, his brother, his bride, and her sister and parents sat down for a last breakfast in the Hoffmans' house, trying to ignore the relentless crackle nearby, the cindery air, and the intense heat. The breakfast was cold, since stove fires were taboo, but everyone had their fill of bread, butter, and fruit. They had barely finished the meal when they heard a loud knock on the door. When it was opened, a fireman standing there delivered a terse message:

"Leave the house immediately! It's going to be dynamited."

General Funston was still destroying whole blocks of buildings in an effort to "starve" the fire. And the family, fearing that the conflagration would eventually reach this house, had already packed all portable items in case the threat grew. The men dragged the baggage out to the street and the whole party strode toward Van Ness Avenue nearby, stopping a block away to watch with tears of agony as the Hoffman home disappeared in a billowing blast of dynamite. Emerson then managed to find a horse-drawn cart, which carried family and baggage to the home of Reverend Adams. As the horse, braving a storm of glowing cinders, plodded over the rubble, the chief operator of the Postal-Telegraph Cable Company, based on Goat Island in the bay, reported at about that time:

"Scores of dead are lying along the street but will be taken care of from now on."

The newlyweds were horrified as they viewed the scene. Would they be honeymooning in heaven? The thought, however, steeled their determination to defy the fire.

They were greeted at the Adams house by twenty-five guests, friends and family, who tried to act as if life were normal. The bride had brought her wedding presents and trousseau, and soon buttoned herself into a white lace wedding gown. Her younger sister, May, who was herself engaged to Reverend Adams's son, Will, would be her bridesmaid. The guests were served frothy cake baked before the earthquake and, since no liquor, juice, or even water was available, they drank imaginary toasts from an empty punch bowl.

As Reverend Adams conducted the ceremony that afternoon and finally pronounced the couple man and wife, the world was digesting in shock a new message tapped out by a telegraph operator in Oakland:

"Fire is still raging in San Francisco and entire city is doomed. . . . The fire cannot be checked until it burns out. Every building in business section and nearly half of residence section destroyed now and not a large building left standing."

The operator didn't bother to report that in the first two days of the disaster, the city was not only burning but was shaking—from 135 aftershocks.

The wedding party went on nevertheless, as the tinkle of glasses competed with the ever louder crackle of fire outside. How close were the flames? Nobody dared to ask. Not at this sacred moment, a moment of triumph over terror. But the terror could only grow for the newlyweds and other San Franciscans as the many fires of the previous day fused into several roaring fronts. The Ham and Eggs Fire north of Market had jumped that street and joined with the blaze south of Market to form one front. And the Nob Hill fire, fanning out north, west, and south, had united with the Delmonico restaurant fire to jump Powell Street and merge with the eastern wing of the Ham and Eggs Fire—through which the newlyweds would have to pass to set out on their honeymoon.

After one more drinkless toast, they prepared to leave. The question on everybody's mind was: Could they get through the flaming maze and out of town?

GETTING OUT of town was no doubt on John Barrymore's mind, too. Especially at this moment, with the militiaman pointing a gun at him in the belief that he and his friend were looters.

"Fortunately," the actor would later say, "the man behind the gun asked questions before he shot."

With a perspiring air of sincerity, he flung himself into the greatest performance of his life. The soldier would be wasting a bullet, he argued. Yes, they had broken a window, but he was simply helping a friend who had lost his key to get into his house so he could save a few things before it was dynamited.

The militiaman, fingering the trigger of his rifle, paused for a moment, then he lowered the weapon and walked on. The two men, heaving sighs of relief, then entered the house and rescued some valuable artwork. Later, Barrymore went to stay with friends in Burlingame, about fifteen miles from San Francisco, hoping once more that his company was already well on the way to Australia. Feeling he should get word to his family, he bicycled back to San Francisco en route to Oakland, from where he would send a telegram, since communication lines from San Francisco were dead.

But on the way he was stopped by some soldiers who were so impressed by his credentials that they put him to work supervising a gang of lesser mortals who were sorting out and piling up debris.

"I knew so little about work myself," he would later remark, "that it was difficult for me to become a good executive."

After about eight hours, the soldiers released him, and he proceeded to Oakland. There, he was greeted by Ashton Stevens, the *Examiner*'s theater critic. He had "good news."

"You're in time to get your boat after all. Word was sent east: 'Everybody found except Barrymore.' The company is going to sail from Vancouver in three days."

Damn it! Why hadn't he stayed lost another three days?

Barrymore finally sent a message to his sister, Ethel, vividly describing his close calls. After Ethel had read the note to their uncle John Drew, she asked him if he believed it.

"I believe every word of it," he replied. "It took a convulsion of nature to make him get up and the United States Army to make him go to work."

HUGH KWONG LIANG, together with other Chinese fleeing Chinatown, finally arrived at the open grassy grounds of the Presidio army post, where canvas tents were being set up amid the great pine trees. The refugees were filled with fear and suspicion. As one of them would say:

"Living precariously in canvas tents among hostile Barbarians on the fog-chilled slopes overlooking the Golden Gate, [we] wondered about the reception [we] might receive, or what unspeakable indignities might be visited upon [us] under the shadows of the fortress's mighty guns. Not even civic disaster with its common misery could wipe out the bitter memory of forty years of ugly persecution of the Chinese in California."

Since each refugee tent had to have at least two inhabitants, Hugh, being alone, shared one with another teenager, Jimmy Ho. There was plenty of room, for Jimmy had no baggage at all and Hugh had only his trunk.

Hardly had the two youths moved in when they heard a woman crying for help in a tent nearby. They rushed over and found that she had just given birth to a baby, but that several women were already taking care of her. When the boys returned to their own tent, they were stunned. Hugh's trunk was missing! Now he had nothing.

"Evidently some heartless persons had stolen it," he would charge. "So that for me was the last straw. . . . I really felt hopeless and downhearted. My friend, Jimmy Ho, felt so sorry for me and perhaps for himself, too, that he broke down and sobbed."

Jimmy then set out to find relatives among the refugees, and Hugh was alone again. Abandoned by his cousin and now by his new friend, threatened by sparks from the fire settling on his tent, Hugh plunged into a deep depression.

"I . . . made up my mind," he would relate, "that eventually I must face death. . . . Strange as it may seem, I was not afraid any longer. The horrors of the day and my personal sufferings throughout the ordeal may have deadened my nerves. But I was thinking, even though my thoughts were wild and morbid. I was willing to accept the cruel fate of death."

But how was he to die? He had three choices, he calculated. He could simply wait to burn to death. He could starve to death. Or he could drown himself. He chose the third solution. So that night he set out for the water-front, where he planned to leap into the water and join his ancestors.

AFTER SITTING on the trunk with her mother for what seemed like eternity, Jessy Wilson saw her husband, Willie, approaching and thanked God that she would finally have help in escaping the fire, which was now crackling hardly a block away. Supporting the older woman, Willie led the way to a cousin's home some distance from the fire, only to find that the cousin had fled for his life.

"My poor dear mother was so fatigued," Jessy would later say, "that she could walk no longer and fell. Willie and I were so worn out we could not lift her, and I had to ask a young man who was passing by to help us. The whole city seemed in flames by then, everybody had deserted their homes and the situation was hopeless."

But somehow they managed to stumble on—until they met a friend who offered them an apartment for the night. The place was dark, except for the reflection of firelight. Jessy's mother thought she had been taken home and threatened to throw herself out of the window if Jessy did not give her her own room, her keys, and her chest of drawers. But she finally went to sleep—until 2 A.M., when soldiers began dynamiting nearby and the structure trembled. One soldier then came to the door and ordered the Wilsons to leave the building at once, as it was about to be blown up.

Minutes later, the family was out on the street again. It appeared that with the fire and explosions ravaging the world around them, they had played their last hand.

CHAPTER 32

Misery, Murder, and Mastery

BERNARD DULBERG thought he had played *his* last hand as the militia dragged him away. They had forced him to leave his three children in the care of some refugees living in a lot on Van Ness Avenue while his wife and newborn infant remained in the hospital. Seven-year-old Etta and her younger sister and brother could hardly stop crying, but the refugee women calmed them down, feeding them and stitching some clothes for them with an old sewing machine. The children, however, wondered if they would ever see their parents again.

To their joy, that evening their father returned and swept them up in his arms. He had been shoveling debris all day, and with great vigor, for he was closely watched by militiamen poised with rifles and bayonets. Now free to leave, Dulberg and the children went to the hospital to pick up Rebecca and her baby, and the family bumped in their wagon over the cobblestones to Golden Gate Park.

The park was a huge expanse of several hundred green acres stretching west to the Pacific Ocean. Some years earlier John McClaren, a municipal engineering icon, had converted it from a desert of sand dunes into an exquisitely landscaped Garden of Eden—studded with eucalyptus, cypress, and Monterey pine trees. It was a place where children joyfully sat on a merry-go-round animal, or rode on a real donkey or in a goat-pulled cart along winding gravel paths; where lovers went rowing in Stow Lake, sipped tea in the exotic Japanese Tea Garden, or sat among the tulips that surrounded an authentic Dutch windmill; and where birds sang merrily in every tree and buffalo grazed peacefully nearby.

The park was now aswarm with tens of thousands of desperate people, including many children. Some lay prostrate on the grass. Others huddled in groups praying. One woman rocked a dead baby in her arms. A child nestled up to her dead mother, "cooing and talking in sweet baby talk" to her, as one refugee would observe. One little girl sat silently in the shade of a tree caressing her doll; she had bolted from a group of children in the charge of nuns to run back to her burning home, risking her life to find the doll.

Many people staggered through the wretched crowds robotlike, glassy-eyed, half-mad; some were in search of their loved ones, people like George and Amelia Horton. The sounds on the street—the scrape of trunks against stone, the chugging of overloaded, overheated automobiles, the clip-clop of overburdened horses, and the incessant roar of the fire— had all faded into an exhausted silence, broken only by quiet sobs and low moans of pain and despair. One reporter would write:

"The horrors of war concern only males who know that the game is death. This was murder and robbery in the dark."

Yet, despair was tempered by a fierce, underlying will to survive.

Even so, for refugees in the park and throughout San Francisco the threat to survival was ominously multifaceted. The earthquake and fire had already taken a grave toll, and the flames were still claiming ever more victims. Many of the wounded lay dying because drugs and treatment centers were scarce. Others were perishing at the irresponsible hands of military and paramilitary men. And then there was the insidious threat of starvation and deadly thirst, especially in a family like the Dulbergs, with a newborn infant and three other children.

Some mothers in Golden Gate Park, to quench the thirst of their young, gave them shots of whiskey surreptitiously supplied by soldiers. Other refugees, one observer would report, "gathered tin cans out of the ruins, rusted, dirty cans, and filled them at the gutters where the fire engines made a stream. Water was carried by loving ones to loved ones, to husbands, wives, babies; in hats and hands, in paper cones and in small bottles, and a mere sip was a Godsend and, after a while, even a sip was not to be had. A drop of muddy water was a testimonial of love and of friendship, or an evidence of charity and mercy, when it passed that day from the hand of one to the lips of another."

Few of the refugees anywhere had the strength to forage for food outside their camping area. In any case, all the grocery stores were soon raided by hungry people, or their owners had simply given away all their stocks. Fortunate was the forager who returned with a can of sardines or a few slices of bread. And not many people, certainly not the Dulbergs, had the money to pay the exorbitant prices demanded by black marketeers, who did business despite the risk of being shot or bayoneted by soldiers for exploiting the refugees.

Not even the city's rich, their pockets now empty, could afford food. When one wealthy man taking refuge with his wife in Golden Gate Park saw a neighbor of small means munching on a loaf of stale bread, he called to the neighbor:

"I'll give you a thousand dollars for a piece of it."

But after a pause, he lamented, "I forgot. I haven't a cent. We must starve."

The neighbor broke his loaf of bread in half and handed half to the hungry couple.

The threat of starvation was ominously reflected in a message General Funston wired to the War Department: "Famine seems inevitable. All large supply stores burned. Most energetic efforts from outside only can prevent frightful suffering. . . . I request that everything possible be done in the way of food, supplies, tentage and blankets."

THOUGH EMERGENCY provisions were rushed from Oakland and Vallejo, they did not immediately reach San Francisco, since almost every vessel afloat in the bay was busy fighting the fire or rescuing refugees.

Even when some relief items were unloaded at a city pier, there were no automobiles or teams of horses to transport them to the refugee centers. Some of these vehicles were carrying wounded people to hospitals or dynamite to burning areas, while many others were waiting outside mansions in case the rich and powerful owners had to make a quick getaway. Nor were many of the debris-covered roads usable.

On the second night of the fire, these obstacles produced a murder.

Provisions had finally reached a point several blocks from Columbia Square Park, an ash-carpeted playground in an already burned area crowded with refugees. But the horse-drawn wagon carrying the food could not be moved farther because the streets in the area were blocked by debris. Jacob Steinman, a militia sergeant, was thus ordered to walk to the square and bring back some of the refugees; they would carry the provisions to their center.

Steinman, who, witnesses would later report, was intoxicated, approached a refugee named Bush, also drunk, and ordered him to gather several men for the work. But the superintendent of the playground, Joseph Myers, stepped in and objected. Popular with the impoverished refugees, he had often served as a baby-sitter for their children at the playground. They trusted him, and he loved their children. Though his burned home on Post Street was far from the playground, he had come here to be with them at this terrible time.

While Myers was delighted that food had finally arrived, he could not imagine that these people, drained, weak from hunger, and bewildered by their narrow escape and loss of their meager possessions, would now be asked to carry heavy cartons for blocks. He volunteered to hire a wagon and secure them, even though transportation was almost impossible to find, especially if one did not have much money.

Sergeant Steinman was furious. Who was giving orders around here? "Keep out of this," he snarled.

Bush then sided with the militiaman, though he himself could not carry any load, since he had only one leg.

"What have you done for the people?" Bush asked Myers.

"I've been going among them," the playground director replied, "doing what I could to encourage them and relieve them."

Steinman then interjected, "You shut up and get out of here."

"Why, you know me, corporal," Myers responded, apparently having met Steinman before the militiaman was promoted to sergeant.

"No," Steinman replied, "I don't know you. I don't want to know you. Shut up and get out of here!"

According to witnesses, Myers reluctantly turned to leave; Steinman, however, would later claim the playground director had been poised to attack. In self-defense, the sergeant would say, he drew his revolver and fired twice. Myers slumped to the ground and died instantly. Then, pointing his gun at the stunned crowd, Steinman shouted:

"If there is anyone who questions my authority, let him say so! I'll come back tomorrow and kill every man in the park!"

And he stalked away.

WHILE THAT ATTEMPT to feed the refugees ended in tragedy, the Committee of Fifty debated how to deliver the food piling up on the docks and in the railroad yards. Finally, a young lawyer named William Denman offered a solution. All he needed was a couple of soldiers to help him, he claimed, and he would provide the transportation. Shortly, he and two soldiers were out on the street stopping every automobile and team of horses that passed, forcing the driver at gunpoint to dump everything out of his vehicle and ordering him into line behind Denman's car.

"If any driver tries to drop out of this line," Denman ordered the soldiers, "shoot him!"

But no one tried, and the procession of vehicles successfully transported the provisions to the camps. Not all of the crates were picked up, however. Many had been stolen from the docks and freight cars by thieves in the night, or more subtly by corrupt officials. On the third morning, however, mass starvation was averted with the arrival of food from army posts and neighboring communities. But would a full stomach be enough to give people renewed strength to fight the lingering flames?

JESSY WILSON had virtually given up hope of saving her own life and that of her mother as they sat, trapped, in the path of the fire. Miraculously, at this crucial moment, her husband found them and managed to pull Jessy's mother in an abandoned cart to the home of two nieces some blocks away. This time, the fire didn't follow.

"It's wonderful how well poor Mama stood all our trials," Jessy would later write a friend. "I did not tell her the house was burned for about three days after it happened. The poor soul broke down and had a good cry over it, but I told her I had saved the paintings she loved so much and that comforted her a bit."

As for herself, "I aged so during those two days that when I took

Mama to my nieces, they did not know me and wondered who that old lady was whom I had engaged to take care of Mama. My hair whitened so and my face shriveled up. I suppose suffering and the intense heat from the fire caused it."

But she had won the clash of wills. She had outlived the fire.

CHAPTER 33

Running a Gauntlet

T HE NEWLYWEDS, George and Josephine Emerson, remained in Reverend Adams's house on the night of April 19, and in the morning set out for the Ferry Building to take a boat to the East Bay. There, if fate permitted, they would spend their honeymoon. Dragging a trunk with one hand and carrying a heavy suitcase with the other, George, his bride at his side, trudged through an almost blinding screen of smoke toward Market Street. After the Ham and Eggs Fire had turned this central thoroughfare into a scorched valley, bordered on both sides by towering walls of fire, police on horseback herded refugees into side streets. But now, with the whole area a desert of smoking ruins, the street had been reopened and thousands were treading this rubble-carpeted pathway to the Ferry Building. An observer would dramatically describe the scene:

> Oakland, the star of hope to which all eyes were turning—such a little distance across a narrow stretch of water, and yet such a great way for the crippled, the fatigued, the exhausted, the footsore and the heartsick; a stretch of continents for the mother trying to carry her dying child to safety, the wife kneeling in the streets alongside her injured and suffering husband; the husband upon whose shoul-

ders were more years than strength could combat and whose gray head was bowed over another lying helpless there on the ground and into whose eyes he did not dare look lest the fear in his heart would prove well founded.

When the newlyweds finally reached Market Street, they were stopped by a squad of soldiers. Glancing at the trunk, the lieutenant in command, rifle in hand, barked:

"You look husky. Let the girl sit on the trunk and you get busy with the bricks."

He pointed to a pile of bricks that a half dozen men were clearing from the Market Street sidewalk.

"But you wouldn't make George work on his honeymoon," the bride wailed. "We were only married last night, and we must get to Mill Valley in time for lunch."

The young lieutenant replied curtly, "All the better. Learn now what you have to expect in married life."

Emerson took off his waistcoat, though not his tie or derby, and, for five hours, worked amid a blizzard of ash, lime, and sand, removing bricks, tangled iron, and other refuse from the ashes. Meanwhile, his bride sat miserably on the trunk watching, her fashionable, floor-length skirt brushing the rubble and her slightly cocked hat protecting her from the blazing sun. Would this wedding day never end? Finally, the lieutenant took pity on them and sent them on.

They soon saw the Ferry Building looming before them, its huge clock, like a one-eyed Cyclops, peering down Market Street from a tower modeled after the majestic Giralda Tower in Seville; the clock had been running three minutes fast, registering 5:16 A.M., when the earthquake stopped it. This gateway to safety with its arcade that suggested the classic Roman, was built in the mid-1890s with reinforced concrete blocks and operated by the Southern Pacific Railroad. It never looked more beautiful—even stripped of its south wall, which had crashed into the bay.

But the trials of the couple were not over yet. Another squad stopped them before they reached the building and at bayonet point forced the groom, though utterly drained, to haul heavy freight. Finally, when Emerson found himself unguarded for a moment, he grabbed his bride and baggage and dashed into the crowd that was trying to board one of the ferries carrying people out of the city at the rate of seventy a minute. As one observer would describe the scene:

"At the iron gates they clawed with their hands as so many maniacs. They sought to break the bars, and failing in that turned upon each other. Fighting my way to the gate like the others the thought came into my mind of what rats in a trap were. . . . When the ferry drew up to the slip and the gates were thrown open the rush to safety was tremendous. The people flowed through the passageway like a mountain torrent that, meeting rocks in its path, dashes over them. Those who fell saved themselves as best they could."

One man struggled aboard with a bundle tightly cradled in his arms. It contained the bodies of his two infants, whom he hoped to revive in a hospital in Oakland. His wife had died in the earthquake.

A woman carrying a birdcage with almost as much tenderness was stopped at the gate by an officer.

Why, he asked, was she taking up precious room with a birdcage?

"I wouldn't let Polly burn if the whole town goes," she replied.

But where was Polly?

The woman lifted up the cage and saw to her horror that the bottom had fallen out. Polly was gone—perhaps already simmering in the pot of some hungry refugee.

So determined were some people to worm their way aboard that, according to one story that circulated after the crisis, a man asked a woman he didn't know to pose as his wife, since married couples were being given priority. When this ruse worked and they were aboard, a young man approached the "husband" and, noting that he was carrying some of the woman's baggage, said:

"I'll relieve you of some of those bundles now."

"No, you won't; they belong to my wife," the "husband" replied, pointing to a large woman at his side:

"But that's my mother!" the young man exclaimed.

"She is?" croaked the elder man after a brief pause. "Then you must be my son. Glad to meet you."

Since the newlyweds could legitimately claim to be married, they managed to join the crowd swarming over the open decks. And shortly, the vessel, veering against one wall of the piling, then squeakily scraping the opposite one, wobbled into the bay like a fish wriggling off a hook. The couple stared at the wall of fire extending the full breadth of the city, reaching up, then melting away into a smoky black sky. The fire they had so brazenly defied with a wedding conducted in its deadly midst. A reporter who had made the ferry trip would write:

"The most dreadful feature of the whole panorama was the intense silence and the intense motion. . . . The colors were neither those of night nor day, but fierce, vivid, frenzied tones unimaginable outside the crater of a volcano. The background was a sickly and lurid glow like the unearthly flush on the face of a dying man."

The couple then looked away toward the east, where a bright sun shone down like a face flushed with the joy of spring in a world they could barely believe still existed.

HUGH KWONG LIANG got lost in the darkness as he headed toward the waterfront where he planned to jump into the water and drown himself. His spirit plummeted ever lower. Was he even bungling his effort to commit suicide? Finally, he saw a light flashing at intervals from some distant object. As Hugh approached the strange glow, the shadowy shape of a boat came into view. Without realizing it, he had nearly reached the waterfront! There, soldiers were unloading something from two trucks and carrying it to the craft.

The light seemed almost like a message from heaven. Where was that boat going? He stole up to the vessel, climbed aboard, and hid under a table in the kitchen, but he was soon discovered and pulled out. What would these soldiers do to him? Throw him in jail?

This seemed the right time to leap overboard and drown himself, as he had intended.

CHAPTER 34

From Prayer to Action

"THE CITY is doomed," General Funston telegraphed the War Department on Friday, the third day of the fire. "Everything will burn."

John Dougherty could only pray that Funston was wrong. Would he be the fire chief of a city in ashes? As he stood on Van Ness Avenue helplessly watching the fire attack on a half-mile front, licking its way ever closer from the east, he was on the verge of collapse. Though his firefighters had fought their hearts out, they had managed to save only a few buildings. The battle line at Powell Street had been breached, terrorizing the thousands of people taking refuge in Union Square, which bordered on the street and had been hemmed in by a ring of towering flames on three sides.

The refugees fled in panic toward the west, the only direction still unblocked by fire, past the St. Francis Hotel, which would later grace the downtown graveyard with a new skeletal silhouette against the roaring red sky. They carried with them all the possessions they could, leaving the rest for the fire or looters daring enough to risk being roasted alive.

Finally, the Flood Building, the last building in the Market Street downtown area to remain largely untouched, shriveled into a skeleton with the silent stoicism, it seemed, of a proud martyr condemned to the stake. The fire then continued to lap its way westward, virtually unimpeded.

With the Powell line broken, a new one would have to hold at Van Ness Avenue, which was 110 feet wide. If the fire leaped westward across that broad boulevard there would probably be no way to stop it before it devoured the Western Addition, the largely residential area beyond that led to refugee-packed Golden Gate Park, the Presidio, and the Pacific Ocean.

And if teeming North Beach and the waterfront docks to the north and east melted away as well, the whole heavily populated eastern part of the city would be almost totally gone, and so would the chances of evacuating the tens of thousands of people packing the Ferry Building and its surroundings who were waiting to cross the bay to Oakland. What would happen to this great multitude in the ensuing panic?

STILL, Dougherty refused to concede defeat, especially since there was some good news from the upper Mission district south of Market—perhaps the best from that area since 1776, when its seed, Mission Dolores, the Spanish Mission of St. Francis d'Assisi, took root and sprouted into a village that would become San Francisco. Salvation began when refugees camped in a park near the heavily damaged mission were seen streaming up a hill to a yellow house south of Twentieth Street and carrying back water to the park.

Water? Where did it come from? The only known source of water south of Mission Street was a pipe running by the shattered Valencia Hotel that had cracked apart and, in towering geysers, released millions of gallons of water. A volunteer fireman sent to investigate the report found a hydrant near the yellow house and turned it on, expecting the usual dribble of liquid, if that. But to his glee, water shot clear across the street. This one worked!

The water could not have been found at a more critical time, for a stiff wind was driving the south-of-Market fire south and east. Though whole blocks in advance of the fire were dynamited, the flames simply leaped over the firebreaks and would, it seemed, soon roar into the residential and refugee-packed hills beyond. Now, with the discovery of water, horses strained to drag two fire engines up the hill leading to the magic yellow house, but lacked the strength. Finally, volunteers managed to pull the engines up using ropes, and hoses connected to the hydrant soon stretched all the way to Mission and Twentieth Street.

On the corner of Mission and Twentieth Street was the Almora, a four-story lodging house. If the Almora could somehow be saved from the approaching flames, the fire would be stopped from crossing Twentieth Street at that point, and the conflagration south of Market might dissipate.

The firemen reached the Almora before the flames did and kept the roof and top floors wet with buckets of water, sacks, and blankets, enduring the almost unbearable heat. Thus, only the bottom floors burned, and the building collapsed inward, smothering its own ruins and ending the southwestward thrust of the fire south of Market.

A voice cried out, "Three cheers for the San Francisco Fire Department and volunteers!" and there was thunderous applause by onlookers. Then, someone pulled an old, screechy piano from his house and played, "Home Never Was Nothin' Like This."

MEANWHILE, John Dougherty, apparently driven by a flash of awareness of his role in history, metamorphosed into a man of action on the evening of April 19. He jumped into his horse-drawn buggy and drove up and down Van Ness lashing out at his men with words like "cowardly bastards," demanding they stop the fire or stand and die. Infuriated by his charges, the exhausted men, just as Dougherty had hoped, somehow found a new strength.

Vowing to make the chief regret his charge, they gripped their hoses with a new firmness—hoses that could now spurt water piped to the area by naval vessels anchored in the bay at Fort Mason—and advanced in their fury toward the fire as if it were an attacking army. At the same time, every soldier, guardsman, and sailor who could be spared was brought to Van Ness to help the firemen meet the conflagration head-on. Many civilian volunteers also helped, carrying hoses, despite military efforts to keep them away. And on the night of April 19, the fire cast an eerie, deadly shadow across Van Ness.

Using doors taken from buildings as heat shields until the doors themselves started to burn, firefighters, throughout the day of April 20, threw horse blankets over embers in a desperate attempt to extinguish the fire, but it continued to work its way slowly against the wind. It seemed unstoppable.

CHAPTER 35

Dynamite and Desperation

EVEN WHILE being widely praised for his tough attempt to keep order, Mayor Schmitz had become little more than an agent of General Funston. But now, as they met on Van Ness Avenue near the fire line, he was determined to overrule the general. The two men were arguing over the best way to stop the fire before it crossed that broad avenue. They agreed, however, on one tactic. With the lack of water, blowing up buildings on or near Van Ness was the only way to stop the fire before it burst into the western part of the city.

But the two men bickered over how to use the dynamite. On the first afternoon of the inferno, Schmitz, fearing future lawsuits, had asked a judge whether dynamiting property was legal if done to prevent a catastrophe. And the judge found a precedent from a ruling made during a fire that raged in 1849.

"The right to destroy property to prevent the spread of a conflagration," the ruling read, "has been traced to the highest law of necessity and the rights of man independent of society or civil government."

Schmitz wanted dynamiters to blow up only those structures just ahead of the fire because they were doomed anyway and also because he would save the homes of his rich, important colleagues, friend and foe; he would need their support after the crisis in case he was tried. But General Funston disagreed. Indeed, he had for many hours been ordering his men to dynamite buildings that lay far ahead of the fire, even those with a chance of surviving, in order to create a wasteland too vast for the flames to hurdle.

Actually, Captain Le Vert Coleman, who had been supervising the dynamite operation, had advised an even more extreme plan: Use dynamite to excavate a trench fifty feet deep all along the side of Van Ness Avenue and extend it to the end of Dolores Street—a gully that the fire, presumably, could never cross. Funston feared that the proposed ravine could become a wind channel that would actually spread the flames, but he reluctantly acceded to Schmitz's wishes. After all, some of his own officers were pleading with him to save their homes. However, as the general had feared, the dynamite as used under the mayor's plan invariably sent fiery debris flying to neighboring blocks, which started new fires. The conflagration had become so violent that even wide wastelands, it seemed, would not be able to deter the advancing flames. One of Funston's battalion chiefs would comment:

"I came to the conclusion that dynamiting is all right provided you have plenty of water to cool off the ruins, but it is almost useless without it, as it only makes kindling wood of the buildings for the flames to feed upon."

When dynamiters arrived at the home of another high-ranking officer, a guard threatened to kill them if they tried to blow it up. Dynamite couldn't stop the fire, anyway, the officer felt, though in the end he submitted to the dynamiters' demands.

Nor was it necessary, some military leaders felt, to risk the lives of their men with such a "useless" tactic, especially since few men were trained to conduct it, and at least one commander was intoxicated while directing the operation. Some soldiers had already been wounded; one lieutenant had been killed by a premature explosion on Van Ness Avenue, and another was maimed when a charge blew up in his face. And a gunner had severely burned himself while firing a cannon being used to destroy buildings. He could not walk or even see very well, but since he was the only man around who was experienced with the gun, he was ordered to continue firing. Carried from place to place with the gun, he aimed the weapon while being propped up, and fired at a selected building. Each time, he was knocked down by the concussion as a great wave of fire and smoke ravaged the sky.

Some civilians were also victims of dynamite, critics noted. In one lodging house near the waterfront, dynamiters who were to blow up a ramshackle structure dragged out several drunks and drug addicts lying unconscious on their dirty sheets, but two who resisted were left to die in the explosion. From the ruins of another dynamited building frequented by opium smokers emerged a "ghost." Observers were startled to see a Chinese man stagger away half awake and apparently unharmed, darkly muttering to himself.

There were other problems, too, especially a shortage of vehicles to carry the explosives, since most impressed automobiles and wagons, and even hearses, were used to carry the wounded and dead to hospitals. Moreover, some car owners found devious ways to keep their automobiles out of service. One such shirker, on being stopped by a policeman, argued that his wife had been injured and persuaded the officer to go with him to pick her up at a prearranged place. The wife feigned injury, and the policeman let the husband take her home—exacting a promise that he would return with the car.

But the policeman never saw him or the car again.

The most bitter opponents of dynamiting were the civilian victims and potential victims who viewed the loss of their homes and businesses as the death of the dreams they symbolized. They were particularly outraged because, they claimed, the dynamiters were inexperienced and seldom checked the direction of the wind or the path the fire was following. Osgood Putnam, who would later take charge of relief work, would write:

"Untold grief would have been spared, and I believe in many cases mental unbalance has resulted from keen personal losses. Hundreds of cases can be duplicated where the senseless proceeding was carried out, keeping people from their homes for many hours before the fire reached them."

Another critic would write with even greater emotion:

Do you know what was the most terrible sight in the burning city? It was the streets by night, vacant, deserted, dreadful; empty of all

human sound; lighted only by the hideous glare of oncoming horror; homes of men, standing dumb and helpless, with blank, staring
windows through which none should ever look; with doors swinging in the wind through which none should ever pass; long, terrible
streets toward which the fire approached with no hand lifted to its
hindering; streets from which the soldiery had driven all men who
might desire to fight bravely to the last in their homes' defense;
streets whose awful silence was even as a cry of agony before
impending doom. . . . The throttling grip of the military [filled]
men with fear of violence, breeding deadly apathy and dumb
despair.

Why, critics asked, couldn't homeowners fight their own battles
against the fire? Soldiers even tried to stop volunteers from coming to the
aid of exhausted firemen pleading for help. Civilians? the soldiers
smirked. They were good only for clearing the streets of debris. But the
critics pointed to homeowners, rich and poor, who successfully fought the
fire armed with only barrels of wine, bottles of vinegar, pitchers of juice,
even collections of urine.

There was, for example, impoverished Telegraph Hill, which, reaching to the top of a two-hundred-foot sheer cliff, overlooked the northern
waterfront. In the mid-1800s the hill was the site of a semaphore—
accounting for its name—that signaled the arrival of ships to merchants
and townspeople awaiting goods and passengers. Now, soldiers and firemen largely ignored this height, apparently feeling the fire would be
feeding on almost worthless property anyway, though two marines
guarded the hundreds of hovel-like homes housing more than a thousand
people—for a while; one was perpetually drunk and the other had disappeared after firing at one of the inhabitants. As one observer would
write:

It was the boys of the hill that saved the hill. It was Toby Irwin, the
prizefighter, and Tim O'Brien who works in the warehouse at the
foot of the hill, and his brother Joe, who works in a lumberyard,
and the Dougherty boys, and the Volse boys, and Herman, the grocery clerk—it was they who saved the hill. It was the old Irish

woman who had hoarded a few buckets of water through the long days of fear and rumor and who now came painfully toiling up the slopes with water for the fire—it was they who saved the hill.

It was the poor Italian with a barrel of cheap wine in his cellar who now sweatily rolled it out, and broke its head in with an axe, and with dipper and bucket and mop and blanket and castoff coat fought the fire till he dropped—it was he who saved the hill. It was Sadie who works in the box-factory and Annie who is a coat finisher and Rose who is a chocolate dipper in a candy shop who carried water and cheered on the boys to the work—it was they who saved the hill.

Thank God there were no soldiers there to drive these humble people from their homes, no soldiers with loot-stained fingers clutching gun-butts to make there a desolation—to lay the feast upon which flames might feed to gorging, unmolested, unchecked, undisturbed.

Neither were there soldiers protecting the Southern Pacific depot and freight sheds at Third and Townsend Streets by the waterfront. Three men armed with a garden hose managed to save the property, spraying a few drops here and there, wherever a spark of fire landed.

And look at what happened—or didn't happen—it was pointed out, when the fire first attacked the Montgomery Block, a downtown historic structure built in 1853. Ignoring the pleas of the building's manager to spare it, the soldiers were preparing the dynamite when, as the Block's historian, Idwal Jones, would write later:

"The eccentric and religious Elder Treadwell . . . leaned out of the large window, arms raised heavenward, prophesying woe upon all who laid impious hands upon the Ark. With his long white beard and black cap, the role of the prophet sat grandly upon the elder. His voice smote down upon them: 'Their visage is blacker than a coal; they are not known in the streets. Their skin cleaveth to their bones; it is withered, it is become as a stick.' "

The soldiers, thunderstruck, paused in their work. Who was this raving madman? Or was he a prophet asking God to bring down his wrath upon them? They packed up their dynamite and vanished into the swirling smoke. The "prophet" had saved the Montgomery Block—at least temporarily.

*   *   *

PRIVATE HOMES and commercial buildings, the skeptics further argued, were not the only structures saved by people who refused to surrender to the flames. At about 8 A.M. on the morning of the quake, soldiers burst into the U.S. Post Office at Mission and Seventh Streets, south of Market, and ordered the forty-six employees who had shown up for work despite the quake to leave immediately. The fire was closing in from all sides on this stunningly designed granite building, which was completed only months earlier when workmen from Italy put the final touches to a Byzantine-style interior featuring bronze, wood, marble, mosaic, and etched glass. Flames had already slipped through the third-floor window from the northeast and turned several rooms into a roaring furnace, then danced into another window from the east.

Assistant Postmaster William F. Burke and nine others, however, refused to leave despite the threat to their lives. Burke would later report:

> [The fire] entered from the Seventh Street front into the money-order division, and the ten men divided and fought it on either side. The windows were broken by the heat, while the window frames and doors took fire. The bricks rained on everything and the smoke was suffocating. Wet sacks were nailed on the doors in an effort to save them at the outset, but finally the doors were allowed to burn until nearly charred through and then were knocked down and beaten [with the sacks, which had been soaked in water from hydraulic elevator tanks] until the flames were put out.

During the ordeal, incredibly enough, not a single letter or other document was lost or destroyed, though many of the addresses no longer existed. Even unstamped letters written on old cuffs, rags, and scraps of paper were accepted by the post office and delivered if at all possible. One survivor, Marshall Stoddard, would write to his mother on a detachable collar:

> Dear Mom,
> This is the closest I can come to paper. . . . Lost all my things, some burnt up and money stolen. Living out of charity out at Presidio. . . .

They thought I was going to have depthiria [*sic*] and just got out of hospital. I got an army shirt, a pair of trousers and my house slippers and a place to sleep.
Marshall

Stoddard's frantic mother received the collar, paying the mailman the two cents due, and read it. . . . Well, at least the boy was alive!

Not all letters, collars, cuffs, et cetera got through. Indeed, some of this mail was demolished in branch post offices as they were gradually consumed, together with valuable records and even gold and silver coins that had been stored in red-hot safes and had melted into solid rolls. Even so, the postal service had conquered the fire.

A FEW BLOCKS from the main post office, at the corner of Fifth and Mission Streets, stood the U.S. Mint, which was built in 1874, a time when great public buildings were supposed to reflect the power and majesty of the nation. But now it seemed the power and majesty were about to vanish in a sea of fire. Peering down from the roof with a sense of doom was a company of troops sent by General Funston to guard this massive brick and sandstone building with its stately portico of granite columns. Looters, he feared, might be tempted to haul away its glittering contents—over $200 million in bullion and coin. And indeed, unconfirmed rumors circulated about a gang of fourteen men who actually stormed the mint and were shot down on the steps by soldiers.

Other reports indicated that bodies were found on the steps, but that they were hardly lifeless. Dozens of heavily made-up, gaudily garbed prostitutes and their pimps, seeking to escape the fire tearing through the nearby Tenderloin district, had gathered on the steps. Supplied with a wagonload of liquor contributed by a bar owner, they were soon drunk and, anticipating the world's end, decided to live out their last minutes in the style to which they were accustomed.

"Prayers gave way to ribald song," one observer reported. "The women began flinging their arms about and showing signs of resurrection. Men cursed and some of them fought. Male and female embraced. Some danced. Soon a wilder, fiercer orgy than the red-light district had ever known was in progress on the broad sweep of the mint steps and the street in front of it. . . . It grew in intensity as the flames grew."

Meanwhile, inside the mint, Superintendent Frank Leach ordered his sixty men to bolt all the steel shutters, clear away the sizzling tar on the roof with pick shovels and iron bars, and pour caustic vitriol over the exposed roof beams. An artesian well in the basement, though damaged by the earthquake, supplied a bucket brigade with water that dampened the walls and exposed rafters.

As the hours of terror passed, embers from the fire streamed into the courtyard like shooting stars, posing a new threat, since the tar torn from the roof now littered the ground. One man climbed down with a bucket of vitriol and poured it on the burning tar, finally assuring the survival of the mint (with its improvised brothel), which, together with the post office and several other buildings, would poke defiantly out of a vast downtown desert of charred ruins.

CHAPTER 36

A Fruit Dish and a Cup of Tea

WHILE IT WAS NOW questionable whether any form of dynamiting could save San Francisco, Mayor Schmitz suddenly had a change of heart. Since his own tactic had failed, he supported Funston's view that only buildings located far in advance of the fire should be blown up to create a gap too wide for the flames to jump.

To keep the fire from gutting the western part of the city, the army would thus dynamite all along the eastern side of Van Ness from Golden Gate Avenue to the bay, a span of twenty-five blocks. Schmitz would write off the whole part of the city east of Van Ness and throw everything into the battle along that superwide avenue. He hoped that his rich, powerful friends who could influence his postfire fate would understand that he had no choice.

Shortly, a three-man demolition team was on its way from Mare Island Naval Shipyard near Vallejo to supervise the blowing up of buildings on Van Ness. But they had little dynamite left, so Schmitz ordered that a launch be rushed to Contra Costa County for some more.

At the same time, soldiers were sent to knock on doors on both sides of Van Ness, ordering people on the east side to leave immediately and on the west side to open their windows or risk having them blown out by dynamite blasts across the street. One sentry, making a megaphone of his hands, shouted up and down the area:

"This street is going to be dynamited; if you want anything in the grocery store, go to it!"

The atmosphere was tense, with firemen nervously sitting on the sidewalk by fire engines lined up along Van Ness trying to pump brine from the bay to wet down the buildings on the west side of the avenue so they wouldn't catch fire. On the east side of the street demolition squads stood by, waiting to stop the fire with dynamite in what could be the decisive battle of the war.

THE PROBLEM was that these squads did not yet have enough dynamite to be effective. And as the minutes passed, the fire crept westward block by block toward Van Ness, as if controlled by some supernatural force. On the north, it had reached Hyde Street, two blocks away, then Polk Street, only one block away. On the south, from O'Farrell Street, it actually reached Van Ness. The throngs of refugees who had fled to the Western Addition resumed their flight westward, convinced the fire would cross Van Ness and follow them. Some fell to their knees in the street blocking traffic and begging for heavenly mercy when a religious fanatic ran up and down the avenue shouting hysterically:

"The Lord sent it, the Lord sent it!"

Why hadn't the launches sent by the mayor to Contra Costa County returned yet with the dynamite? Lieutenant Raymond W. Briggs, an army officer in charge of dynamiting, rushed on horseback to the waterfront to find out. In shock, he found that the launches had not even left the dock! He then hurried to Fort Mason, where General Funston was now based, and the two men raced to a military dock, arriving just as the army tug *Slocum* was about to leave for Oakland.

Get everybody off! Funston ordered.

And in minutes the *Slocum* was headed for Pinole to pick up some dynamite.

Too late, it seemed, as the heat from the fire curled asbestos roofs along Van Ness and became almost unbearable to the firemen who, with brows and hair singed, were now trying to douse the flames with the little water dribbling through hoses that naval vessels had pumped in from the bay. At some points the fire ebbed, at others it thrust ahead, spitting smoke as a darkened, choking Van Ness became a scene of utter chaos, confusion, and near panic.

At about this time, Franklin K. Lane, a former city attorney and a member of the Committee of Fifty, was watching the struggle from Russian Hill nearby when he told a friend: "It could be stopped right here. . . . I'd take the chance myself if we could get any explosives."

"Well," replied his friend, who was unaware of the shortage of explosives, "there's a launch full of dynamite from Contra Costa County lying right now at Meiggs Wharf."

The launch that Schmitz had ordered had arrived, but no one had bothered to inform the mayor or anyone else!

As Lane absorbed this shocking news, another attorney and his wife whom Lane knew drove by. Lane quickly described the situation and sent the couple to Meiggs Wharf to pick up the dynamite and take it to Van Ness.

But would they arrive too late to save the rest of the city? It seemed so. When no dynamite had arrived by 3 P.M. on Thursday, Funston and Dougherty felt they could wait no longer. To hell with the dynamite! They would have to gamble; instead of dynamiting the houses on the eastern side of Van Ness, they would set fire to them with guncotton, an explosive used in smokeless powder. The gap between the two sides had to be widened one way or the other so the flames moving west would have little to feed on. Hopefully, the new fire would burn out before the flames coming from the east could fuse with it. In describing the "backfire" plan, one observer would report:

". . . a soldier would, with a vessel like a fruit dish in his hand, containing some inflammable stuff, enter the house, climb to the second floor, open the front window, pull down the shade and curtain, and set fire to the contents of his dish."

The soldiers would then break windows with bricks and stones to create a draft that would spread the fire. And in about half an hour, most of the houses along the eastern side of Van Ness would be aflame.

ONE OF THE DOOMED HOMES belonged to John F. Merrill and his wife, who headed the San Francisco Red Cross Society. Mrs. Merrill, whose husband was out of town, had thrown open their magnificent mansion at the corner of Van Ness and Washington to nearly a hundred refugees, asking only that they make as little noise as possible, since an aged relative lay seriously ill upstairs. And she didn't ask about their economic status, pedigree, or college degree. All were welcome.

Most of the guests had never before set eyes on so luxurious a home. It was filled with treasures from many lands, prized by Mrs. Merrill not only for their intrinsic value, but as souvenirs of happy days in faraway places. And she was only too glad to share the joy of such beauty with her guests, though they came literally off the street. But then came a chilling knock on the door. A messenger delivered the devastating message:

"Everybody must leave this house. . . . We're going to destroy it within half an hour."

Half an hour? Only that much time before a cherished part of her life would be sacrificed to the ruthless necessity of the moment?

Mrs. Merrill thanked the messenger as prosaically as if he were delivering her laundry. But as she turned away, she uttered, almost in a whisper:

"My beautiful home!"

Her guests heard this remark and, though now homeless themselves, felt a deep compassion as they gazed around at the priceless treasures everywhere. Several people stepped toward her, as if expecting her to faint. But she remained the composed, dignified hostess. And in a calm, conversational tone, she told her guests:

"I do not want anybody to leave until you have all had some tea and toast."

She quietly gave her servants orders to place all the family silver, crystal, lace, jewelry, and other valuables in a newly purchased fireproof safe she was sure would survive both dynamite and fire. They immediately obeyed, and even threw into the safe a small, inexpensive watch the family would never have missed. Then, after a short, almost surreal tea party, the guests filed out with their tension cloaked in silent dignity.

Finally, when all the guests and servants had left, Mrs. Merrill, with her arm around her sick relative, emerged and closed the door behind her. In minutes, the house was reduced to rubble that would become fodder for the fire.

Later, she returned to check on the safe that lay buried in the debris, and all she found in it were ashes and a lump of bullion. Only one item survived in its orginal shape—the cheap little watch. It kept perfect time, too, engraving in Mrs. Merrill's mind the moment a lifetime's collection of precious memorabilia disappeared amid the glowing cinders.

AND SO, it seemed, might most of the northeastern part of the city as the backfire joined with the fire lurching ahead from the east to form a solid mass of flames. They spread east to ravage Telegraph Hill once more, swallowing mansions still standing, as if impelled by a contemptuous afterthought, and greedily gobbling up everything else not already digested, down to the asphalt paving on the streets.

So intense were the flames that sparks, as feared, flew over the growing divide of Van Ness Avenue from the eastern to the western side at some points and started fires there, including one in the steeple of St. Mary's Cathedral. The building was saved when two priests climbed up to the steeple and, with an axe, sheared away the burning parts of the roof.

But then the flying sparks set fire to a stable on the grounds of the Claus Spreckels estate, also on the western side of the street, and gradually turned the mansion itself, though solidly made of stone, steel, and tile, into a burned-out skeletal ruin. As the firestorm roared on westward, tears dripped down the sooty cheeks of the firemen, the soldiers, and the civilian volunteers as they crowded behind one another, swinging a single leaky hose in one direction, then in another as required. But they refused to give up. To contain these flames some climbed up on burning roofs and pulled off blackened shingles barehanded, even as the fire at one point edged westward six blocks beyond Van Ness on its drive into the Western Addition and toward the ocean.

General Funston was devastated. He had already been irritated by a telegram from Washington asking him to check on whether certain friends or relatives of his superiors were safe. San Francisco was burning down, and they expected him to stop his work and ease their personal concerns? He had replied with repressed anger:

"Account confusion it has been impossible to locate individuals inquired for but attention will be given to the matter as soon as possible."

Now anger turned into bitter resignation, reflected in another wire to Washington:

"Fire crossed Van Ness Avenue to the west. Almost certain now entire city will be destroyed."

DYNAMITE FINALLY ARRIVED, but apparently too late. With the east side of Van Ness already afire, and the west side beginning to burn, soldiers rushed to Franklin Street, a narrower thoroughfare one block west of Van Ness, and set up a new fire line, though they would continue to defend Van Ness where possible. With Van Ness breached, throngs of people in the Western Addition fled in panic to Golden Gate Park or other safer areas in the west.

The dynamiters then set off explosions all along Franklin and the western side of Van Ness—an operation they had hoped to avoid—injuring several soldiers in the process. But whenever the fire receded at some point, it would break through at another. Gradually some firemen, drained from hours of fighting the fire with just a dribble of water and wet blankets, almost overcome from the heat, frustrated by a sense of hopelessness, and worried about the fate of their families, left the scene to return home, if home still existed. Others simply went to sleep on the street or even in a haystack in some empty lot.

At least that is where Franklin K. Lane, the attorney who was instrumental in delivering dynamite to the army, found several firemen asleep several blocks west of Van Ness.

"They lay like dead men," Lane would say.

And though many firemen continued to fight with great courage, the army viewed the firemen in general as dead men. As one army officer would say—with questionable justification:

"The fire department at this place and time was utterly helpless and unable to meet the situation."

IT WAS NOW TIME for other city magnates to abandon the symbols of their life at once. Fulton G. Berry, who lived on Van Ness, was resigned to fate when a dynamite squad rapped on his door. Yes, he lived in a virtual palace, but he would build a new one.

"Blow her to blazes, boys!" he exclaimed.

And he slouched away without looking back.

Gordon Blanding, who lived nearby on Clay Street, three doors from

Van Ness, greeted his callers more cautiously. How could he leave his invaluable art treasures, including a fine pipe organ and opulent furnishings that identified his home as one of the most luxurious mansions in San Francisco? Especially after it had already been saved by a stroke of luck; a notorious gambler saw a fire starting on the roof and, telling a companion that "if that fire isn't put out the whole Western Addition will go," climbed up and smothered the flames with a couple of sofa cushions. The man won his most important gamble.

Now Blanding would engage in a gamble of his own. Unlike Mrs. Merrill and Fulton Berry, he had no intention of welcoming the messengers with words of understanding. Understand the destruction of his home? No, he did not understand. But there was more than one way to welcome people.

Blanding led the dynamiters down to the cellar, where they would lay explosives and prepare for the detonation. There, before their astonished eyes, ranged a magnificent sight—row upon row of bottles containing the finest vintages of France's Champagne and Burgundy districts, the soft but exhilarating wines of the Rhine river region and the heavier fermentations of Duoro and Oporto.

The men were worn out after dynamiting the Merrill mansion and other homes, and Blanding observed the sparkle in their eyes. How they longed to sit down, relax, and quench their thirst with this wealth of liquid joy.

Before destroying the house, he asked, wouldn't they like to taste some of the wine? They would probably never have the opportunity again. Well . . .

And the dynamiters sat down and quaffed the most delightful stimulants they had ever tasted. They tasted and tasted and tasted, constantly remarking on the quality of each sip, then of each bottle. Blanding kept glancing at his watch. Time was passing, and who knew. . . .

JOHN DOUGHERTY and his firefighters thought they knew—but they wouldn't admit it. All Thursday night, April 19, and early Friday morning, they fought with dynamite and a small flow of water from their hoses to stop the fire at Franklin Street. If it sprang across the street to the west side, could they possibly save the Western Addition? No, it seemed, but they would keep on fighting—if necessary all the way to the sand dunes stretching from the ocean beach.

CHAPTER 37

The Lure of Rare Wine

I T'S OUT! The fire's out!"

Close to 5 A.M., Friday, a miracle seemed to occur. In frenzied joy, firemen shouted to Captain Coleman, who was supervising the dynamiting of houses on Gough Street, a block west of Franklin, to stop the demolitions. They had extinguished the fire where it had crossed to the west side of Franklin, though it still continued to rage east of Van Ness. People still living on Franklin ran into the street, wept, screamed with joy and embraced one another.

At 5 A.M., Friday, General Funston reported to the War Department: "Fire is making no progress to the west of Van Ness. A wind of considerable force now beginning. Indications now that all of that part of the city east of Van Ness Avenue and north of the bay will be destroyed. Some considerable apprehension is felt as to Fort Mason, but it is believed we can save it."

Time had been on Gordon Blanding's side as he had hoped. Thanks to the heroics of John Dougherty and his men—including the many civilian volunteers who joined in the struggle despite military opposition—the fire had been conquered. When the dynamiters in Blanding's basement went outside half-drunk and saw that the flames were receding, they happily wobbled away, leaving his house intact. Blanding quietly thanked God for giving him such discriminating taste in wine.

ARNOLD GENTHE, one of the nation's most famous photographers, best known for his superb portraits of life in Chinatown, could only hope that his discriminating taste in *whiskey* would save his home on Sutter Street just east of Van Ness Avenue. Actually, he had not thought much about the danger, since he had been too busy snapping pictures of the horror around the city.

"I have often wondered," he would later muse, "what it is in the mind of the individual that so often makes him feel himself immune to the disaster that may be going on all around him. So many whom I met during the day seemed completely unconscious that the fire which was spreading through the city was bound to overtake their own homes and possessions. I know that this was so with me."

Even as the whole east side of Van Ness from Golden Gate to Greenwich was being dynamited a block deep, Genthe dropped in on some friends living on Van Ness for a drink.

"While we were raising our glasses," he would recall, "there occurred another shock. Everyone but my hostess and I ran outside."

"Let us finish anyway," the woman said.

"Sure," Genthe replied and he quoted a line from Horace: " 'And even if the whole world should collapse, he will stand fearless among the falling ruins.' "

Genthe then went to the Bohemian Club for another drink, only to meet a friend who exclaimed: "You dummy. What are you doing here? Don't you know that your house is going to be blown up?"

Suddenly struck by this reality, the photographer rushed to his house but was stopped at the door.

"You can't get in here," a militiaman guarding the house told him, playing with the trigger of his rifle.

"But it's my home," Genthe said.

"I don't care whether it is or not," the militiaman grunted. "Orders are to clear all houses on the block. If you don't do as I say, I shoot, see?"

Genthe saw. And he answered—quickly. He had to save his hundreds of prized photos, documents, and letters.

"How about a little drink?" he asked.

"Well, all right," the man responded.

The pair walked down to the cellar, where Genthe produced a "precious bottle"—Johannisberger Schloss 1868. He had been saving this rare wine for a special occasion—and this was it. But why squander it on this crude, would-be "killer"?

"I knew that to my unwelcome guest [the wine] would mean nothing," Genthe would explain, "so I brought out for him a bottle of [undistinguished] whiskey and while he poured himself drink after drink, I sipped the wine, if not with the leisurely enjoyment that it called for, at least getting some of its exquisite flavor without having to gulp it down with barbarous haste."

But the taste turned a bit sour when the militiaman, his thirst sated, ordered, "Now you have got to get out of here or I'll have to shoot you, see?"

Thus, the ruse would not work this time, and dynamiters, who were less convinced than Gordon Blanding's guests that the fire had been stopped, went to work. Genthe watched from a safe distance as his house collapsed, turning a near lifetime's collection of invaluable memorabilia into a pile of ashen debris. His only consolation was that his cherished liquid gold from 1868 had not gone to waste.

But if Genthe's pain was perhaps eased by the wine, it was not abated by any stoic philosophy accepting fate. Instead, he would say, "I rather believe that the shock of the disaster had completely numbed our sensibilities. . . . If I had shown any sense, I might easily have saved some of the things I valued most—family papers, letters and photographs of my parents and brothers, books written by my closest relatives, and of course my more important negatives, which I could have carried away in a suitcase. As it was, practically everything I possessed had gone up in smoke."

Genthe was not the only great photographer to meet this fate. "More than any other photographer," writer Kevin Starr would state, "[Carleton] Watkins documented the rise of nineteenth-century San Francisco . . . unobtrusively, indirectly, by suggestion. . . . Twenty years before Arnold Genthe, Watkins photographed the Chinese in a spirit of respect and dignity."

Now an old man, his eyesight almost gone, he had to be led from his burning studio with no time to save thousands of invaluable negatives. The shock would help to drive him mad, and he would end his days in the Napa State Hospital for the Insane.

Hardly had the fruit of these two artists' genius vanished in the inferno when, ironically, General Funston wired the War Department: "Fire has been stopped practically at Franklin."

The ordeal was over—or was it?

CHAPTER 38

The Ghoulish Lion

A THUNDEROUS EXPLOSION suddenly rent the air. People who had been hugging one another and dancing in the street suddenly froze in shock. It couldn't be true! Had some madman set off more dynamite to fan the flames again and destroy them all? Typically, a policeman who had been watching the flames on Van Ness die out would agonizingly say to a friend:

Men, women, and children were thanking God that the disaster that had rendered them homeless and penniless was ended at last.

Then suddenly, "Boom!" . . . And the great Viavi Building at the northeast corner of Van Ness Avenue and Vallejo Street went hurtling skyward. For some unthinkable reason it had been dynamited, and ten minutes later the whole district was again in flames.

The dumbfounded [firefighters], who had felt their toil was done, gaped speechless in their amazement. Presently, when they found their tongues, you could hear such exclamations as "For God's sake! What did they do that for?"

The only answer was the roaring of the flames.

A citizen [who had been hauling hoses] came up to me, covered with sweat and smoke and dirt, and panting from his exertions. He cursed solemnly in an educated way. Then he began to explain himself, and at first I thought the excitement had put him out of his wits.

"Officer," said he to me, "a distinguished cabinet officer recently made the announcement that service in the army disqualified men from using their brains and properly directing their energies."

Then he waved his hand at the new blaze that spread roaring from the Viavi Building.

"If you doubt that gentleman's word," said he, "look at that! Look at that!"

The fire had surged again. Why? General Funston, his critics charged, hadn't taken account of the capricious nature of dynamite. The force of the explosives used to blow up the Viavi Building with its warehouse of inflammable chemicals thus hurled burning timbers and rafters into a fire-free area. And even as word spread in the refugee camps that the fire was at last snuffed out, by late morning the conflagration was raging once more along Van Ness Avenue.

At the same time, a wing of the blaze, nudged by a rising smoke-laden western wind, was veering northeastward with "indescribable fury," as an observer would note, toward North Beach and the docks along the seawall with its boats that offered the only means of whisking people to the East Bay and supplying the city with essential goods.

Thus, with both the dock area and the residential Western Addition facing destruction, the fire would, it appeared, soon be claiming virtually the whole eastern part of San Francisco, most of the built-up city.

En route to North Beach, it ravaged Russian Hill—except for a cluster of frame houses at the crest of the hill whose owners had fought off the flames with brooms, wet towels, and buckets of water from an old cistern. Shortly, however, the fire would return and devour even these holdout houses.

As the blaze neared densely populated North Beach, panic broke out; terrorized residents were hemmed in by a wall of flame sweeping in from three sides and forcing them virtually to the water's edge. No amount of dynamiting would open an escape passage, though some were able to leap into launches. They were among about twenty thousand refugees along the seawall who were evacuated after General Funston, from his office in Fort Mason, ordered every craft afloat in the bay to rush to the rescue in what some experts believe ranked as one of the largest evacuations by sea in history. But many more people in North Beach could not be saved before the wall of fire closed in on them.

Appropriately, while the flames whipped toward one defiant musician, he sat at a piano in the middle of the street atop deserted Jones Street hill, his long hair flowing and his red tie flying, tapping away Saint-Saëns's "Danse Macabre"—the dance of death. No one knows if this Nero, one of several to musically dare fate, ever finished the piece.

THE SCREAMING, panicky people in North Beach who could not squeeze onto the overpacked crafts fled in all directions like mice in a maze, trying to find a passage through the inferno. Hundreds died, overrun by the relentless blaze or the hot gases it emitted. Del Crespi and his family managed to escape to a fire-free area and survived the deadly storm, though their house did not. Throughout the following day, Saturday, wagons from the coroner's office would retrieve the charred remains of the victims amid the ruins of fifty blocks of buildings.

After rampaging through North Beach, the fire swept southeast along the seawall, destroying every obstacle in its path—oil tanks, lumber yards, iron foundaries, grain warehouses, and other buildings. Spreading farther south over territory already scorched, the fire rumbled across the Barbary Coast again, leveling the last of Jerome Bassity's whorehouses, among other palaces of joy.

As the fire once again raged farther south, chewing up like a ghoulish lion the remains of prey it had left for later, it appeared that the two-square-block cluster of buildings downtown—dominated by the Montgomery Block and including a liquor warehouse, Hotaling's Whiskey—was doomed. But as the flames approached at about noon on Friday, firemen, soldiers, and sailors from tugs anchored in the bay stood on the roofs of the threatened buildings and fought the fire with buckets of water, wet mops, and sacks, and even the contents of chamber pots found under the beds of one hotel.

Meanwhile, sailors under the command of Navy Lieutenant Freeman laid a mile-long line of hose from a tug across Telegraph Hill, up Broadway to the Montgomery Block area where, amid cheers from those who had been fighting the fire for hours, the craft's powerful pumps sent a stream of water into the flames. The Montgomery Block, whiskey warehouse and all, thus remained standing like a fortress in the desert.

A local poet, Charles K. Field, would later pen a poem that would especially delight San Francisco's secularists:

> *If as some say, God spanked the town*
> *For being over frisky,*
> *Why did He burn the churches down*
> *And save Hotaling's Whiskey?*

The firefighters didn't know, but they appreciated their reward. A naval officer would report:

"We were exhausted by this hard fight, and extremely thirsty, so we gratefully accepted several cases of canned tomatoes offered us by an official of the Hotaling Company."

Suspicion was widespread that the cases contained something a little more stimulating than canned tomatoes.

Another liquor store owner nearby had no tomatoes to hand out, or any whiskey either. As businessman Lester Sheeline stood across from the store with an acquaintance, he said:

"There's going to be a fire here in a few minutes and it's going to make one of the grandest fires in San Francisco."

"Why?" his friend asked.

"That's my store across the street," Sheeline replied. "There are barrels and barrels of the finest whiskey in the State of California and it's going to make one damn fine fire."

He then burst into laughter. How else could he bear the misery of seeing the fruit of all those years of struggle suddenly turn rancid?

BY MIDNIGHT on Friday, firemen were fighting the blaze on a wharf at the foot of Kearny Street with the help of the state fireboat *Governor Irwin* and other naval vessels, which spewed large quantities of water into the air so that the spray would form a blanket over the piers against the burning cinders.

Since few uniformed policemen could be found, Lieutenant Freeman assumed complete control of the entire waterfront district. According to one of his officers, "He looked all in, with the sweat streaking down through the grime on his weather-beaten face onto the dirty white handkerchief he had tied around his neck. . . . He was a born leader of men, a skipper whose men would go to hell and back for him. I can hear him now, 'Come on, men, sock it to 'em!' And they did."

Freeman would later report:

"My men were on the verge of collapse and were in a hysterical condition. They were too weak to handle the hose. They had then been without sleep for seventy hours, and had very little food save occasional scraps they commandeered. The hardest fight we had during the entire fire was at this point. . . . The wind was blowing a gale from the northwest, and showers of burning cinders, some three and four inches square, made this place a purgatory."

Most of the sailors in the ships involved in the struggle had been thrust into this purgatory. On one of the craft, the USS *Perry,* naval history took a unique turn. Since a Chinese cabin steward, Sing Hoy, was the highest ranking man left aboard—even the ship's cook was on the fire line—the steward became the first member of his race to command a United States war vessel in full commission. This extraordinary promotion was a measure, nevertheless, of the desperation driving the fire-fighting members of a normally prejudiced society.

On the tug *Slocum,* the men, their feet painfully blistered, had to hose down their deckhouse so that it wouldn't catch fire from the falling cinders and intense heat, which created a miniature cyclone and caused the street cobbles ashore to pop like popcorn. But the wharf could not be saved. Would all of those farther south now burn?

DIRECTLY in the path of the fire as it roared along the seawall was the brick residence of O. D. Baldwin, who headed an important real estate firm. Determined to save his splendid home, Baldwin ordered his servants to extinguish the tongues of flame shooting over from a neighboring house before they could set his own frontal woodwork on fire; he thanked heaven that when the earthquake struck, his wife had had the foresight to fill all available vessels with water, even the porcelain vases in the drawing room, and to place them around the house.

But while the blazing cornices of the house were being chopped off, a military officer accompanied by several dynamiters came and ordered Baldwin and his helpers to leave the house instantly.

"No," Baldwin replied. He would not leave, and he couldn't legally be forced to do so.

The officer stared at Baldwin, and suddenly his severe demeanor melted into a smile. He knew this man; he was a one-time neighbor, an old friend.

"Mr. Baldwin!" he exclaimed. "What can I do for you?"

"Drive out this rabble!" Baldwin replied. "And help me!"

The officer ordered the men to leave, and Baldwin's servants continued to fight the blaze furiously—until the house was saved and stood almost alone on the ravaged block. Once more, a determined citizen defied his leaders, as well as the fire, to defend the fruit of his dreams.

Meanwhile, some of the firefighters and soldiers, almost delirious from fatigue, injuries, and hunger, had become apathetic again, resigned to the worst and determined to pass the last deadly hours of the city indulging in illusions of normalcy. They looted the remains of grocery and liquor stores and casually ate breakfast washed down with beer while watching the progress of the fire, as detached from the scene as they would be at a movie.

WHEN HUGH KWONG LIANG, who had been planning suicide, was discovered as a stowaway in the kitchen of the boat he had boarded, he was about to jump overboard. But he was caught in time and soon lost his suicidal urge. For, to his astonishment, the soldiers who found him listened sympathetically to his tale of misery. They even gave him a meal—meat, vegetables, coffee—his first food in over twenty-four hours. He had only to clean up the kitchen.

The next morning, when the boat arrived in Napa, the men took up a collection and gave Hugh some money. With that, the dark shadows in his mind faded away completely and would never return. Indeed, this event helped to change his life.

"I shall never forget . . . their kindness," Hugh would later say. "I awakened to the fact that these men were the real Americans. They were so nice and considerate. It was a far cry from the . . . prejudice and harsh discrimination I had previously known."

This statement reflected a glimmer of hope, fostered by the catastrophe, that both Chinese and whites were starting to realize that they were really part of the same world. That it was possible for the Chinese to slowly integrate themselves into American society without sacrificing their cultural ties to China. And that it was possible for Americans to welcome such integration as an enrichment of their society.

Eventually, Hugh Kwong Liang would help to realize this hope. Saved by the sudden light in the darkness, he achieved the American dream he had thought was beyond reach. Several decades after Chinese gambling clubs were compared to "the wailings of a thousand lovelorn cats, the screams, gobblings, brayings, and barkings of many peacocks, turkeys, donkeys and dogs," Hugh won acclaim in clubs around the country as a singer and entertainer. No one could imagine that a man who brought such joy to people's lives had once decided to take his own.

MEANWHILE, newly married Ida Harrington saw her dream dissolve into dread. As soon as she realized that her former "husband," John McMahon, had kidnapped their daughter, Ruth, she went on a frenzied search for the young girl. She hunted for Ruth in every refugee camp in the Bay Area, waving a photo of her before hundreds of eyes. Finally, in San Francisco she found the tent that housed her daughter and McMahon.

Mother and child embraced, and shortly McMahon emerged from the tent.

Ida begged him to let her take their daughter home.

No, the child was his, McMahon replied. And that day he would leave with her for his home in St. Louis.

In a panic, Ida rushed to see a police official and urged him to prevent her daughter's departure, but he advised her to see a lawyer. Through a charity organization she found one, and he managed to secure a writ of habeas corpus that would keep McMahon from leaving the state with Ruth. She flagged down a carriage and rushed to the railroad station, with only minutes until the train to St. Louis would pull out.

Too late. The train had just chugged away—and the writ now was worthless.

Ida was shattered. But thanks to the fire, she now had her personal savior to help heal her wounds and lead her into the future.

CHAPTER 39

The Deadline and the Doorknob

S ETTLING DOWN in Golden Gate park on a patch of grass that soldiers would shortly cover with a tent, the Dulbergs tried to ignore their hunger and thirst. They had little choice. But like many refugees suffering great hardship, they found some therapeutic comfort in reading a remarkable newspaper distributed around the city on Thursday, the second day of the fire. It recorded the extraordinary experiences of other people during the first day in a special edition put out jointly by San Francisco's three leading newspapers—the *Call,* the *Chronicle,* and the *Examiner*—all of whose plants had been gutted by fire.

A fourth, less damaged, newspaper, the *Daily News,* with its press able to produce papers by hand, had alone published an edition on the first day, its banner headline crying "Hundreds Dead! Fire Follows Earthquake, Laying Downtown Section in Ruins—City Seems Doomed for Lack of Water." But reporters of that paper had little time to gather details. Indeed, shortly the *Daily News* office was dynamited into rubble by soldiers trying to stop the progress of the fire. So people knew little of what was happening outside the range of their own vision, giving rise to the spread of fantastic rumors—though the incredible reality of the disaster coincided in many respects with their frightened imaginations.

The editors of the other three papers had gone to bed dejected on

April 17 because there was so little news that day. The headlines had dealt with the splendor of the opera crowd, rumors that President Roosevelt might run for the Senate when he left the White House, the deterioration of race relations in the South. Who would buy their newspaper? They could never have imagined that one of the biggest stories in the nation's history would break in their backyard—and they would be unable to report on it because the disaster had swallowed up their offices and presses.

But refusing to miss this huge story, they met at the offices of the last surviving city newspaper, the *Bulletin*. Perhaps they could use the *Bulletin*'s presses. But the flames soon reached that building as well.

Now the *Oakland Tribune*, across the bay, was their only hope. Without consulting their publishers, the editors took a boat to Oakland and, with the help of a few reporters, set up shop at the *Tribune*. Soon, a one-shot joint issue rolled off the presses on Thursday with huge headlines blaring "San Francisco in Ruins" and "Entire City of San Francisco in Danger of Being Annihilated."

They stretched across the front page over stories describing the horrors of the catastrophe. Though some were exaggerated, they reflected the big picture of what was happening to the city and its people. The lead story breathlessly began:

"Death and destruction have been the fate of San Francisco. Downtown, everything is in ruin . . . theaters are crumbled into heaps . . . on every side there was death and suffering. . . . Men worked like fiends to combat the laughing, roaring, onrushing fire demon."

The editors were determined to conquer their own perceived adversity. Yes, they had gone to press despite enormous difficulties. But what newspaperman could thrive, or even survive, without competition? One unified edition was enough. The *Examiner* thus arranged for an exclusive deal with the *Oakland Tribune* to use its presses, and the *Chronicle* for a similar deal with the *Oakland Herald*. The two San Francisco papers, rushing to beat each other to the street, raced across the bay from Oakland in launches loaded with their respective editions. The *Chronicle* won the race to San Francisco, but the horse and buggy carrying the papers from the dock to its temporary distribution office there was stopped by a soldier.

"Get down and start shoveling those bricks!" he ordered the coachman, rifle and bayonet in hand.

The coachman's arguments about freedom of the press only induced the soldier to jab the air with his bayonet. And so bricks soon flew—even as excited readers like the Dulbergs pored over the news in the victorious *Examiner*. The full, almost unimaginable scope of the tragedy burned indelibly into their minds helped to ease their pain and turn self-absorption into compassion for their fellow sufferers. The tales of horror also, it seems, stirred dreams of a new, shining, almost fairy-tale city springing magically out of the ashes once again, even as the clouds of disaster swirled menacingly overhead.

YOUNG DEL CRESPI would not soon recover from the close call he and his family had when the fire ravaged its way through his North Beach district, leaving hundreds dead and injured. But even so great a shock did not rid him of his obsession. Hardly had the Crespis returned to the ruins of their home from the crest of Russian Hill, where they had escaped the flames, when Del clambered over mountains of debris to Lillian's house.

"There wasn't a soul around for blocks," he would recall, "and nothing was standing except a few brick chimneys. It was so quiet you could hear a pin drop, and I stayed there gazing into the ruins of Lillian's home."

Suddenly, Del saw something shiny in the ruins. He bent down and picked up the doorknob from the front door of the house—the door that had been slammed in his face. He stared at the object as if hypnotized by some secret force. Then he pulled back his arm and threw it as far as he could into the ashen wasteland. He had a strong arm. So strong that one day he would pitch for the Cleveland Indians, the Detroit Tigers, and the Washington Senators.

But Del wasn't thinking of the future now, a future he could hardly imagine without Lillian. He still harbored hope of seeing her again. For shortly after the fire, school would reopen somewhere, and perhaps she would be there.

CHAPTER 40

A Last Stand

A T 3:30 A.M. ON SATURDAY, April 21, the fire that had devoured the first pier at the waterfront in the north now threatened to sweep all of them along the seawall—unless the flames could be stopped in a final stand at the Belvedere Ferry slip near Sansome Street. Acting Fire Chief Dougherty drew up in his buggy to personally direct the battle, as he had on Van Ness Avenue. He had to turn his men's apathy into frenzy.

He had one last chance to save at least a bit of the downtown area. He would change his tactics and no longer browbeat his men, leading them instead by example. And he would have help from the *Governor Irwin* and the tugs *Leslie, Active,* and *Pilot.*

At the same time, another climactic battle was brewing on Van Ness Avenue. Once again, along the east side of the street, fire engines were lined up, pumping water from the bay into a wall of fire that seemed determined to roar now all the way through the Western Addition to the sand dunes. Firemen, military men, and volunteers rushed from one dynamited building to another, stamping out glowing firebrands and smoldering embers with wet blankets, and, when necessary, taking over hoses dropped by men overcome by heat or exhaustion. One fireman, Stephen Russell, would later write in a letter to his sister:

It took two firemen to hold the hose while two more sheltered them with a wet blanket. And many, many times we would lie down in the gutter and roll in the water, but it would not be two minutes till we were perfectly dry again. Our coats fell from our backs. . . . Our caps were burned or baked on our heads. Our feet were blistered by the heat on the rubber boots. . . . The doctors and nurses injected strychnine into us so we could go on. And one volunteer citizen . . . went up and down the line with a sack and dipped it in the gutter, then applied it to the back of our neck. . . . The horses were exhausted also and could not pull the engines at times. One place in particular up a steep hill, we put a rope on the engine and about five hundred people got hold and dragged horses, engine and all up the hill. Many of our men were delirious.

But their efforts seemed to be in vain. Some of the flames that had been driven west by a strong east wind were suddenly turned around by a western wind and retraced their path eastward. They gathered momentum as they devoured leftovers and joined flames coming from the west.

With the fire apparently on the verge of victory, Mayor Schmitz was alarmed. He would lose not only his city, but perhaps also his freedom. For would he appear heroic enough to impress those who would later judge him? He needed the support of an influential paramilitary group person-ally loyal to him, especially since Funston would certainly not support him. Nor could he use the militia to counter the general's influence, since it was widely condemned for its military crimes and, anyway, was primarily under Governor Pardee's control. The vigilante and other paramilitary groups acted independently and were also notorious for their violence and lawlessness. So what he needed was a personal police force—a Protection Committee.

Schmitz thus wanted to swear in a thousand special policemen, but how would he find rifles for them? Having no choice, he would have to obtain them from the general whose power he wanted to neutralize.

More policemen? Funston was perturbed. Why would the mayor want his own "army"? Anyway, he was preoccupied with more important mat-ters. The fire on Van Ness was edging toward Fort Mason, his refugee-packed headquarters at the northern end of the avenue on the waterfront, and he was directing its defense. Soldiers and sailors were demolishing some outlying buildings to create a firebreak and manning rooftops with hoses, ready to spout water pumped in from the bay. The general had just sent a telegram to Secretary of War Taft ominously reading:

"Fort Mason . . . may go but we will know in an hour."

And at this critical time, the mayor wanted a "private army"!

No, not a single rifle, Funston responded. Besides, he didn't have the authority to issue army supplies to civilians.

But hadn't he sent army rations to the people—without authorization?

Funston could not explain this contradiction and apparently feared that Schmitz, in his nervous resolve, might go straight to Washington with his request. So he headed the mayor off.

He would consult with the secretary of war who, he hoped, would be too worried about the fire to pay much attention to Schmitz's request.

But the secretary approved it shortly, asking Funston to "kindly detail some noncommissioned officers to instruct the citizens sworn in to properly use the rifle."

Schmitz was joyous. He would finally have a handpicked paramilitary force he could rely on to support him during and after the fire. And he had shown the "dictator" who the real boss was in San Francisco. A few hours later, his joy would soar when Funston wired Secretary Taft:

"At this hour, 11 P.M., remainder of residential section known as Western Addition seems out of danger."

Perhaps. But the war was not over. In fact, the whole dock area, including the Ferry Building, which was being abandoned by thousands of terrified refugees, was about to dissolve in smoke.

AT THE BELVEDERE FERRY SLIP, which only rescue craft would now dare approach, an army of firefighters had gathered—twenty engine companies, six ladder companies, three chemical companies, and naval teams aboard four vessels offshore, all pumping water from the bay into the fire. But all seemed helpless to put it out. They faced a defeat that would surely spell doom for the other docks as well. The city would then be sealed off from the East Bay and the world, trapping thousands in the waterfront area.

In desperation, John Dougherty leaped from his buggy and grabbed a hose from one of his firemen. He then scrambled toward the pier, almost penetrating the wall of fire, and, though nearly overcome by the heat, spurted a stream of water into it. His young firefighters—mesmerized by this remarkable act of courage by their elderly chief—rushed to help him, determined now to make a last stand, even to the death.

"The men were an inspiration," James Hopper, the *Call* reporter, would say, hopeful that the world might survive after all. "When they dropped, exhausted, in the gutters, somebody would always be there to pull them to their feet and help them to carry on. Their helmets were baked to their heads and their turn-out rig was peeling off their backs. More than one of the fire horses had collapsed in its harness."

Yard by yard, the firemen edged forward, their faces sweaty, their ears resonating with the crackle of hell. Soldiers who had rebuffed volunteers before now grabbed men off the street to help in the struggle and shot about twenty who refused to obey. Finally, a U.S. government observer would report to his headquarters:

"We saved the ferry slip and stopped the fire."

THE GREAT FIRE thus finally hissed to a steaming halt at 7:15 A.M., Saturday, April 21, after seventy-four hours of geological and incendiary rage that generated a peacetime cataclysm probably unmatched in American history. While buglers on horseback galloped through the streets announcing that the fire was finally out, Mayor Schmitz, in a sleepless daze, stumbled into his temporary office at Franklin Hall and confirmed the news to members of the Committee of Fifty. Almost immediately, the United States Army band at the Presidio emerged in full force and played martial music while refugees listened and wept. Schmitz, meanwhile, triumphantly wired President Roosevelt:

"We are determined to restore to the nation its chief port on the Pacific."

The following day, the heavens, no longer black with smoke, took a final, mocking shot at the San Franciscans; they exploded with rain—rain that, had it arrived a day or two earlier, might have saved much of their city. Now it soaked the refugees clinging together in leaky tents or under trees and turned their camps into swamps—though it could not dampen the joy of the people that the "war" had finally been won and that they could now try to piece back together their shredded lives. When someone expressed sympathy for an aged, crippled woman who lay on the wet ground, she retorted with a touch of prideful sarcasm:

"I am the widow of a Union soldier. The sufferings endured by my husband at Vicksburg were as nothing compared to mine. I am very comfortable, thank you."

CHAPTER 41

Rise from the Ruins

URING THE CALAMITY, San Francisco, in a sense, regressed into its infancy. One observer who visited the city after the fire felt as if he were stepping back into time.

"On emerging from the Ferry Building," he would say, "one was accustomed to the full-toned voice of a big town, intensified by traffic over the cobbles of Market Street and the confused shouts of hotel runners, the strident cries of newsboys, and the clanging of car bells. All of these are silent; the noises are those of a village; the wagons, express carts, and men on horseback partially screen a ghastly background."

Shadowy figures, crazed, hungry, blindly in search of lost mementos, wandered tentatively across the scorched landscape in scenes that suggested man's last destitute days on earth. An *Examiner* columnist would describe such a scene:

"Three old women, faces smudged, hands blackened from picking about in the charred ruins, came toiling with frequent halts and loud panting up the almost perpendicular hill. One of them had lost her home and three of her family were victims of the fire that hemmed in the poor on two sides. She had refused to seek refuge across the bay and now spent her time prowling among the embers. She seemed like some hideous vampire."

In the residential areas where some homes were still livable and in the parks, military reservations, and empty lots were more than 200,000 homeless refugees, as compared to 98,000 in the Chicago fire. They lived mainly in tents, where rich and poor together would cook meals on fallen brick chimneys or on weedy grass for weeks. Heating indoors was forbidden because fires could easily restart in the scorched, wind-swept homes with their broken gas pipes. The worst-off refugees crowded into the Southern Pacific Railroad station. A relief worker would report:

"I will never forget the awful sight and smell [in the station]. It was filled with women and children who apparently had just sat there in their own filth for the past three days."

But all refugees would soon eat the same food provided by relief groups and chatter about the same topic—the future of their beloved city. A future, one reporter noted, that seemed to bode well for a new civic society when a baby daughter was born to the wife of Rudolph Spreckels behind screens set up on the sidewalk in front of the heavily damaged family mansion—while "on a similar sidewalk in the next block that same night a lost cat who had no home brought forth a litter of kittens."

SOON AFTER the fire, General Funston's urgent plea for aid bore fruit, though the trains were delayed by detours because of twisted tracks buried in the earth and geysers of boiling-hot mud spurting through sand and loam along the way. The Dulbergs and other refugees would now stand in breadlines sometimes extending for blocks, where soldiers would dole out small rations of food from army trucks loaded with canned meat, fish, soup, vegetables, and condensed milk for children. Food flowed from other sources as well. Bread and pasta would come from a bakery half-buried in ashes; five thousand pounds of beef would be found in the ruins of a wholesale market; and a trainload of provisions from Los Angeles would be distributed. The people shared not only the food, but also makeshift stoves, pots, pans, utensils, can openers, and other items.

Eventually, food and relief supplies would stream in from thousands of individual donors throughout the country, the Red Cross, the army, which supervised a ration system, and the navy, which provided tons of water, as any water left in San Francisco's pipes had been polluted by sewage. William Randolph Hearst, whose *Examiner* building lay in ruins, was perhaps the foremost unofficial donor, with his *New York American* organizing charity benefits and pleading with readers for help.

Hearst arranged for all relief provisions to be carried free by trains of the Southern Pacific Railroad—whose sheds on Townsend Street by the bay would survive the fire—even though the railroad's vast, corrupting economic and political power in California was one of the publisher's principal editorial targets. The trains left jammed with a total of 226,000 nonpaying refugees wishing to leave the city temporarily. But they had one-way tickets; city leaders wanted to reduce the population until the city was rebuilt and people could earn their own way.

One relief camp leader, Colonel J. W. Lake, who had been a regimental commander in the Spanish-American War, could, oddly, thank the disaster for bringing him the happiest moment of his life. Twenty-six years earlier his wife had separated from him in Maine and disappeared with their son. For many years the devastated colonel searched for the boy but was unable to find him. Eventually, he moved to California and volunteered to help the refugees when the disaster occurred. One day a young man came to him and requested food and shelter for his wife and himself.

Name?

Lake.

The colonel stared at the young man in shock.

Lake? Could it be? . . .

It was.

And that night and thereafter his son and daughter-in-law would not go hungry or homeless.

In at least the burned-out south-of-Market district thirsty residents could choose wine over water, despite the official ban on alcohol. When the earthquake destroyed the California Wine Association warehouse, thousands of barrels of wine had drained into the basement, where a six-foot-deep pool of the prohibited liquid formed. When it was discovered, people ran with buckets to this magic pool, the panacea to all the horror they had experienced.

But if there was not enough of either water or wine, there was soon enough bread for everybody. Rabbi Jacob Voorsanger of the demolished

Temple Emanu-El, who headed the mayor's subcommittee on relief of the hungry, supervised the distribution of thirty-five thousand loaves of bread on the third day of the disaster. And additional donations from outside the city were sometimes sent not only to appease hunger but also to ease worry about relatives; refugees might bite into a loaf only to chew on a piece of paper with a scribbled plea for information about some loved one.

And more aid would soon be on the way. Secretary of War Taft, after conferring with President Roosevelt, had already asked Congress to appropriate $500,000 for relief, and the House of Representatives had passed the bill in ten minutes. Many San Franciscans nevertheless resented the President for refusing offers of aid from foreign countries, feeling this rejection reflected false pride at their expense.

But they displayed a bit of false pride of their own when they protested Roosevelt's decision to route all food and goods sent by Washington through the Red Cross, a decision rooted in the President's distrust of the city's corrupt leaders. Those refugees who dared make the precarious trek to the ferry and managed to get to Oakland would find camps there, too, and would not lack food, warm clothing, or adequate shelter. In fact, so great was the flow of aid that on May 1, only about a week after the fire was snuffed out, the *Chronicle* complained in an editorial that the refugees were receiving too much!

"Thousands of our people have been living far better than they ever before lived in their lives," the newspaper stated, "as the result of too lavish generosity which will prove fleeting, and the unwise expenditure of relief funds by local committees."

Who needed so many tents and blankets? Why were ski caps being distributed when nobody could remember when the snow last fell in the Bay Area? Interlaced with such carping about how aid money was spent was criticism that many refugees did not receive their rightful share of the aid they really needed. An outraged physician, Margaret Mahoney, would report:

"Our crowning sorrow was the relief distribution. The whole world rose to the occasion. San Francisco was supplied with every necessity. . . . But a small part has reached the refugees, for whom the relief was sent. Red tape and system have prevented those who lost their all from receiving proper care. May all other stricken communities be spared the combination of Red Cross, trained charity workers, and a relief committee composed of wealthy men."

But not only the wealthy were at fault; so were the poor, some of whom snatched more of the supplies than they were entitled to. A relief worker would report on a melee that took place in one storeroom:

"There was a regular riot going on. The clothing had all been dumped out of the sacks and men and women were grabbing and fighting for choice articles. I remember seeing a very old man fight his way out of the crowd with a bundle and when he held it up to see what he had, it was a pair of ladies' panties."

Though hunger and thirst were no longer major problems, despite such negligence, inefficiency, and theft, the threat of epidemics remained, especially since the city's sanitation system had been demolished and numerous bodies were decomposing in the ruins. Still, while some cases of typhus, scarlet fever, and smallpox were reported, they would not reach epidemic levels. On the other hand, rat-carried bubonic plague would take its heavy toll the following year.

AS THE DULBERGS languished in Golden Gate Park, they were like stitches in the tapestry of a classless society utterly alien to San Francisco's traditional caste culture. The rich and the poor, the whites and the nonwhites, the haughty and the humble, the honest and the dishonest were brought to one level, living in neighboring tents, standing in the same breadlines. Laborers mingled with businessmen, and a Chinese laundryman sat next to a millionaire's wife clad in a velvet cloak she had worn to Caruso's performance. Many of the rich had lost everything, while some of the poor earned what they regarded as fortunes charging exorbitant prices for carrying the household goods of the rich in carriages or wagons, or on beefy shoulders.

Still, tradition finally conquered, at least in one respect: Police ordered all Chinese to gather in a separate corner of the park. If they were to die, they would have to do so among their own. And while the Chinese were permitted to get in the breadlines, most were afraid to do so, whether in Golden Gate Park or elsewhere.

In some cases, soldiers "confiscated" the rations that some Chinese managed to accumulate. One private walked up to a group of Chinese who were eating and asked one of them if he would like to work, the *Chronicle* would report, and the man replied that he was too sick. The soldier would then relate:

"I made a pass with my gun and he moved with a jump. We took away their board of supplies, put the whole bunch to work, and when we thought they needed food again, gave them plenty to eat. This pleased them very much and they were all right and appeared to be satisfied."

Satisfied that they had to depend on the soldiers' generosity in doling out food belonging to them?

But after relief supplies arrived, many of the refugees were as satisfied as life in the park would permit, and children like Etta indeed loved "picnicking" every day. Doctors hung up shingles on trees noting their availability. And one family hung up a sign with the inscription GOD BLESS OUR HOME, and another announced IF YOU ARE THIRSTY, GO INSIDE, THERE ARE SPRINGS IN EVERY BED. Still another rhythmized:

> *The cow is in the kitchen,*
> *The cat in the lake,*
> *The children in the garbage pail,*
> *What difference does it make?*

This lighthearted mood became a bit curdled only when soldiers tramped from tent to tent, calling out the names of missing people, reminding everyone of the immense tragedy of the disaster.

After several months, the shingles and signs would be nailed to two- and three-room cottages that refugees would rent at a nominal rate and later own. Never in the history of San Francisco would so many of the working classes own their homes—homes with gardens where children who once played in dark alleys or cold cellars would romp among the flowers and vegetables.

THIS INDOMITABLE SPIRIT would change the lives of the survivors, including the Dulbergs, who would move into one of the new cottages, and then into a larger home in Daly City. They may have lost everything, but they had triumphed over the earthquake, the fire, and the militia under the most horrific circumstances. And in the midst of it all, a baby was born—as if God wanted to compensate them for their terrible ordeal.

But God, for reasons beyond mortal comprehension, can take away, too. Exactly three years later, the little girl born on that day, who had so miraculously survived one of the most devastating fires in history, was celebrating her birthday when she set her dress on fire while playing with a match—and burned to death.

Even this tragedy did not deter the Dulbergs. Was not misfortune, however, unbearable, the supreme challenge? Like San Francisco itself, they would recover and prosper.

RESCUE PARTIES threading their way through the ruins responded to the cries of many people trapped in the wreckage, but they could not hear those of fisherman Antonio Compania through the thick walls of the refrigerator in which he had inadvertently locked himself. Not until eight days after the great fire did fellow employees in the meat and fish market remember seeing him run into the refrigerator. Turned into a stifling prison, it remained standing alone after virtually every wall within a mile had been leveled by the earthquake, fire, or dynamite. Now a rescue team used dynamite to scatter bricks and other wreckage in which the refrigerator was partly ensconced.

The door was then wrenched open and there lay a skeletal figure—Antonio Compania. He appeared to be unconscious but still alive. How had he survived? Teeth marks in the rotting beef hanging on hooks gave some clue, but he had had no water after the ice melted in the fire that enveloped the refrigerator. He must have futilely screamed and rapped on the zinc wall for hours and days at a time, even though dynamiters had been only a few feet away.

When rescuers broke in, they dragged Compania into the street and tried to resuscitate him. They were hopeful when he opened his eyes slightly. His throat tightened when he tried to talk, but he managed to utter some unintelligible gibberish. Had he gone insane? Nobody could be sure, for he soon closed his eyes for the last time.

Other rescuers digging in huge piles of wreckage around the post office expected to find the bodies of postal workers believed to have been killed in the triumphant struggle to save the building three days earlier.

How could anyone buried under tons of rubble still be alive? But after shoveling bricks and stones for hours, the men saw debris moving slightly. Was it possible? . . .

The workers frantically thrust their shovels deeper into the pile, and finally they stared into the hollowed eyes of a decrepit figure. In joy, the diggers pulled him out. They had saved at least one life. One? The earth moved again, and again. . . . Finally, it stopped—after eight men had been pulled from what should have been their graves. And all with only minor injuries! Soon there were eight more postal clerks sorting out letters—many from people pleading with recipients to find loved ones even if they had to perform miracles.

YOUNG DEL CRESPI was also hoping for a miracle.

"With my shoes shined, hair slicked back with my mother's olive oil, and a new suit of clothes on, and with all my wealth, made gathering junk," Del Crespi would recall, "I attended the opening day of school. The new teachers and principal looked us over and decided we were getting so big by this time that they jumped us up a couple of grades on account of those we had missed during the catastrophe. They started me off in the high seventh grade, which was quite a skip from the fourth grade."

But delusion finally dissolved into reality. Lillian was not there. Not there to play games with him, help him with his homework, and stand by him when the gang called him the "teacher's pet." Why had he bothered to buy all those new clothes—knickerbockers, long black stockings, high laced shoes with hooks on them, a shirt with a Buster Brown collar? Or to slick back his hair? All for Lillian. Yet one more time he had failed to find her. He had tried so hard after the fire, searching every refugee camp in the Bay Area.

"I had just about run out of camps," Del would agonizingly recollect, "and I almost gave up hope of ever seeing Lillian again."

But not quite—until one terrible moment. Noting that a local shop-keeper was rebuilding his shattered store near the ruins of Lillian's house, he asked the man if he knew what became of his beloved's family.

"Yes," the shopkeeper replied, "they all perished in the earthquake and fire."

Del was stunned. He went home, tearfully tracing the Bridge of Sighs, and locked himself in his room. His life, he felt, was at an end, and he refused to go back to school.

"I played truant for four days," he would say, "until Sweeney, the hookey cop, came after me and made me go back."

But Del became an indifferent student and, without Lillian to inspire him to study hard, failed even to graduate from grammar school. He found peace only in playing baseball, though eventually he would marry a former classmate who reminded him of Lillian. His baseball career took off when, after jobs with semipro teams, he signed with the San Francisco Seals of the Pacific Coast League, a stepping-stone to the majors.

But not even professional success and marriage to another could blot out the memory of Lillian. She would forever live in his heart, and was cheering him on, he surely felt, when he delivered his finest pitches. Cheers that may have helped to drown out the slam of the door that would still occasionally, and torturously, echo through his mind.

HARDLY WAS the fire over when Mayor Schmitz decided it was time to make it clear to General Funston just who was running San Francisco. He had scored a victory when Secretary of War Taft agreed to his request that rifles be issued to a new special force under his control. But that wasn't enough. Funston was still making decisions on his own involving security—impressing people for work, sending his troops, who were often unruly, to any part of the city he wished.

This problem only added to the mayor's fear that his own leadership would be tarnished by the behavior of the militia when he desperately needed public support in the upcoming criminal case against him. Only hours after the fire was out, a militiaman punctuated victory with a final shot; when a young man refused to throw away a pint of whiskey he carried, the militiaman casually raised his rifle and shot him dead.

Hoping to free himself from the albatross of the militia, Schmitz went to Fort Mason for a showdown with Funston.

Would the general, he urged, please assume control of the militia.

Funston was taken aback. How could he? He didn't have the authority. He wouldn't dare say that he was having a hard enough time controlling his own troops; nor would he explain why the question of authority had not kept him from illegally sending these troops into the city.

As word of the friction between the two men leaked out, Secretary Taft grew concerned and demanded an explanation. Both were now alarmed. The general had falsely assured Taft that he took actions only in consultation with the mayor. And the mayor feared that the public would react against him for opposing the wishes of a highly respected war hero on security matters.

Friction? "The excited imagination of some overworked newspaper correspondent," Funston would reply.

"Absolutely without foundation," Schmitz would wire the secretary. "We are not only without difficulties but are cooperating in the utmost friendship and harmony." And in a second telegram he called the report "remarkably malicious and decidedly untruthful."

Why continue the feud, Schmitz apparently felt, when his own future was at stake? Especially since Funston was about to bow out anyway as military "dictator" of San Francisco. On April 23, a day after the fire was extinguished, General Greely returned from leave and took over the military command from Funston.

That same day, the municipal record would read, the Committee of Fifty passed a motion "authorizing that a resolution be sent to the governor requesting the withdrawal of the militia from the city and county of San Francisco, and tendering a note of thanks to the militia for their efficient services in maintaining law and order."

A few days later, on April 28, the office of the National Guard's judge advocate admitted that the militia's services were not always as efficient as the Committee of Fifty politely, if insincerely, stated in seeking to rid the city of these services. That office would write superiors:

"Within the last three days between fifteen and twenty members of the National Guard of California had been arrested by . . . [militia] sentries for looting. . . . They frequently threaten to make resistance when ordered . . . to desist looting. . . . Many respectably dressed women were also digging in the ruins and said to the sentries . . . that the soldiers had told them that this was a good time to loot."

Governor Pardee, however, was reluctant to withdraw the militia and thus concede that *his* force was guilty of flagrant misconduct. Instead, he asked General Greely to take control of the force. But Greely, like Funston before him, refused. The militiamen thus remained in the city with the backing of Mayor Schmitz, who wanted Pardee's support in the coming corruption trial. They stayed, even though nearly 10 percent of the standing army needed to keep order would shortly converge upon San Francisco and remain for months as part of the largest joint army-navy operation in the country up to that time. Criminal members were free to continue making life miserable for the city even during the recovery period.

SOME MONTHS LATER, the city made life miserable for Mayor Schmitz. For all his efforts to scrub clean his public image, he became, officially, a public enemy. Together with Abraham Ruef, he was, as he had feared, tried and convicted on graft and bribery charges and sentenced to prison for several years. The two men, for example, were found to be secretly in the pay of United Railways, an especially shocking revelation since they led a party that had supported a strike against the railroads. The mayor had earned the money by approving an illegal United Railways streetcar franchise that Ruef, in his role, tried to have legalized.

The judge growled to Schmitz that "by your conviction you will lose the respect and esteem of all good men." But he was wrong. The mayor's popularity only grew among good as well as bad men. He may have been a "crook," but he was a good-natured, well-meaning one in the true San Francisco political tradition who, moreover, showed his courage during the catastrophe.

And so, because of his "heroic" role in it, Schmitz, unlike Ruef, managed to have his sentence suspended, just as he had hoped. Eventually he would regain some of his political power as a city supervisor. When he died in 1928, several mayors and other city officials served as pallbearers, and companies of firemen and policemen as a guard of honor. The funeral service and procession to the cemetery drew crowds of mourners.

Even Ruef, languishing in prison, would find much of the public ready to forgive his crimes and to support a reduction of his fourteen-year sentence. He convinced many people, among them Fremont Older, his most relentless critic and editor of the *Bulletin,* that his greed had understandably resulted from disillusion with his failed efforts to reform the graft-ridden political system he would ultimately embrace. Was Ruef not, in his frustration, the victim of a poisonous cynicism that diverted his great intellectual energy into the odious channels he had found so tempting?

Shortly after Ruef was imprisoned, in part because of the *Bulletin's* crusade, Older would lament:

> I have tried to repent for the bitterness of spirit, the ignorance I displayed in pursuing the man Ruef, instead of attacking the wrong standard of society and a system which makes Ruefs inevitable. I may not have entirely succeeded, but at least I have reached the point where I can see the good in the so-called bad people, and can forgive and plead that mercy be shown to Abraham Ruef. . . . [He] and the others had merely been found out and caught. Being found out was Ruef's chief crime. I feel sure that if he had escaped detection, even though we were possessed of a general knowledge of all that he had done, he would still be honored and respected in this community. So Ruef, after all, was punished for his failure, not for what he did.

He was, after all, a typical, if especially brilliant, San Francisco politician with gold-rush impetuosity flowing through his veins. A man whose earth-shaking political impact would end, appropriately, with the earth-shaking disaster that destroyed the city he robbed. After spending seven years in San Quentin—where, with impassioned humility, he pressed for prison reform—Ruef was released and returned to his real estate ventures, only to die in 1936 awash in bankruptcy.

IF THE CATASTROPHE helped to produce cleaner government, it also helped many criminals, blue and white collar, to avoid punishment. For with court records destroyed, little evidence of wrongdoing survived. And in the postdisaster chaos, prosecution of crime was pursued with little vigor.

So hundreds of civilian criminals and sightseers-turned-looter (not counting the hungry, impatient poor who grabbed more than their share of items in storehouses) ransacked freight cars and Red Cross trucks carrying relief supplies. One man was found driving away from a relief station with a wagonload of provisions under cover of a Red Cross flag, hoping to stock his grocery store without cost. Others dug among the ruins for booty, spurred by a government ruling that looters should no longer be shot but simply be put to work clearing the streets.

Nor could property owners depend on the military to prevent looting. The question remained even after the catastrophe: Who would prevent the *military* from looting? When Southern Pacific officials asked the army to send them soldiers to guard boxcars loaded with relief supplies, the soldiers pilfered the cars themselves!

Bureaucrats took their share as well. For example, when eighty thousand barrels of flour rolled in from the Midwest, they proved to be of little use to people still cooking primitively in the street. Instead, they were auctioned to commercial bakers at extremely low prices, suggesting graft.

Among those seeking to profit from hard times were five fashionably dressed ladies who called at the few homes still standing and asked the owner if they could rent a room. Living in a refugee camp was unbearable, they said, and they would be willing to pay the owner well. After examining a room, they departed, promising to return soon. They didn't. And the owner soon learned why: Drawers containing valuables had been cleaned out.

ORGANIZED CRIME in the Barbary Coast and Chinatown, however, never fully recovered its power and gradually dissipated. Still, Jerome Bassity did manage to build what he claimed was the world's largest whorehouse—too large, it turned out, to survive very long.

More than eighty known criminal offenses were committed within three months after the calamity, with the sprouting of about a thousand illegal makeshift saloons in the ashen wasteland. (Liquor could be legally sold only after the three months.)

Cliff Graves, a patron of a bar in a boardinghouse called The Phoenix, which had sprung up south of Market, would relate what typically happened at a poker game in the bar:

"A row started [and] . . . the crowd surged out the double door onto the sidewalk. There was [*sic*] at least two hundred men surging around. . . . They fought for a few minutes when someone yelled, 'He's murdered.' The crowd ran in all directions. . . . In just a few seconds there was only one man left. He waved his arms, turned and run [*sic*] up the street. . . . We found he had his throat cut from ear to ear. He gave one grunt, and turned over."

Later, Graves heard shots coming from another saloon and ran "to see the fun." He asked several policemen nearby "why they didn't go over and stop the fight. They said that when the fight and shooting stopped, they would go over and count the dead. We waited a few minutes. . . . [Some] girls stopped screaming and the cops went over. I was right behind them. Five men and two women were dead. The old madam told the cops to call the wagon, that business had to go on."

IRONICALLY, the immediate resurgence of criminal enterprise mirrored the optimistic spirit of San Franciscans, whether virtuous or not. Some cynics doubted that the city would ever rise again. Thus, Will Irwin would write in the *New York Sun*:

"The old San Francisco is dead. The gayest, lightest-hearted, most pleasure-loving city of this continent, and in many ways the most interesting and romantic, is a horde of huddled refugees living among ruins. . . . San Francisco was the city that was."

Some San Franciscans were even more pessimistic about the future. Thus, after fleeing the city one man wrote a letter to "My dear Carl":

This is Sunday—the Lord's day of rest! His week's work is ended and he did it well. The doom of San Francisco has been branded with unrelenting, uncompromising ferocity on the face of the darkest history of all mankind. I am so utterly physically and mentally unstrung that my mind and body refuse to act. The use of the pen is a hardship to me. Given the last four days and experiencing and seeing what we had to encounter before our hastened flight from the city of hell and devastation has left its indelible imprints of despair on everybody's vision haunting him to the rest of his days.

These gloomy outlooks, however, did not truly represent the spirit of San Francisco after the disaster. In fact, the city began to rise again even before the ashes were cool. Writer Gertrude Atherton would philosophize:

"Frivolity, the most unpardonable and far-reaching of all vices, is at an end in San Francisco for years to come. . . . Everybody looks back upon the era 'before the earthquake' as a period of insipidity, and wonders how he managed to exist. If they are appalled at the sight of a civilization arrested and . . . treasure gone up in smoke, they are equally aquiver with a renewed sense of individuality, of unsuspected forces they are keen to pit against Nature."

In the same spirit, Charles Page, a survivor, would write to his son: "We saw no crying women or downcast men. There was an exhilaration in the desperation of the moment. What it was I do not know but surely men forgot the past, seemed to overlook the present and to face only the future, the future which would repair the disaster. There were smiles on people's faces at times; there was seriousness all the time, but the determination to overcome the disaster was universal."

This attitude was apparent even among some visitors who were in the city on business when the earthquake struck. One man from New York who decided to remain would explain to newsmen:

"The calamity has put all men as nearly on a level, in the matter of wealth, as a community can be. The rich have lost the greater part of their fortunes and most of their advantages. All of us are starting from scratch and the race is to the best man. If I cannot rise to the top under these conditions then I will acknowledge that the fault lies in me, not in circumstances or conditions."

Besides, some visitors felt, there had to be something special about a city that was loved with such passion by its residents. As one of them, "Ross," would write to his friend "Max" on June 12, 1906:

"I have never seen people with such a genuine love for their city as the San Franciscans possess; it is a *real* affection. . . . The people say: 'Dear old San Francisco, even in ruins, dearest old city.' They seem to love even the cobblestones of the streets. I like these Californians, their ways are different from those of New Englanders."

Perhaps even more reflective of the city's spirit was a poem scratched on the back wall of a sidewalk kitchen:

> *Don't cast round that look of gloom,*
> *Like you've stepped out of a tomb.*
> *Hide your heartache if you're sad,*
> *Make believe you're feeling glad.*
> *Chase the mean look from your eye,*
> *Things will boom up bye and bye.*

This poem could have been scrawled by almost any San Franciscan, perhaps by the woman interviewed by writer Annie Laurie, who would report:

She was standing in a funny little square tent made partly of boards and partly of ragged bits of cloth. She wore a dress that had been through the fire with her, but her bright hair was brushed neatly back from her rosy face. She was washing dishes, petting a dog, talking baby talk to a baby and bossing some half-dozen of boys, all at the same time.

"Run down to the edge of the pavement with these beans," she said to one boy, "and see if you can't find somebody's fire to warm 'em a little by. Hike over to the commissary wagon; they're giving out eggs there. The baby can't eat these beans. Where are those blankets? Didn't I tell you rascals to put them out to air?

"Oh, yes; I've got thirteen boarders. Yes, we all sleep in this tent. No, they don't pay me a cent. Burnt out? Who isn't? What's the use of being blue about it, though? Didn't you see our totem at the door? Allow me to present you. This is our friend, Happy Hooligan."

And there on the ridgepole of the tent was perched a little wooden Happy Hooligan on top of a crudely painted sign that said, as did the poem on that kitchen wall:

"Cheer up."

Actually, more than courage, ambition, and a cheery outlook would be needed to energize and define the new San Francisco—a new sense of social justice and civic brotherhood would be necessary as well. Thus, the rigid class system would gradually break down and racism would recede. As one observer, Pauline Jacobson, would enthuse:

"Everybody was your friend and you in turn everybody's friend. The individual, the isolated self, was dead. The social self was regnant. Never even when the four walls of one's own room in a new city shall close around us again shall we sense the old lonesomeness shutting us off from our neighbors. Never again shall we feel singled out by fate for the hardships and ill luck [we may have]."

Immediately after the fire, some San Franciscans saw the destruction of Chinatown as the one happy result of the catastrophe. In the *Overland Monthly,* a writer declared that the "fire has reclaimed to civilization and cleanliness the Chinese ghetto, and no Chinatown will be permitted in the borders of the city. Some provision will be made for the caring of the Orientals."

Abraham Ruef, who served as Mayor Schmitz's director of Chinese affairs before both men were tried and convicted on corruption charges, agreed at first. The military did as well, and an article soon appeared in the press reporting:

"The military authorities, it is generally understood, have decided to deport all homeless Chinamen to a general rendezvous on Angel Island, there to remain until ways and means can be found by which they can find occupation and be housed. Many of the woman campers surrounding the Chinese camps at the Presidio and North Beach have requested their removal to some distant points."

The Chinese refugees were thus herded from one outlying area to another. City leaders tried to confiscate their valuable property in the center of town, and some even wanted to keep Chinese who had fled to Oakland from returning to San Francisco. Interestingly, the Chinese replied to these signs of prejudice with pride: They were the only ones who submitted lists of salvaged items to the hard-pressed fire insurance companies.

The legal system finally restored their traditional Chinatown to them. Abraham Ruef even helped, his lawyerly instincts toward justice surprisingly overruling any dreams he may have had of a real estate bonanza at the ravaged site. There was no legal way, he concluded, to force the stubbornly defiant Chinese to move from the land they owned. At the same time, China's empress-dowager personally protested against the city's racist policy, embarrassing city leaders internationally. Finally, these leaders relented.

But the new Chinatown would no longer lure sinners with underground dens of iniquity. And the Chinese, who had shared the terror and the moments of prayer and hope with their white-skinned neighbors, would seldom again be feared or regarded with contempt by most of them.

At the same time, the Christian and Jewish communities grew closer than ever before. After the Jews—almost a fourth of the city's population—lost almost all their synagogues, the Calvary Presbyterian Church offered temporary sanctuary to the Temple Emanu-El congregation. In gratitude, Rabbi Voorsanger, the gutted temple's spiritual leader, would write:

"It is not only an act of grace to let the children of the old Covenant of Israel have asylum in the home of one of the oldest Christian congregations of California, but also a striking evidence to what extent humane sentiment has superseded the consideration of purely theological differences. We are one people at the present time, and sectarian lines are very faint indeed."

In fact, residents of whatever origin, having survived and conquered the catastrophe together, would view themselves with greater pride as San Franciscans, and not simply as members of a particular ethnic or class community. Of course, some level of community identity would always exist and would even spur spirited, even bitter, conflict. Nevertheless, a feeling of camaraderie unknown since the early days of the gold rush now permeated society. Charles Page would marvel to his son:

"San Francisco has had the name of a bad city. If it is, it has received punishment in the extreme. The good in it has never been known until now. Its inhabitants are of all kinds; but neither race, or education, or condition in life could be distinguished in the spontaneous outburst of bravery, generosity, and self-sacrifice. All were alike."

Not really all. For some of frailer character would be forever haunted by guilt-filled memories of screaming victims they ignored as they fled in terror, of loved ones they abandoned to save themselves. Others viewed the disaster as an opportunity to profit from the misery of their fellows, or were simply indifferent to their agony. Thus, some greedy landlords who normally rented rooms for $25 a month were now demanding $350 for the few rooms that had survived the disaster. But these social misfits were the exceptions and could be found mainly among the rich.

As Florence Mabel Sylvester, a nurse who cared lovingly for many of the injured, would comment:

"The vultures preyed on those that had money, and when I came to the Western Addition, and near the fashionable homes, I felt an air of coldness and selfishness all about; but those who were first ruined by the fire, who lost all and had no chance to save things, they were the ones who gained the greater view, who saw in truer proportions, who felt and showed the brotherhood and sisterhood of man."

IT WAS this spirit of fairness and compassion combined with a keen business sense—the justly proportioned ingredients of the American dream—that would drive Amadeo Peter Giannini, founder of the Bank of Italy. Hardly was the fire under control when he opened a temporary bank at the home of his brother, Dr. Attilio H. Giannini, on Van Ness Avenue. Other larger banks, also demolished and with their funds locked in vaults that remained white–hot for weeks, would delay reopening. But the Bank of Italy, with its ash pit of coins worth $80,000, cashed checks for limited amounts, accepted deposits, and made loans for rebuilding. Nor did Giannini have to worry about the credit rating of his customers, most of them from Italian North Beach; he knew virtually all of them personally.

A gamble? Yes. He had $80,000 to cover deposits of $846,000. But, he calculated, since the money would be used to encourage the rebuilding of homes and businesses, and would be loaned at fair interest, the people would jump at his offer. He knew his San Franciscans. They would not make a run on his bank and break the one institution that could help them to immediately begin rebuilding their lives.

And Giannini was right. He sat himself down on a plank resting on two barrels and began doing business again with his trusted, and trusting, customers. Business that would soar into the stratosphere, to the shock of the big bankers, as a new San Francisco sprouted from the ashes. Gradually, his fireplace Bank of Italy grew into one of the world's banking giants—renamed the Bank of America.

IF OPTIMISM had always been a San Franciscan trait, this feeling after the catastrophe was reflected not only in public resolve to resurrect the city but also in personal resolve to pursue dreams relentlessly. George and Amelia Horton never gave up their dream of finding each other, even after both moved to Oakland soon after the fire. Yet, each surely recognized the irrationality of the dream—hadn't they checked with every possible government office, relief organization, hospital, neighbor, and friend?

A few weeks after the disaster, George was walking down a busy street

in Oakland, his mind idle, when a strange thing happened. Someone passing by caught his eye. He stopped and glanced back, as did the passerby, and found himself staring into the face of a young woman who seemed just as startled. In a second, they were clasped in each other's arms and weeping openly.

The nightmare of George and Amelia Horton was over.

SO, TO SOME EXTENT was the nightmare of George and Josephine Emerson. Still shaken by their terrifying experience, they cut short their honeymoon in Mill Valley and went to stay at a friend's apartment in Berkeley. There, a few days later, Josephine's sister, May, wed the son of Reverend Adams, who had joined the Emersons in marriage in the middle of the raging fire. The ceremony seemed almost to be a happy replay of their own surreal wedding—without the horror that time would never erase from their memories.

Instead of a claustrophobic room sealed to keep out fiery ashes, a cool breeze drifted in through open windows. Instead of terror written on every face, a calm joy lit up each. Instead of a desperate prayer on trembling lips, there were songs of hope and happiness. Instead of a smoke-soiled wedding dress, the bride wore a sparkling white gown.

When the ceremony was over, guests lifted a glass and toasted the couple. While at the Emerson wedding the glasses had been empty, now they were full—a symbolic measure, it seemed, of San Francisco's loving tenacity and courage in its struggle to rebuild itself into a safer, more open-hearted, even more beautiful metropolis than the one that vanished in a storm of earth and fire.

Epilogue

THE DEATH TOLL from the earthquake and fire was staggering. Although the official number was 498, a figure repeated in many accounts of the disaster, it was absurdly and, it seems, deliberately miscalculated to reassure potential business investors that San Francisco was a safe place to live and work. At least that many people alone were summarily executed for seeming to loot, hesitating to obey the most inconsequential order, or simply annoying someone carrying a gun.

This is the conclusion of Gladys Hansen, a former San Francisco Public Library official who now heads the Museum of the City of San Francisco. She has done extensive research on the question of casualties and destruction, examining health, cemetery, probate, orphanage, and coroners' records, and communicating with survivors and their descendants as far away as Europe. While she has been able to confirm three thousand deaths, the catastrophe, she estimates, probably claimed between five thousand and ten thousand victims—one out of every forty to eighty people trapped in the city. Thousands more were injured.

"Whole families disappeared," Ms. Hansen says. "Not even bones were left."

The number of casualties may have been this great because the fire, spreading almost immediately after the earthquake, prevented rescuers from digging for people trapped in the wreckage. The fire thus not only incinerated victims killed in the quake, but also apparently burned alive most of those who might have been saved if a more immediate effort had been made to find them. Nor was there a serious attempt to investigate their disappearance. Some observers believed that the fire might have created less havoc and killed fewer people if firemen, deprived of water, had doused the flames with the estimated 35 million gallons of wine stored in vats and barrels in the San Francisco area.

Mayor Schmitz and his political and business cronies not only conspired to fictionalize the death toll, it would appear, but they also falsely minimized the earthquake's role in the catastrophe, attributing most deaths and almost all the damage to the fire. As a result, many desperate homeless, accepting these claims, built new dangerously unstable wood-frame houses, even on "made" ground, though many such predisaster structures had collapsed in the earthquake, with only the wreckage devoured by fire. Again, why frighten away investment with tales of natural disaster that only God could control? Fires, on the other hand, could be controlled with better fire-safety measures.

A member of the State Earthquake Investigation Commission charged that geologists were "advised and even urged over and over again" not to release geological data on the earthquake to the public, and condemned the "general disposition that almost amounted to concerted action for the purpose of suppressing all mention" of the earthquake.

"Owners of property along the faults," the expert maintained, "kept geologists from publishing their knowledge by threatening them with lawsuits."

Consistent with this charge, which was most forcefully pushed by the earthquake-battered Southern Pacific Railroad, James Horsburgh Jr., the company's general passenger agent, wrote to every California Chamber of Commerce: "We do not believe in advertising the earthquake. The real calamity in San Francisco was undoubtedly the fire."

To support such self-serving declarations, artists were hired to doctor photos so that the fire was seen burning otherwise undamaged buildings, which, in reality, had been damaged by the earthquake. Even years later, in the March 1911 issue of the *Bulletin of the Seismological Society of America,* Professor Andrew Lawson wrote that a discussion of earthquakes was as welcome in San Francisco as a discussion of the plague. As a result, funds for earthquake research could not be obtained, helping to explain why the city would adopt strong earthquake-bracing laws only in 1947.

So effective was this deceptive effort that San Franciscans would almost always refer to events as having taken place either "before" or "after" the *fire,* seldom referring to the earthquake, though it triggered the fire. Yet, Gladys Hansen's research has indicated that most victims died in the quake, which measured the equivalent of 8.3 on the Richter scale and was exceeded in magnitude by few recorded earthquakes in history.

In any event, there is likely to be a long pause between great earthquakes in the San Francisco Bay Area. Karl V. Steinbrugge, of the University of California at Berkeley, would write:

"The frequency of major or great earthquakes strongly affecting at least large sections of the San Francisco Bay Area may reasonably be assumed to be from sixty to a hundred years. . . . Further, the forces released by the 1906 San Francisco shock appear to be a reasonable maximum for future great shocks."

A prognostication that offers little comfort to San Franciscans seared with the horrors of the 1906 calamity that have passed down through the generations via diary, letter, and legend.

THOUGH THOUSANDS of people were no longer alive to enjoy the final triumph, the survivors reveled in this treasured moment as the sky cleared and the red sun turned to gold once more, with the pall of smoke finally dissipating into history. It cast its rays now on a different city, a city with its forty-seven square miles largely ravaged. For three miles west from the Ferry Building to Van Ness Avenue, almost half the way to the ocean beach, and for six miles north and south, the land was a desolate field of dying embers, a wilderness of red bricks, hot, glowing rubble, and twisted iron beams. Chimneys stood in lonely isolation like scorched trees after a forest fire, and a few shells and tottering walls obscured by lime dust dotted the grotesque landscape. The burned-out vestiges of a once–thriving metropolis now smelled nauseatingly of decomposing bodies pinned under steaming ruins.

For all the wreckage, "buildings created upon good foundations," an engineering report would say, "withstood the ordeal well, even when the streets around them were depressed and fissured." But even most of these buildings were gutted by the fire.

In destroying 490 city blocks and portions of 32 others, the earthquake and fire consumed about twenty-eight thousand buildings worth from $350 million to $500 million, a sum representing about two-thirds of the property values of the city and nearly one-third of the taxable property in California. The twin culprits completely demolished the business district, the transportation and communications systems, and three-fifths of the city's homes and lodging houses.

Almost every bank, all the principal hotels, all wholesale houses, and nearly all public and private libraries and art galleries burned. With virtually all retail stores gone, most food had to come from other cities and states. Some of the oldest, most scenic, and most notorious districts, including Telegraph Hill, Russian Hill, Nob Hill, Chinatown, and the Barbary Coast, had become ash-blanketed slopes or valleys. The gas and water systems were disabled, and nearly every street was clogged with debris, which blocked almost all traffic.

Some insurance companies would go bankrupt trying to pay unverifiable claims amounting to some $300 million, about half the true value of the insured property, and many of their clients, suffering unrecoverable losses, would experience the same fate. It was not uncommon for compensation to be at 5 to 10 percent of a policy's value, or for a foreign company to simply refuse to pay anything. And since the companies would not offer earthquake insurance and it was often unclear whether damage to a property was caused by earthquake or fire, some people committed arson on their own homes to obtain compensation.

Perhaps the most unsurprised beneficiary of insurance was a police sergeant, R. Leonard Ingham, who, long before the disaster, worried that the shoddy buildings he passed on his beat south of Market, together with the rest of the city, would one day go up in smoke. Finally, on April 16, he walked into the office of the Hartford Fire Insurance Company and asked for a $2,000 fire insurance policy. To the shock of company officials, he predicted that two days later, on April 18, they would owe him $2,000.

On that day, Ingham prophesied, San Francisco would burn down in the greatest fire the world will have ever known.

He then drew a diagram of the area that would be destroyed—and he was exactly right!

Death, injury, and material loss were not the only terrible legacies of the catastrophe. Smallpox and typhoid fever claimed some victims, and the bubonic plague would soon break out. The spread of disease might have been worse, however, but for an order, however belated, that all able-bodied men had to look for bodies in the ruins and bury them as swiftly as possible.

Finally, with almost every document in the offices of the county clerk, the recorder, the assessor, and other government bureaus demolished, San Francisco was robbed, in an administrative sense, of about forty years of an extraordinary past that would have served as an invaluable guide on the road to a new municipal future.

YET, SOMEHOW San Francisco began sprouting anew even while the earth still emitted steam. R. B. Hale, who headed the Hale Brothers department store, is one example. The store began burning at 11 A.M. on the first day of the fire, and by 2 P.M. Hale told an aide to see about a wrecker and to send a telegram ordering steel for a new building "as soon as it was possible."

Reconstruction of the city started with the mushrooming of eight thousand barrackslike "refugee houses." Each contained six or eight family units, one of which would house the Dulberg family. Shortly new, more permanent earthquake-proof and fireproof buildings took root in the scorched soil, and within eighteen months there was more office space within the burned area than before the fire. Business centers spilled over into undamaged areas, and walled stores, restaurants, and theaters featuring ten-cent vaudeville shows replaced the canvas-covered accommodations that had sprung up after the fire.

Also, a finely designed civic center burgeoned from the charred wilderness encompassing a magnificent new City Hall, a well-supplied library, and other public buildings. Additional structures, including a Hall of Justice, a county hospital, and numerous schools, cropped up, while parks and playgrounds soon stretched across acres of burned land. The building trades, which had employed fewer than twenty thousand people at the start of 1906, employed three times as many by the end of the year.

To make sure San Francisco would never again see homes, factories, and skyscrapers reduced to heaps of flaming debris and fleshless skeletons, the city built new, modernly equipped fire stations and a high-pressure auxiliary water supply. The system included two reservoirs, holding 500,000 gallons and 750,000 gallons, respectively, which were to be kept filled with water from a larger supply reservoir near the summit of Twin Peaks. A pumping station with both electric and motor power was built to pump water from city mains to the Twin Peaks reservoir at the rate of 1,400 gallons per minute.

Other pumping stations sprang up elsewhere to supply the high-pressure system with salt water from the bay. In addition, the city provided 135 undergound cisterns with an average capacity of 75,000 gallons beneath street crossings. A new fire-alarm system was also installed, operating from a public square in fireproof and shockproof quarters.

Despite all these measures, however, San Francisco, according to some experts, remains vulnerable to another great firestorm. The severe wind drafts created by a fire could swiftly spread the flames across the city, as they did in 1906. And since the western sand dunes have since been built up into a densely populated residential area, a new conflagration would have far more kindling wood, escaped gas, and chemical spills to feed on today than it had in that fateful year.

The danger is especially great since many of the building and pipeline defects contributing to the 1906 disaster remain, including the lack of space between many side-by-side structures, the widepread use of synthetic materials in modern homes, and many still-deficient water-distribution mains and household water connections.

In a 1987 engineering report by the insurance industry, the writer, Dr. Charles Scawthorn, states that at least seventy-nine fires might start in San Francisco after another great earthquake, and that there would not be enough fire equipment and personnel to deal with thirty-nine of them. The fire would destroy from 22,500 to about 48,000 buildings, depending on weather and fire-defense conditions, and private property losses would reach two billion to five billion dollars.

*   *   *

NOR CAN SAN FRANCISCANS rely on efforts already made to mini-
mize earthquake damage, especially since only the major buildings are
earthquake-proof. Though the building code of the city and county was
revised in 1909 to enforce safer construction through official inspection, a
noted engineer would write of San Francisco's helter-skelter rise from the
ruins that "all grades of workmanship, good and bad; all types of design,
scientific and unintelligent; all degrees of construction, from honest to dishonest examples, were to be seen on every hand."

Even today worrisome safety problems exist. In fact, some experts
believe that modernization could actually increase casualties in a future
earthquake, especially with the near-doubling of the city's population
since 1906. For example, high-rise buildings, even those that are supposedly earthquake-proof, would be more vulnerable to tremors than many of
the older and shorter structures. Additionally, the plate glass windows now
common in many buildings could crumble into a deadly rain over heavily
populated areas. Combined with an unstoppable fire, a major quake could,
it is felt, cause immeasurable damage to the city.

Without mentioning fires, a report by the National Oceanic and
Atmospheric Administration estimates that another 8.3 earthquake in the
Bay Area would result in more than 50,000 casualties—10,360 deaths and
40,000 hospitalized injuries.

IS SAN FRANCISCO thus a dangerous place to live? Some experts
believe so, at least over the long term. This danger was most recently
demonstrated by the Loma Prieta earthquake that struck the Bay Area in
1989. Fortunately, that one was weaker than the 1906 upheaval, and the
destruction—while considerable—was less serious, with few threatening
fires breaking out. It was, however, the first major earthquake along the
San Andreas fault since 1906, registering a whopping 7.1 on the Richter
scale.

Centered along a segment of the fault in the southern Santa Cruz
Mountains, this quake reruptured the southernmost thirty-five miles of the
1906 upheaval and was the country's costliest natural disaster, the total
loss exceeding $6 billion. Casualties and damage, however, did not com-
pare with the 1906 figures, largely because of better-built structures and

more modern fire preventive and fire-fighting measures. Sixty-two people died and more than 3,700 were injured, while almost one thousand homes were destroyed and eighteen thousand damaged, leaving twelve thousand residents homeless. Especially hard hit, as in 1906, was the Marina District, which rested on unstable "made" ground. Not surprisingly, many of the wood-frame houses there and elsewhere that were built after the 1906 disaster collapsed. The 1989 quake was also powerful enough to split apart the San Francisco–Oakland Bay Bridge.

Though the Bay Area survived that disaster without blanket destruction, it still served as a warning: Another quake and fire on the scale of the 1906 calamity could overcome even the best safety measures. Still, according to Carol S. Prentice of the U.S. Geological Survey, this dread prospect is not likely to materialize for at least another century. The Survey has calculated, however, that there is a 70 percent chance of at least one 6.7 earthquake striking the Bay Area between 2000 and 2030.

Nevertheless, as in 1906, few San Franciscans would live elsewhere. Earthquake? Fire? Perhaps. But they would ride it out. Like their ancestors did whenever the city bounced around or burned to the ground. Besides, why think darkly about the future? It was always good.

SO DETERMINED were the survivors of the disaster, especially the business community, to rebuild their city swiftly that they ignored much of the intricate, long-term "Burnham Plan" for a new San Francisco that had been developed before the cataclysm. As one observer would explain:

"Majority opinion was overwhelmingly opposed to any 'impractical' or aesthetic considerations. Among the ruins, 'adornment' seemed only a grim joke to all but the most idealistic citizens."

A good thing, too, many people think, for with a strict adherence to such a plan, San Francisco might have lost some of its singularly exciting character. Now, the new downtown streets would continue to climb straight up the steep hills rather than wind around in a more practical ascent. A few proposals, however, were salvaged from the Burnham Plan: A splendid Civic Center built around a spectacular new City Hall would spring up in the ruins, while some streets would be widened and graded. San Franciscans would thus go to work rebuilding a city upon its parched, fissured foundation, as reflected in this popular rhyme:

Hear the hammers click and clatter? Hear the donkey-engines snore?
We are making San Francisco four times bigger than before;
Four times bigger, four times better for a thousand years to come;
Four times best of all creation, and we guess that's going some!"

By 1915, a modern, reconstructed San Francisco had risen, phoenix-like, from the ashes of a past sprinkled with gold dust that clung now only to cherished memory. That year the city held a Panama-Pacific International Exposition and invited the world to revel in its regained splendor and ingest the unique spirit that inspired its rebirth.

Twenty-one years later, in November 1936, another wonder gave new meaning to this spirit: The eight-and-a-quarter-mile-long San Francisco–Oakland Bay Bridge, the world's longest bridge, opened to traffic, an event that marked the end of San Francisco's physical "isolation." Then, several months later, in May 1937, another engineering marvel was opened—the one-and-a-quarter-mile-long Golden Gate Bridge connecting San Francisco with Marin County, the world's longest single-span bridge.

Just as Joshua A. Norton, the revered, slightly mad, self-proclaimed Emperor of North America and Protector of Mexico, had predicted more than seventy-five years earlier. Strutting through town dressed in his gold-braided uniform and plumed beaver hat, he had reminded his skeptical yet inveterately optimistic subjects of the maxim ingrained in their city's soul:

Nothing was impossible.

Notes

PROLOGUE

1–2   Emerson: *San Francisco Bulletin, San Francisco Chronicle,* 5/1/06; *Call,* 5/4/06.

2–3   Early San Francisco history: Issel, William, and Robert W. Cherny, *San Francisco, 1865–1932,* Berkeley, Calif.: University of California Press, 1986, pp. 7–14; Lewis, Oscar, *San Francisco: Mission to Metropolis,* Berkeley, Calif.: Howell-North, 1966, pp. 1–25; Sutherland, Monica, *The Damndest Finest Ruins,* New York: Coward-McCann, 1959, pp. 21–46.

5   Burnham: Olmsted, Roger, and T. H. Watkins, *Here Today: San Francisco's Architectural Heritage,* San Francisco: Chronicle Books, 1968, pp. 1–5.

5–6   Atmosphere on earthquake eve: Tracy, Grover, *My Experiences in the Great San Francisco Earthquake,* Bloomington, Calif.: San Bernardino County Museum Association, 1968, pp. 1–8.

     San Francisco profile: Keeler, Charles, *San Francisco and Thereabout,* San Francisco: California Promotion Committee, 1903, pp. 1–7.

6   Nightlife: *San Francisco Progress,* "Theaters Were Full the Night Before the 1906 Earthquake," 4/19/79; *What Was Happening on San Francisco's Stages the Night Before the 1906 Earthquake,* San Francisco Archives for the Performing Arts.

1: CARUSO AND THE ODOR OF ROSES

7–11   Caruso: Jackson, Stanley, *Caruso,* New York: Stein and Day, 1975, pp. 141–42; Scott, Michael, *The Great Caruso,* New York: Alfred A. Knopf, 1988, pp. 191–92; Ybarra, T. R., *Caruso: The Man of Naples and the Voice of Gold,* New York: Harcourt, Brace, 1953, pp. 125–26; Greenfeld, Howard S., *Caruso: An Illustrated Life,* North Pomfret, Vt.: Trafalgar Square, 1991, pp. 71–75; Kennedy, John Castillo, *The Great Earthquake and Fire;* New York: William Morrow, 1963, pp. 1–5; Thomas, Gordon, and Max Morgan Witts, *The San Francisco Earthquake,* New York: Stein and Day, 1971, pp. 17–18, 44–45, 50; Goerlitz, Ernest, memoir, *Story of the San Francisco Earthquake and Conflagration as Far as It Affected the Conreid Metropolitan Opera Company April 18th, 19th and 20th, 1906,* San Francisco: California Historical Society.

2: BARRYMORE SLEPT HERE

11   Barrymore: Fowler, Gene, *Good Night, Sweet Prince,* New York: Viking, 1944, pp. 129–30.

12–13   Barrymore: Kobler, John, *Damned in Paradise: The Life of John Barrymore,* New York: Atheneum, 1977, pp. 84–85; Barrymore, John, *Confessions of an Actor,* New York: Arno, 1980, ch. 3.

13   Hortons: *Bulletin,* "Husband and Wife United," 5/10/06.

3: SULLIVAN'S NIGHTMARE

14–16   Sullivan: Blake, Evarts I. (ed.), *San Francisco,* San Francisco: Pacific, 1902, p. 210; *San Francisco Monitor,* "Honors to Dead Chief," 4/20/07; Thomas and Witts, *San Francisco Earthquake,* pp. 24–25, 53.
           Sullivan and Dougherty: *San Francisco and Its Municipal Administration,* San Francisco: City of San Francisco, 1902–4, pp. 210, 212.

16–19   San Francisco fire history: Burks, John, *Working Fire,* Mill Valley, Calif.: Square Books, n.d., pp. 19–22; Kenoyer, Natlee, *The Firehorses of San Francisco,* Los Angeles: Westernlore Press, 1970, p. 20; Conlon, J. J., *Tale of a San Franciscan,* Bancroft Library, Berkeley, Calif.; Derneter, Richard, *Irish America: The Historical Travel Guide,* vol. 2, Pasadena, Calif.: Cranford Press, 1996, pp. 110–11; Barnes, John A., *Irish American Landmarks: A Travel Guide; The Exempt Firemen of San Francisco,* San Francisco: Exempt Fire Company, 1900, pp. 121–49; "The San Francisco Story," *International Fire Fighter,* 6/59; Gould, Milton S., *A Cast of Hawks,* La Jolla, Calif: Copley, 1985, pp. 51–77; Sutherland, *The Damndest Finest Ruins,* pp. 47–49; Bowlen, J. J., "San Francisco Fire Department History," *San Francisco Chronicle,* 5/15, 5/20, 5/31, 6/1, 8/12, 8/15, 8/21, 8/28/03; Wyatt, David, *Five Fires,* New York: Addison-Wesley, 1997, pp. 51–77; "Reports of Fire Officers of the San Francisco Fire Department on the Fire of 1906," Bancroft Library.

4: THE NECTAR OF CORRUPTION

21–28   Schmitz and Ruef: *History of the New California,* pp. 792–93; *San Francisco and Its Municipal Administration,* San Francisco: City of San Francisco, 1905, 1902–4; *The Bay of San Francisco,* Chicago: Lewis Publishing Company, 1892, pp. 348–54; *History of the Bench and Bar of California,* Los Angeles: Commercial Printing House, 1908, p. 1064; Van der Zee, John, *The Gate,* New York: Simon & Schuster, 1986, pp. 23–24.

R. Spreckels: Steffens, Lincoln, *Upbuilders,* New York: Doubleday, Page, 1905, pp. 245–84; *The San Francisco Bay Region,* San Francisco: San Francisco Regional Planning Association, 1926, pp. 10–11; *California and Californians,* Chicago: Lewis Publishing Company, 1926, pp. 148–49.

Older: Duffus, R. L., *The Tower of Jewels,* New York: W. W. Norton, pp. 23–25, 220–25.

Government corruption: Lewis, Oscar, *San Francisco: Mission to Metropolis,* pp. 181, 207–12; *Report on the Causes of Municipal Corruption in San Francisco,* San Francisco, Board of Supervisors, City and County of San Francisco, 1/5/10; *Star* (*San Francisco*), "These Charges Cannot Be Ignored," 8/4/06; Dickow, Henry W., *My Early Life,* San Francisco Public Library; Perrin, Helen Huntington, memoir, *Early Years in San Francisco,* San Francisco Public Library; Hichborn, Franklin, *"The System": The San Francisco Graft Prosecution,* San Francisco: James H. Barry, 1915; *Corruption in City Government During the Decade 1900–1910,* San Francisco Public Library; Ruef, Abraham, *San Francisco Bulletin, The Road I Traveled,* April 5–September 10, 1912 (several chapters each week); Bean, Walton, *Boss Ruef's San Francisco,* London: Cambridge University Press, 1952 (including quotes involving Schmitz and Ruef); Thomas, Lately, *A Debonair Scoundrel,* New York: Holt, Rinehart & Winston, 1962.

5: THE BANKER AND THE BOY

29–30   Giannini: James, Marquis, and Bessie Rowland James, *Biography of a Bank,* New York: Harper, 1954, pp. 21–22.

30–31   Aurelio Delbert Crespi: Memoir, San Francisco Public Library.

6: COOK'S TOUR OF A CATACLYSM

32–33,   Jesse Cook: Memoir, 3/1/25, San Francisco Public Library (including quotes
35–36   regarding Cook).

33–35   Earthquake: Heppenheimer, T. A., *The Coming Quake,* New York: Times Books, 1988, pp. 19–23; *Scientific American,* "The San Francisco Earthquake," 5/19/06, pp. 419–20; *Geological Society of America Bulletin,* "San Andreas Fault: History of Concepts," vol. 92, M. L. Hill, pp. 112–31; "The Great San Francisco Earthquake of 1906 and Subsequent Evolution of Ideas," (by Carol S. Prentice), Lawson, Andrew C., ed., *The California Earthquake of April 18, 1906,* Report of the State Earthquake Investigation Commission, vol. 1, pt. 1, ch. 5 Washington, D.C.: Carnegie Institution of Washington, 1908; Clarke, Thurston, *California Fault,* New York: Ballantine, 1991, pp. 174–210; Svenson: Thomas and Witts, *The San Francisco Earthquake,* p. 64.

7: THE END OF THE WORLD

37–39   James Hopper: Memoir, San Francisco Public Library (including quotes involving Hopper).

39–40   Emerson: *Bulletin, Chronicle,* 5/1/06; *Call,* 5/4/06.

40–42   Jesse Cook: Memoir, 3/1/25.

42–43   H. C. Schmitt: *Argonaut* (San Francisco), "The Great Fire of 1906," 5/1/26.

43   Compania: 5/4/06.

8: BIRTH AND DEATH

44–45   Etta Siegel: Memoir, 7/18/77, Bancroft Library, Berkeley, Calif., and taped memoir in author's possession (including quotes involving Siegel); Baumgarten, Edward, Siegel's grandson, interview; Baumgarten, Juanita, Siegel's daughter, interview; Perada, Rita, Siegel's granddaughter, interview.

45   Gimpy Bill: *Bulletin,* "How "Gimpy Bill" Escaped Death on His Four Wheels," 4/28/06.

46   Harry F. Walsh: *Argonaut,* 5/15/26.

46–47   Jessy Wilson: Letter to friend, 7/19/06, San Francisco Public Library.

9: THE MISER AND THE MELTING POT

49–50   Crespi: Aurelio memoir (including quotes).

10: THE ACCORDION AND THE COPS

51–52   Valencia Hotel: *Argonaut,* 10/16, 10/23/26; Hansen, Gladys, and Emmet Condon, *Denial of Disaster,* San Francisco: Cameron, 1989, pp. 24–25.

52–55   City Hall: *Argonaut,* 9/18, 9/25/26.

11: THE DISHWARE AND THE DRAGONS

56–60   Chinatown culture and history: Leong Gor Yun, *Chinatown Inside Out,* New York: Barrows Mussey, 1936; Pan, Erica. Y. Z., *The Impact of the 1906 Earthquake on San Francisco's Chinatown,* New York: Peter Lang, 1995; Dillon, Richard H., *The Hatchet Men,* New York: Coward-McCann, Comstock, 1962, pp. 215–70; Dobie, Charles C., *San Francisco's Chinatown,* New York: D. Appleton-Century, 1936, pp. 289–99; Salter, Christopher L., *San Francisco's Chinatown: How Chinese a Town?* San Francisco, 1978, pp. 1–6; Chinese women: Yung, Judy, *Unbound Feet,* Berkeley, Calif.: University of California Press, 1995, pp. 25–37.

60–62   Liang diary: Chinn, Thomas W., *Bridging the Pacific,* San Francisco: Chinese Historical Society of America, 1989, pp. 197–205.

12: THE CRACKLE OF TERROR

63, 66   Emerson: *Bulletin, Chronicle,* 5/1/06; *Call,* 5/4/06.

64–66   Description of refugees: Wilson, Letter to friend; Alexander, W. E., memoir, California Historical Society; Withering, Fred, San Francisco Public Library; Page, Charles, Letter to son, 4/21/06, San Francisco Public Library.

66–67   Compania: *Bulletin,* 4/26/06; McMahon: *Bulletin,* 5/12/06; Gimpy Bill: *Bulletin,* 4/28/06.

13: THE CRUEL TRAP

69–71   Wilson: Letter to friend.

14: NAPOLEON TO THE RESCUE

72   Sullivan dies: *Argonaut,* 9/18/26; Hansen and Condon, *Denial of Disaster,* p. 40. Funston: *Argonaut,* 1/29/27, 2/5/27; Crouch, Thomas W., *A Yankee Guerrillero,* Memphis, Tenn.: Memphis State University, 1975; Clark, H. C., ed., *Journal of the United States Infantry Association,* "The Army in the San Francisco Disaster," Washington, D.C.: United States Infantry Association, 1907; Funston, Frederick, *Cosmopolitan Magazine,* "How the Army Worked to Save San Francisco," 7/06; Funston, Frederick, *Memories of Two Wars,* London: Constable, 1912; Thomas and Witts, *The San Francisco Earthquake,* pp. 25–28.

15: INOCULATING THE MAYOR

81–88   Schmitz: *Argonaut,* 1/15/07 (including statement by John T. Williams); 1/22/07 (including remarks by Mayor Schmitz); Bronson, William, *The Earth Shook, The Sky Burned,* New York: Doubleday, 1959, p. 42.; Kennedy, John Castillo, *The Great Earthquake,* pp. 63–67.

Ruef in bed: Levison, Alice Gerstle, memoir, *Family Reminiscences,* Berkeley, Calif.: Judah Magnus Museum.

16: THE LORD, THE KING, AND THE EXECUTIONERS

89–90   God and earthquake: *Signs of the Times,* Mountain View, Calif., 5/2/06; *Current Literature,* "Providence and the San Francisco Disaster," 6/06; *Bulletin,* "Compares Disaster to the Fall of Babylon," 4/24/26.

McDermitt: Thomas and Witts, *The San Francisco Earthquake,* p. 218.

Schmitz: "It was a revelation . . ." Kennedy, John Castillo, *The Great Earthquake,* p. 64.

Remarks by Schmitz: *Argonaut,* 1/22/07.

17: SUCCUMBING TO CATASTROPHE

94–98   Fire spreads: Reports of Fire Officers of the San Francisco Fire Department on
the Fire of 1906, Bancroft Library; Hansen and Condon, *Denial of Disaster*,
pp. 72–73.

18: THE PUNY MILLIONAIRES

99–103   The Big Four: Riesenberg, Felix, Jr., *Golden Gate*, New York: Alfred A. Knopf,
1940, pp. 183–93; Moffat, Frances, *Dancing on the Brink of the World*, New
York: Putnam, 1977, pp. 35–55.

19: NOT EVEN THE DEAD WERE SAFE

104–5   Police evictions: *Argonaut*, 8/14/26.
105   Relief problems: Mahoney, Margaret, memoir, *The Earthquake, The Fire, The
Relief*, San Francisco Public Library, 7/28/06.
105–7   Ketring, Stehr: *Argonaut*, 10/9/26.
Edna Ketring: *Bulletin*, 5/3, 5/4/06.

20: THE VENGEFUL DEMONS

108   Laundry fire: *Argonaut*, 8/6/27.
108–9   Palace Hotel: Hansen and Condon, *Denial of Disaster*, p. 64; *The Palace Hotel*,
booklet.
109–12   Caruso: *Illustrated Digest*, "First-Hand Account of Earthquake Havoc by
Enrico Caruso," 1906; Goerlitz, Ernest, *Story of the San Francisco Earthquake
and Conflagration*, California Historical Society; Thomas and Witts, *The San
Francisco Earthquake*, pp. 74–75; Kennedy, *The Great Earthquake*, p. 19;
Jackson, Stanley, *Caruso*, p. 141; Ybarra, *Caruso*, pp. 124–25.
112–114 Stehr: *Argonaut*, 10/9/26.

21: THE TONGUE OF A POISONOUS SNAKE

115–118 Mechanics Pavilion: *Argonaut*, 1/22/27; Hansen and Condon, *Denial of Disaster*, pp. 55, 57–58; Hansen, interview; Condon, interview; Stetson, James B.,
memoir, 6/22/06, Bancroft Library.
Windsor deaths: *Oakland Tribune*, "Shot to Death to Escape Cremation," 4/20/06.

22: THE ANGEL AND THE NEWBORN

120–21   McMahon: *Bulletin*, 5/12/06.
121   Car barn: *Argonaut*, 9/3/26.
121–22   Aultman: *Oakland Tribune*, 4/30/06.

122–23   Dulbergs: Siegel, taped memoir; Baumgarten, Edward and Juanita, interviews; Perada, interview.

23: CRIMINALS IN UNIFORM

124–25   Army aid: *Presidial Weekly Clarion,* San Francisco, 4/27/06; Funston, *Cosmopolitan Magazine,* p. 248; Clark, *Journal of the United States Infantry Association,* pp. 69–70.
125–26   Vinegar: *Bulletin,* "Politician Hugs Bottled Vinegar to His Breast, Thinking It Whiskey," 5/13/06.
125–27   Drunks: United States Naval Institute Proceedings, *The United States Navy and the San Francisco Fire,* John E. Pond, 2/1953, p. 985.
127   Militia dynamite crimes: *Argonaut,* 3/19/27, Henry A. Lafler.
127–28   Army looters: California State Senate, Special Committee on Governmental Administration, Disaster Protection of Public Records, Senate Resolution No. 157, 1953.
128–29   Schmitt robbed: *Argonaut,* 5/8/26.
129   McArrow: McArrow, Charles Drummond, *The San Francisco Earthquake and Fire as Remembered by Charles Drummond McArrow,* San Francisco Public Library.
130   Military killings: Berg, Halvor H., Letter to family, San Francisco Public Library; Kester, Frank, *Memories of the San Francisco Earthquake and Fire, April 1906,* California Historical Society; Bales, Clifford, *Sunday Punch* (San Francisco), 4/12/81. Man hanged from pole: Tyron, Tom, Letter to friend, California Historical Society. Looter digs own grave: *Chronicle,* "The Military Took Over," 4/18/86.
130–31   Drayman bayoneted: Spalding, Alfred, San Francisco Public Library.
131   Soldier threatens woman: Perrin, *Early Years.*
          Red Cross official killed: *Argonaut,* 5/28/27, 6/4/27.
          Commissary wagon killing: Reithead, Charles, San Francisco Public Library.
          Reckless fire: *Oakland Tribune,* "Arrest Militiaman for Reckless Firing," 4/28/06.
132   Soldier shoots dog: *Argonaut,* 3/26/27, Fichtner,
          "Shoot That Man": *Oakland Tribune,* "Thrilling Story of a Night of Terror," 4/23/06.
132–33   Dog returns to boy: *Argonaut,* 4/2/07.
133–34   Boy risks life saving dog: *Call,* "Boy Saves Dog and Records," 4/27/06.
134   Stealing from corpse: Lund, R. F., San Francisco Public Library.
134–35   Denicke kills man: *Argonaut,* 6/4/27.

24: BRINGING OUT THE BEST

136   No policemen present: United States Navy Proceedings, 9/52, p. 985.
137–38   Policeman and candy store: Lesser, Sol, *My Experiences During the Earthquake and Fire in San Francisco,* April 18, 1906, California Historical Society.
137   Five cats burn: *Argonaut,* 8/14/06.
138–39   Ross, including quotes: *Argonaut,* 5/15/26.

25: THE CASE FOR THE FIRE

141–42   Giannini: James and James, *Biography of a Bank,* pp. 21–24.

143–44   Ward and his mother: *San Francisco Examiner,* "Policeman Saved by Earthquake," 4/25/06.

144   Jack Brown: *Call,* "Actor Vows Earthquake Cured Friend of Paralysis," 5/14/06. Gimpy Bill: *Bulletin,* 4/28/06.

145   Concert: *Chronicle,* "Orchestras in Cemeteries," Race Whitney, 5/6/06. Dogs: *Bulletin,* "Dogs Devour Bodies Pulled from Ruins," 4/25/06.

145–46   Candy box: *Call,* "Leaves Her Jewelry . . ."

26: A PROUD ENDING

147–48   See notes for Chapter 1 relating to Caruso.

149–50   Dewey: *Argonaut,* 11/27/26.

27: RAVAGEMENT, RACISM, AND RATS

151   Crespi: Memoir.

152–55   Chinese flee: Chinn, *Bridging the Pacific,* Liang diary, pp. 197–205.

153   Stevens's socks; soldier betrays trust: *Oakland Tribune,* "He Escaped Barefoot," 4/23/06.

154–55   Police chase out Chinese roomers: *Argonaut,* 8/14/26.

153–57   Atmosphere during disaster; looting of Chinatown: Pan, *The Impact of the 1906 Earthquake.*
Sword-armed Chinese: *Hartford World,* "San Francisco Quake Changed Lives," John A. Gilliland, 4/85.

155–59   Plague: *History,* "Dealing with the Plague," Tro Harper, 7/24/77; *Call,* "Plague of Rats Only Pestilence Following Fire," 5/5/06; *Annals of Internal Medicine,* "Plague in San Francisco in 1900," Loren George Lipson, 8/72; Lewis, *San Francisco: Mission to Metropolis,* pp. 203–5; Todd, Frank Morton, ed., *Eradicating Plague from San Francisco,* San Francisco: C.H.C., 1909; *Yesterday's Paper, 1900—Black Death in San Francisco!,* University of California, San Francisco for the 1976 Twin Bicentennial Science & Industry Exposition, Dr. John B. deC. M. Saunders; *The Coast Review,* "The Bubonic Graft," 12/07; *Harper's Weekly,* "Shutting Out Bubonic Plague," 7/11/14; Report of the Commission Appointed by the Secretary of the Treasury for the Investigation of Plague in San Francisco Under Instructions from the Surgeon-General, Marine Hospital, Washington, Government Printing Office.

28: THE PERSIAN CAT

160   "Wickedness invited": *Sign of the Times,* "The 'Queen of the West' Laid Low," Mountain View, Calif., 5/2/06.

160–62   Bassity: *Bulletin,* "A Study in Moral Depravity," Pauline Jacobson, 5/14/10; Asbury, Herbert, *The Barbary Coast,* New York: Capricorn, 1933, pp. 236–39.
162–63   Coffman: Dillon, Richard H., *Embarcadero,* New York: Coward-McCann, 1959, pp. 308–13.

29: BLACK NEWS AND WHITE TAILS

166–67   Hortons; child asks mayor to find father, *Bulletin,* 5/10/06.
167–70   Barrymore: Fowler, *Good Night, Sweet Prince,* pp. 130–31; Kobler, *Damned in Paradise,* pp. 84–85; Barrymore, *Confessions of an Actor,* ch. 3.

30: THE HOME BANK AND THE BURNED HOME

171   Giannini: James and James, *Biography of a Bank,* p. 25.
172   Liang diary: Chinn, *Bridging the Pacific,* Liang diary, pp. 197–205.
172–74   Crespi: Memoir.

31: A VOW TO LOVE AND A VOW TO DIE

175–77   Emerson: *Bulletin, Chronicle,* 5/1/06; *Call,* 5/4/06.
177–78   Barrymore, *Confessions of an Actor,* ch. 3; Fowler, *Good Night, Sweet Prince,* pp. 131–32.
178–79   Liang diary: Chinn, *Bridging the Pacific,* Liang diary, pp. 197–205.
179   Wilson, Letter to friend.

32: MISERY, MURDER, AND MASTERY

180   Dulbergs: Siegel, memoir and tape; Baumgarten, E., interview; Baumgarten, J., interview.
180–81   Golden Gate Park: Conlon, memoir.
182   Stale bread: Perrin, memoir.
183–84   Myers murder: *Argonaut,* 6/4/27.
184   Denman and trucks: Kennedy, John Castillo, *The Great Earthquake,* pp. 182–83, 202–3.
184–85   Wilson: Letter to friend.

33: RUNNING A GAUNTLET

186–89   Emerson: *Bulletin, Chronicle,* 5/1/06; *Call,* 5/4/06.
188   Man poses as husband: *Call,* 5/14/06.
189   Liang diary: Chinn, *Bridging the Pacific,* pp. 197–205.

34: FROM PRAYER TO ACTION

191   Yellow house and hydrant: *Argonaut,* 10/30/26.
192   Almoro fire put out: Edwards, F. Ernest, San Francisco Public Library.
       Quoting reporter Paul Ditzel regarding Dougherty: Thomas and Witts, *The San Francisco Earthquake,* pp. 233–34.

35: DYNAMITE AND DESPERATION

193–94   Schmitz and dynamite: *Argonaut,* 1/22/27.
195   Shirker fools police: *History,* 3/67, 4/67.
195–97   ". . . most terrible sight . . ." and "It was the boys of the hill . . .": Lafler, Henry A., *How the Army Worked to Save San Francisco*, San Francisco: Calkins Newspaper Syndicate, 1906.
197   Montgomery Block: Jones, Idwal, *Ark of Empire,* Garden City, N.Y.: Doubleday, 1951.
198–99   Post office saved: *Argonaut,* 12/11, 12/18, 12/25/26.
199–200   Mint: *Call,* "Carouses on Mint Steps," 5/12/06; *Chronicle,* "Brave Men Saved Mint from Fire," 4/22/06.

36: A FRUIT DISH AND A CUP OF TEA

201   Struggle at Van Ness: Hansen and Condon, *Denial of Disaster,* pp. 80–81; Kennedy, John Castillo, *The Great Earthquake,* pp. 125–26, 137–39.
203, 206 Lane and sleeping firemen: Kennedy, *The Great Earthquake,* pp. 129–30.
203–5   Merrill: *Call,* "Refugees Tell of Courage Shown by Mrs. J. W. Merrill," 5/7/06.
206–7   Blanding: *Examiner,* 5/9/06.

37: THE LURE OF RARE WINE

209–10   Photo finish: Genthe, Arnold, *As I Remember,* New York: Reynal & Hitchcock, 1936, ch. 10.

38: THE GHOULISH LION

212–13   Policeman and Viavi fire: *Argonaut,* 8/21/26.
213–15   North Beach burns: Hansen and Condon, *Denial of Disaster,* p. 82; Kennedy, John Castillo, *The Great Earthquake,* pp. 161–62; Reports of Fire Officers.
214–15   Hoteling Whiskey: *Argonaut,* 7/24/26.
215   Montgomery Block saved: Jones, *Ark of Empire.*
215–16   Freeman: United States Navy Proceedings, 9/52, pp. 992–93.
216–17   Baldwin: Lafler, *How the Army Worked,* pp. 4–5.
217–18   Liang diary: Chinn, *Bridging the Pacific,* pp. 197–205.
218–19   McMahon: *Bulletin,* 5/12/06.

39: THE DEADLINE AND THE DOORKNOB

220–22   Press defies fire: *Argonaut,* 4/30/27.
222   Crespi: Memoir.

40: A LAST STAND

223   Dougherty at docks: Thomas and Witts, *The San Francisco Earthquake,* p. 240.
223–24   Firefighter's experience: Russell, Stephen, Letter to sister, Society of California Pioneers.
224–25   Threat to Fort Mason: Funston telegram to Washington, 4/20/06.
         Schmitz seeks rifles: Kennedy, John Castillo, *The Great Earthquake,* pp. 183–86.
225–26   Fire at docks: Reports of Fire Officers.

41: RISE FROM THE RUINS

228–29   Conditions in park: Siegel memoir and tape.
230   Father and son reunited: *Call,* 5/6/06.
231   China offers aid: Prince Ch'ing, Letter to State Department official Rockwell, 4/23/06.
231   Aid rejected: Rockwell, Letter to Prince Ch'ing, 4/25/06.
231–32   Relief problems: *Argonaut,* 2/19, 2/25, 3/5/06; Greely, Adolphus W., *Reminiscences of Adventure and Service,* New York: Scribner's, 1927, pp. 221–24; Smith, Edgar C., *Relief Work in San Francisco,* California Historical Society.
233–34   Dulberg baby dies: Siegel memoir and tape.
234   Compania found: *Bulletin,* 4/26/06.
235–36   Return to school: Crespi, Memoir.
236–38   Schmitz, Funston, and militia: Kennedy, John Castillo, *The Great Earthquake,* p. 183.
236–39   Schmitz and Ruef convicted: Older, Fremont, *My Own Story,* New York: Macmillan, 1926.
239–40   Thieves: "Women Burglars Reap Rich Harvest," *Bulletin,* 5/7/06.
240–41   Saloon murders: Memoir, Cliff Graves, San Francisco Public Library.
241   Letter to "Carl": San Francisco Public Library.
242, 245 Charles Page: Letters to son, San Francisco Public Library.
244   New Chinatown: Pan, *The Impact of the 1906 Earthquake.*
246   Giannini: James and James, *Biography of a Bank,* pp. 21–22.
246–47   Hortons: *Bulletin,* 5/10/06.
247   Emerson: *Bulletin,* 5/1/06; *Call,* 5/4/06.

EPILOGUE

248–50   Casualties and damage: Interview, Gladys Hansen; Clarke, *California Fault*, pp. 200–210 (including statement of member of the State Earthquake Investigation Commission); Lawson, Andrew, *Bulletin of the Seismological Society of America*, 3/1911.

250   Future quakes: Steinbrugge, Karl V., *Earthquake Hazard in the San Francisco Bay Area*, Berkley, Calif.: Institute of Governmental Studies, University of California, 1968, pp. 44–46.

251–52   Insurance problems: *The London Assurance*, "A Payment That Made San Francisco History," pamphlet; *Congressional Record*, p. 1811, 1/28/07.
Ingram's insurance: flyer, Hartford Fire Insurance Co., Society of California Pioneers.

252   "A Résumé of the Work Performed by the Committee for Housing the Homeless After the Destruction of San Francisco by Fire, April 18–20, 1906," Bancroft Library.
Reconstruction: Lewis, *San Francisco: Mission to Metropolis*, pp. 215–23; *Overland Monthly*, "Concerning San Francisco," T. B. Wilson, 9/08; *Collier's*, "A Stricken City Undismayed," Frederick Palmer, 5/12/06; *Collier's*, "San Francisco Rising Again," Frederick Palmer, 5/19/06.

253–55   Future earthquake and fire danger: *Fire Following Earthquake—Estimates of the Conflagration Risk to Insured Property in Greater Los Angeles and San Francisco*, Charles Scawthorn, 1987, San Francisco Public Library; Hansen and Condon, *Denial of Disaster*, pp. 135–53; Bay Area Regional Earthquake Preparedness Project (BAREPP), Hazardous Buildings, Case Study, Oakland, Calif., in Lawson, *California Earthquake*, vol. 1, pt. 1; Interviews: Condon and Hansen, Carol S. Prentice of U.S. Geological Survey, Menlo Park, Calif.

Bibliography

BOOKS

Adams, H. Austin. *The Man, John D. Spreckels*. San Diego: Frye & Smith, 1924.

Aitken, Frank. *A History of the Earthquake and Fire*. San Francisco: E. Hilton, May 1906.

Alden, C. H., Jr. *Burnt Clay Construction at San Francisco*. Brick Builder, May 1906.

Allen, Clarence R. *Earthquakes and Mountains Around the Pacific*. Pasadena, Calif.: California Institute of Technology, 1963.

Alt, David D., and Donald W. Hyndman. *Roadside Geology of Northern California*. Missoula, Mont.: Mountain Press, 1975.

Altrocchi, Julia Cooley. *The Spectacular San Franciscans*. New York: Dutton, 1949.

American Guide Series. *San Francisco: Its Bay and Its Cities*. New York: Hastings House, 1947.

Andrews, Allen. *Earthquake*. London: Angus & Robertson, 1963.

Asbury, Herbert. *The Barbary Coast*. New York: Capricorn, 1933.

Atherton, Gertrude. *Golden Gate Country*. New York: Duell, Sloane & Pearce, 1945.

———. *My San Francisco*. Indianapolis: Bobbs-Merrill, 1946.

Bain, David H. *Sitting in Darkness: Americans in the Philippines*. New York: Houghton Mifflin, 1984.

Bancroft, Hubert Howe. *Some Cities and San Francisco*. Resurgam, New York: Bancroft, 1907.

Banks, Charles E. *The History of the San Francisco Disaster and Mount Vesuvius Horror*. San Francisco: C. E. Thomas, 1906.

Barker, Malcolm E. *San Francisco Memoirs*. San Francisco: Londonbord, 1994.

———. *Three Fearful Days*. San Francisco: Londonbord, 1999.

Barnes, John A. *Irish American Landmarks: A Travel Guide.*

Barrymore, John. *Confessions of an Actor.* London: Robert Holden, 1926.

Barth, Gunther. *Bitter Strength: A History of the Chinese in the United States, 1850–1870.* Cambridge, Mass.: Harvard University Press, 1964.

Bean, Walton. *California.* New York: McGraw-Hill, 1968.

———. *Boss Ruef's San Francisco.* London: Cambridge University Press, 1952.

Berry, James. *The Earthquake of 1906.* Privately printed, 1907.

Bicknell, Ernest P. *Pioneering with the Red Cross.* New York: Macmillan, 1935.

Boardman, Mabel T. *Under the Red Cross Flag at Home and Abroad.* Philadelphia: Lippincott, 1915.

Bolt, Bruce. *Earthquakes.* New York: W. H. Freeman, 1988.

Bonnet, Theodore. *The Regenerators: A Study of the Graft Prosecution.* San Francisco: Pacific Printing Co., 1911.

Borel, Antoine. *San Francisco Is No More.* Menlo Park, Calif., 1963.

Bowlen, Frederick J. *Fire Horses: Farewell, Good and Faithful Servants!* San Francisco, 1939.

———. *Roster of Exempt Firemen.* 1940.

Bronson, William. *The Earth Shook, the Sky Burned.* New York: Doubleday, 1959.

Brook, James, Chris Carllsson, and Nancy J. Peters (eds.). *Reclaiming San Francisco: History, Politics, Culture.* San Francisco: City Lights, 1998.

Brooks, George W. *The Spirit of 1906.* San Francisco: The California Insurance Company of San Francisco, 1921.

Brown, Helen Hillyer. *The Great San Francisco Fire.* San Francisco: Leo Holub, 1956.

Brown, Mrs. Hugh. *Lady in Boomtown.* Palo Alto, Calif.: American West, 1968.

Brownell, Blaine A., and Warren E. Stickles (eds.). *Bosses and Reformers: Urban Politics in America, 1880–1920.* Boston: Houghton Mifflin, 1973.

Buckingham, Clyde E. *Red Cross Disaster Relief.* Washington, D.C.: Public Affairs Press, 1956.

Burchell, R. A. *The San Francisco Irish.* Berkeley, Calif.: University of California Press, 1980.

Burks, John. *Working Fire.* Mill Valley, Calif.: Square Books, n.d.

Burnham, Daniel H. *Report on a Plan for San Francisco, 1905.*

Byerly, Perry. *Earthquakes in Northern California.* Berkeley, Calif.: University of California, 1940.

Byington, Lewis. *The History of San Francisco.* Chicago: S. J. Clarke, 1951.

Camp, William. *San Francisco, Port of Gold.* New York: Doubleday, 1947.

Carghill, Oscar. *The Big Four: The Story of Huntington, Stanford, Hopkins, and Crocker.* New York: Alfred A. Knopf, 1941.

Caruso, Dorothy. *Enrico Caruso: His Life and Death.* London: J. Werner, Laurie, 1946.

Cather, Helen Virginia. *The History of San Francisco's Chinatown.* Master's thesis, Berkeley, Calif.: University of California, 1932.

Chandler, Arthur. *Old Tales of San Francisco.* Dubuque, Iowa: Kendall/Hunt, 1977.

Chinn, Thomas W. *Bridging the Pacific*. San Francisco: Chinese Historical Society of America, 1989.

The Church in San Francisco: How It Suffered from Fire and What Can Be Done to Rebuild It. New York: Domestic and Foreign Missionary Society of the Protestant Episcopal Church, 1906.

Clark, H. C. (ed.). *Journal of the United States Infantry Association*. Washington, D.C.: United States Infantry Association, 1907.

Clarke, Thurston. *California Fault*. New York: Ballantine, 1991.

Clary, Raymond H. *The Making of Golden Gate Park*. San Francisco: California Living Books, 1980.

Cleland, Robert G. *A History of California*. New York: Macmillan, 1923.

Coblentz, Stanton A. *Villains and Vigilantes*. New York: Yoseloff, 1936.

Coffmann, Jerry L., and Carl A. von Hake, eds. *Earthquake History of the United States, U.S. Department of Commerce Publication 41-1*. Washington, D.C.: U.S. Government Printing Office, 1973.

Cogan, Sara G. *The Jews of San Francisco and the Greater Bay Area, 1849–1919*. Berkeley, Calif.: Judah I. Magnes Museum, 1973.

Coleman, Charles M. *P.G. & E. of California*. Garden City, N.Y.: Doubleday, 1980.

Coolidge, Mary. *Chinese Immigration*. New York: Henry Holt, 1909.

Crown Zellerback Corporation. *The City of Gold: The Story of City Planning in San Francisco*. San Francisco: Crown Zellerback Corporation, 1960.

Dana, Julian. *A. P. Giannini: Giant in the West*. New York: Prentice-Hall, 1947.

———. *The Man Who Built San Francisco*. New York: Macmillan, 1937.

Davidson, C. *Great Earthquake*. London: Murby, 1936.

Davis, Robert, as told to John Connor. *Incidents in the Life of Major General Frederick Funston, USA* (manuscript). Sacramento: California State Library, 1949.

Deacon, J. Byron, *Disasters and the American Red Cross in Disaster Relief*. New York: Russell Sage Foundation, 1918.

Derleth, Charles, Jr. *Destructive Extent of the California Earthquake*. San Francisco: Robertson, 1907.

Derneter, Richard. *Irish America: The Historical Travel Guide*, vol. 2., Pasadena, Calif.: Cranford Press, 1966.

Dickelmann, William. *San Francisco Earthquake Fire, April 18, 1906*. San Francisco, 1906.

Dicker, Laverne Mau. *The Chinese in San Francisco*. 1979.

Dickson, Samuel. *San Francisco Is Your Home*. Palo Alto, Calif.: Stanford University Press, 1947, 1957.

Dillon, Richard H. *Embarcadero*. New York: Coward-McCann, 1959.

———. *The Hatchet Men: The Story of the Tong Wars in San Francisco's Chinatown*. New York: Coward-McCann, 1962.

———. *North Beach*. Novato, Calif.: Presidio Press, 1985.

———. *Shanghaiing Days*. New York: Coward-McCann, 1961.

Dobie, Charles C. *San Francisco: A Pageant*. New York: D. Appleton-Century, 1933.

———. *San Francisco's Chinatown*. New York: D. Appleton-Century, 1936.

Douty, Christopher M. *The Economy of Localized Disasters: The 1906 San Francisco Ca-tastrophe*. New York: Arno Press, 1977.

Downey, Arthur D. *After the Earthquake*. Privately printed.

Downey, Fairfax. *Disaster Fighters*. New York: Putnam, 1938.

Duffus, R. L. *The Tower of Jewels: Memories of San Francisco*. New York: W. W. Norton, 1960.

An Earthquake Chronicle, Journal of the Military Institute, 9/06.

The Exempt Firemen of San Francisco. San Francisco: Exempt Fire Company, 1900.

Farwell, Willard B. *The Chinese at Home and Abroad*. San Francisco: A. L. Bancroft, 1885.

The Fate of the San Francisco Grafters. San Francisco: Cubery, 1908.

Fowler, Gene. *Good Night, Sweet Prince*. New York: Viking, 1944.

Fried, John J. *Life Along the San Andreas Fault*. New York: Saturday Review Press, 1973.

Funston, Frederick. *Memories of Two Wars*. London: Constable, 1912.

Genthe, Arnold. *As I Remember*. New York: Reynal & Hitchcock, 1936.

Gentry, Curt. *The Madams of San Francisco*. Garden City, N.Y.: Doubleday, 1964.

Gilbert, Grove Karl. *The San Francisco Earthquake and Fire of April 18, 1906, and Their Effects on Structures and Structural Materials*. Washington, D.C.: Government Print-ing Office, 1907.

Gilliam, Harold. *San Francisco Bay*. Garden City, N.Y.: Doubleday, 1957.

Gilliam, Harold, and Michael Bri. *The Natural World of San Francisco*. Garden City, N.Y.: Doubleday, 1966.

Goodrich, Mary. *The Palace Hotel*. San Francisco: Crandall, 1950.

Gould, Milton S. *A Cast of Hawks*. La Jolla, Calif.: Copley, 1985.

The Great Earthquake, April 18, 1906. Views of Its Calamitous Results in San Francisco and Vicinity. Mountain View, Calif.: Pacific, 1906.

Greely, Adolphus W. *Earthquake in California, April 18, 1906*. Washington, D.C.: U.S. Government Printing Office, 1906.

————. *Reminiscences of Adventure and Service*. New York: Scribner's, 1927.

Greenfeld, Howard. *Caruso*. New York: Putnam, 1983.

Grover, Tracy. *Earthquake*. Bloomington, Calif.: San Bernardino County Museum Associ-ation, 1968.

Gumina, Deanna Paoli. *The Italians of San Francisco, 1850–1930*. New York: Center for Migration Studies, 1978.

Hansen, Gladys. *Who Perished?* San Francisco: San Francisco Archives, 1980.

Hansen, Gladys, and Emmet Condon. *Denial of Disaster*. San Francisco: Cameron, 1989.

Harlan, George. *San Francisco Ferryboats*. Berkeley, Calif.: Howell North, 1967.

Hayler, Guy W. *The San Francisco Bay Region of the Future*. San Francisco: Regional Plan Association, 1926.

Heck, Nicholas H. *Earthquakes*. Princeton, N.J.: Princeton University Press, 1936.

Henry, Neil. *Complete Story of the San Francisco Earthquake*. Chicago: Bible House, 1906.

Heppenheimer, T. A. *The Coming Quake*. New York: Time Books, 1988.

Hewitt, R. *From Earthquake, Fire and Flood*. New York: Scribner's, 1957.

Hichborn, Franklin. *"The System": The San Francisco Graft Prosecution*. San Francisco: James M. Barry, 1915.

Himmelwright, A. L. A. *The San Francisco Earthquake and Fire*. New York: Roebling Construction Co., 1906.

History of the Bench and Bar of California. San Francisco, n.d.

History of San Francisco's Police Chiefs. November 1922.

Hittell, John S. *A History of the City of San Francisco*. San Francisco: Bancroft, 1878.

———. *The Commerce and Industries of the Pacific Coast of North America*. San Francisco: Bancroft, 1882.

Holliday, J. S. *The World Rushed In: The California Gold Rush Experience*. New York: Simon & Schuster, 1981.

Hopper, James. *Our San Francisco*. New York, 1906.

Hoy, William. *The Chinese Six Companies*. San Francisco: Chinese Six Companies, 1942.

Hunt, Rockwell D. *California and Californians*. Chicago: Lewis, 1926.

Iacopi, Robert. *Earthquake Country*. Menlo Park, Calif.: Lane, 1964.

Irvine, Leigh H., and associated editors. New York: Lewis Publishing Co., 1905.

Irving, Robert. *Volcanoes and Earthquakes*. New York: Alfred A. Knopf, 1962.

Irwin, William. *The City That Was*. New York: Huebosch, 1908.

———. *Old Chinatown*. New York: Mitchell Kennerley, 1913.

Irwin, William, and William Marion Reedy. *San Francisco: 1906 and Before*. Oakland, Calif.: Osborne, 1973.

Issel, William, and Robert W. Cherny. *San Francisco, 1865–1932*. Berkeley, Calif.: University of California Press, 1986.

Jackson, Joseph Henry. *My San Francisco*. New York: Crowell, 1953.

Jackson, Stanley. *Caruso*. New York: Stein and Day, 1975.

Jacobson, Pauline. *A Fire-Defying Landmark*. San Francisco, 1912.

James, Marquis, and Bessie Rowland James. *Biography of a Bank*. New York: Harper, 1954.

Johnson, Paul. *San Francisco: As It Is, As It Was*. Garden City, N.Y.: Doubleday, 1979.

Jones, Idwal. *Ark of Empire*. Garden City, N.Y.: Doubleday, 1951.

Jordan, David S. *The California Earthquake of 1906*. San Francisco: Robertson, 1907.

Kahn, Edgar M. *Cable Car Days in San Francisco*. Palo Alto, Calif.: Stanford University Press, 1940.

Keeler, Charles. *San Francisco and Thereabout*. San Francisco: California Promotion Committee, 1903.

———. *San Francisco Through Earthquake and Fire*. San Francisco: Paul Elder, 1906.

Kemble, John Haskell. *San Francisco Bay*. Cambridge, Md.: Cornell Maritime Press, 1957.

Kennedy, John Castillo. *The Great Earthquake and Fire, San Francisco, 1906*. New York: William Morrow, 1963.

Kennedy, Lawrence Joseph. *The Progress of the Fire in San Francisco, April 18th–21st, 1906*. thesis, Berkeley, Calif.: University of California, 1908.

Kenoyer, Natlee. *The Firehorses of San Francisco*. Los Angeles: Westernlore Press, 1970.

Key, Pierre Van Rensselaer. *Enrico Caruso: A Biography*. Boston: Little, Brown, 1922.

Kobler, John. *Damned in Paradise: The Life of John Barrymore*. New York: Atheneum, 1977.

Lafler, Henry A. "How the Army Worked to Save San Francisco." San Francisco: Calkins Newspaper Syndicate, 1906.

Lawson, Andrew. *The California Earthquake of April 18, 1906*, 2 vols. Washington, D.C.: Carnegie Institution of Washington, 1969 (reprint).

Lee, Rose Hum. *The Chinese in the United States of America*. Hong Kong: Hong Kong University, 1960.

Leet, Don. *Disasters and Disaster Relief*, vol. 309. Philadelphia: American Academy of Political and Social Science, 1957.

Leong, Gor Yun. *Chinatown Inside Out*. New York: Barrows Mussey, 1936.

Lewis, E. M. *Historical Sketch of the 20th United States Infantry, from December 31, 1905, to January 1, 1907*. San Francisco, 1907.

Lewis, Oscar. *The Big Four*. New York: Alfred A. Knopf, 1938.

———. *San Francisco: Mission to Metropolis*. Berkeley, Calif.: Howell North Books, 1966.

———. *Silver Kings*. New York: Alfred A. Knopf, 1947.

Lewis, Oscar, and Carroll D. Hall. *Bonanza Inn: America's First Luxury Hotel (the Palace)*. New York: Alfred A. Knopf, 1939.

Linthicum, R., and T. White. *The Complete Story of the San Francisco Horror*. Chicago: Hubert Russell, 1906.

Livingstone, Alexander. *Complete Story of San Francisco's Terrible Calamity*. San Francisco: Continental, 1907.

Longstreet, Stephen. *The Wilder Shore*. Garden City, N.Y.: Doubleday, 1968.

Mack, Gerstle. *1906: Surviving the Great Earthquake and Fire*. San Francisco: Chronicle Books, 1981.

Mahoney, Margaret. *The Earthquake, the Fire, the Relief, July 28, 1906*.

Marks, G. H. *The San Francisco Story*. London: London Assurance Corporation, 1909.

Maxwell, Elsa. *R.S.V.P., Elsa Maxwell's Own Story*. 1954.

McGloin, John Bernard. *San Francisco: The Story of a City*. San Rafael, Calif.: Presidio Press, 1978.

McPhee, John. *Assembling California*. New York: Farrar, Straus & Giroux, 1993.

Mechanics' Institute. *One Hundred Years of the Mechanics Institute in San Francisco*. San Francisco: Mechanics' Institute, 1955.

Meng, Chih. *Chinese American Understanding: A Sixty-Year Search*. New York: China Institute in America, 1981.

Meyer, Larry. *California Quake*. Nashville, Tenn.: Sherbourne, 1978.

Millard, Bailey. *History of the San Francisco Bay Region*. San Francisco, American Historical Society, 1924.

Mississippi Wire Glass Company. *Earthquake and Fire, 1906*. San Francisco and New York, 1907.

Moffat, Frances. *Dancing on the Brink of the World*. New York: Putnam, 1977.

Moran, D. F. *Earthquake and Fire*. San Francisco: Earthquake Engineering Research Institute, 1958.

Morgan, Roland. *San Francisco: Then and Now*. San Francisco: Bodima, 1978.

Morris, Charles. *The San Francisco Calamity by Earthquake and Fire*. Philadelphia: Winston, 1906.

Moses, Bernard. *The Establishment of Municipal Government in San Francisco*. Baltimore: Johns Hopkins University Press, 1889.

Motely, James Marvin. *San Francisco Relief Survey*. New York: Survey Associates, 1913.

Muscatine, Doris. *Old San Francisco*. New York: Putnam, 1975.

Myrick, David. *San Francisco's Telegraph Hill*. Berkeley, Calif.: Howell North Books, 1972.

Myers, John. *San Francisco's Reign of Terror*. Garden City, N.Y.: Doubleday, 1966.

Narell, Irene. *Our City: The Jews of San Francisco*. San Diego: Howell North, 1981.

Neal, Henry. *Complete Story of the San Francisco Earthquake*. Chicago: Bible House, 1906.

Neville, Amelia Ransome. *The Fantastic City*. Boston: Houghton Mifflin, 1932.

Norris, Kathleen. *My San Francisco*. Garden City, N.Y.: Doubleday, Doran, 1932.

O'Brien, Robert. *This Is San Francisco*. New York: McGraw-Hill, 1948.

Older, Cora Miranda. *San Francisco, Magic City*. New York: Longmans, Green, 1961.

Older, Fremont. *My Own Story*. New York: Macmillan, 1926.

Olmsted, Roger, and T. H. Watkins. *Here Today: San Francisco's Architectural Heritage*. San Francisco: Chronicle Books, 1968.

Otis, Leon S. "Can Animals Predict Earthquake?" Menlo Park, Calif.: SRI International, 1982.

Palmer, P. and J. Walls. *Chinatown: San Francisco*. Berkeley, Calif.: Howell and North, 1960.

Pan, Erica Y. Z. *The Impact of the 1906 Earthquake on San Francisco's Chinatown*. New York: Peter Lang, 1995.

Paul, Rodman W. *California Gold*. Cambridge: Harvard University Press, 1947.

A Payment That Made San Francisco History. The London Assurance (pamphlet).

Phillips, Catherine Coffin. *Portsmouth Plaza*. San Francisco: John Henry Nash, 1932.

Pough, Frederick H. *All About Volcanoes and Earthquakes*. New York: Random House, 1953.

Purdy, Helen Throop. *San Francisco As It Was, As It Is, And How to See It*. San Francisco: Paul Elder, 1912.

Reedy, William Marion. *The City That Has Fallen*. San Francisco: Book Club of California, 1933.

Reid, Whitelaw. *The Story of San Francisco for English Ears*. London: Harrison & Sons, 1908.

Riesenberg, Felix, Jr. *Golden Gate*. New York: Alfred A. Knopf, 1940.

Rink, Paul. *A. P. Giannini*. Chicago: Encyclopaedia Britannica Press, 1963.

Salter, Christopher L. *San Francisco's Chinatown: How Chinese a Town?* San Francisco, 1978.

San Francisco and Its Municipal Administration. San Francisco: City of San Francisco, 1902–04.

Saul, Eric, and Don Denevi. *The Great San Francisco Earthquake and Fire, 1906*. Millbrae, Calif.: Celestial Arts, 1981.

Saxton, Alexander P. *The Indispensable Enemy: Labor and the Anti-Chinese Movement in California*. Berkeley, Calif.: University of California Press, 1971.

Schussler, Hermann. *The Water Supply of San Francisco*. New York: M. B. Brown, 1906.

Scott, Mellier G. *The San Francisco Bay Area*. Berkeley, Calif.: University of California Press, 1959.

Scott, Michael. *The Great Caruso*. New York: Alfred A. Knopf, 1988.

Searight, Frank T. *The Doomed City*. Chicago: Laird & Lee, 1906.

Starr, M. B. *The Coming Struggle, or What the People of the Pacific Coast Think of the Coolie Invasion*. San Francisco: Bacon, 1873.

Steele, Rufus. *The City That Is: The Story of the Rebuilding of San Francisco in Three Years*. San Francisco: Robertson, 1909.

Steffens, Lincoln. *Upbuilders*. New York: Doubleday, Page, 1905.

Steinbrugge, Karl V. *Earthquake Hazard in the San Francisco Bay Area*. Berkeley, Calif.: Institute of Governmental Studies, University of California, 1968.

Stetson, James B. *Narrative of My Experiences in the Earthquake and Fire at San Francisco*. Palo Alto, Calif.: Lewis Osborne, 1969.

————. *San Francisco During the Eventful Days of 1906*. San Francisco: Murdock Press, 1906.

Stewart, George R. *Committee of Vigilance: Revolution in San Francisco*. Boston: Houghton Mifflin, 1964.

Strother, French. *The Rebound of San Francisco*. New York: Doubleday, Page, 1906.

Sutherland, Monica. *The Damndest Finest Ruins*. New York: Coward-McCann, 1959.

Swanberg, W. A. *Citizen Hearst*. New York: Scribner's, 1961.

Taper, Bernard (ed.). *Mark Twain's San Francisco*. New York: McGraw-Hill, 1963.

Tebbel, John. *The Life and Good Times of William Randolph Hearst*. London: Victor Gollancz, 1953.

Thomas, Gordon, and Max Morgan Witts. *The San Francisco Earthquake*. New York: Stein and Day, 1971.

Thomas, Lately. *A Debonair Scoundrel*. New York: Holt, Rinehart & Winston, 1962.

Thompson, Erwin. *Presidio of San Francisco*. San Francisco: Golden Gate, 1992.

Tilton, Cecil G. *William Chapman Ralston, Courageous Builder*. Boston: Christopher House, 1935.

Todd, Frank Morton (ed.). *Eradicating Plague from San Francisco*. San Francisco: C.H.C., 1909.

Tong, Benson. *Unsubmissive Women: Chinese Prostitutes in Nineteenth-Century San Francisco*. Norman, Okla.: University of Oklahoma Press, 1994.

Tow, J. S. *The Real Chinese in America*. New York: Chinese Consulate General, 1923.

Tracy, Grover. *My Experiences in the Great San Francisco Earthquake*. Bloomington, Calif.: San Bernardino County Museum Association, 1968.

Turner, Patricia (ed.). *1906 Remembered,* San Francisco: Friends of the San Francisco Public Library, 1981.

Tyler, Sydney. *San Francisco's Great Disaster*. Philadelphia: Ziegler, 1906.

United States Geological Survey. *The San Francisco Earthquake and Fire of April 18, 1906, and Their Effects on Structures and Structural Materials*. Washington: Government Printing Office, 1907.

Vance, James, Jr. *Geography and Urban Evolution in the San Francisco Bay Area.* Berkeley, Calif.: Institute of Governmental Studies, 1964.

Van Der Zee, John. *The Gate.* New York: Simon & Schuster, 1986.

Valentine, Alan. *Vigilante Justice.* New York: Reynal, 1956.

Walsh, James P. *The San Francisco Irish 1850–1976.* San Francisco: Smith McKay, 1978.

Waltham, Tony. *Catastrophe: The Violent Earth.* New York: Crown, 1978.

Weatherred, Edith Tozier. *San Francisco on the Night of April 18, 1906.* San Francisco: Bachrach, 1906.

Wells, Evelyn. *Champagne Days of San Francisco.* Garden City, N.Y.: Doubleday, 1939.

————. *Fremont Older.* New York: Appleton Century, 1936.

Wijkman, Anders, and Lloyd Timberlake. *Natural Disasters: Acts of God or Acts of Man?* Philadelphia: New Society, 1988.

Williams, Edward Thomas. *China: Today and Yesterday.* New York: Crowell, 1923.

Wilson, James Russel. *San Francisco's Horror of Earthquake and Fire.* Philadelphia: Percival Supply Co., 1906.

Winkler, John K. *W. R. Hearst: An American Phenomenon.* New York: Simon & Schuster, 1928.

Wirt, Frederick M. *Power in the City: Decision-Making in San Francisco.* Berkeley, Calif.: University of California Press, 1974.

Wollenberg, Charles. *Golden Gate Metropolis.* Berkeley, Calif.: University of California Press, 1985.

Wood, Robert Muir. *Earthquakes and Volcanoes.* New York: Weidenfeld and Nicolson, 1987.

Wyatt, David. *Five Fires.* New York: Addison-Wesley, 1997.

Ybarra, T. R. *Caruso: The Man of Naples and the Voice of Gold.* New York: Harcourt, Brace, 1953.

Yanev, Peter. *Peace of Mind in Earthquake Country.* San Francisco: Chronicle Books, 1991.

Young, John P. *San Francisco: A History of the Pacific Coast Metropolis,* vol. 2. Chicago: S. J. Clarke, n.d.

Yung, Judy. *Unbound Feet.* Berkeley, Calif.: University of California Press, 1995.

Zeigler, Wilbur G. *Story of the Earthquake and Fire.* San Francisco, Osteyee, 1906.

NEWSPAPERS AND MAGAZINES

All local newspapers devoted virtually their entire issues from April 19, 1906, to at least the end of May to the disaster and its aftermath. In view of this vast daily record, only the most important articles appearing in the *San Francisco Bulletin*, the *San Francisco Call*, the *San Francisco Chronicle*, the *San Francisco Daily News*, the *San Francisco Examiner*, the *Oakland Tribune*, and less prominent newspapers are included in this list.

Aiker, E. "The Builders." *Out West*, 3/07.

Atherton, Gertrude. "San Francisco and Her Woes." *Harper's Weekly*, 11/2/07.

Austin, Mary Hunter. "The Temblor," *Out West*, 6/06.

Averbach, Alvin. "San Francisco's South of Market District, 1850–1950; The Emergence of a Skid Row." *California Historical Quarterly*, Fall 1973.

Baker, Ray S. "A Corner in Labor: What Is Happening in San Francisco, Where Unionism Holds Undisputed Sway." *McClure's*, 2/04.

Bentley, C. H. "The New San Francisco." *Grizzly Bear*, 9/07.

Blackmar, Frank W. "San Francisco's Struggle for Good Government." *Forum*, 1/26/1899.

Boden, Charles B. "San Francisco's Cisterns." *California Historical Society Quarterly*, vol. 15, no. 4, 1937.

Bowker, Michael. "Can Animals Really Predict Earthquakes?" *Los Angeles Times*, 2/1/88.

Bowlen, Frederick. "San Francisco Fire Department History." *San Francisco Chronicle*, 45 chapters, from 5/15/39 to 7/13/39.

Briggs, Arthur R. "San Francisco, the Wonder City." *Grizzly Bear*, 7/07.

"The Bubonic Plague." *The Coast Review*, 12/07.

Burnham, Daniel H. "San Francisco: The City Beautiful." *Architecture and Engineering*, 6/06.

Cahill, B. J. S. "The New City Hall, San Francisco." *Architecture and Engineering*, 8/16.

"Caruso on Trial Historically." *San Francisco Progress,* 4/13/80.

"Caruso's Plight at the Palace." *San Francisco Magazine*, 4/67.

"The Clash of Classes in San Francisco." *American Magazine*, 11/07.

Cowles, Paul. "What Really Happened." *Out West*, 6/06.

Craig, W. T. "The Fire Insurance Situation in San Francisco." *Grizzly Bear*, 11/07.

"Death of Funston." *Army and Navy Journal*, 2/24/17.

Dickey, Charles W. "Lessons of the San Francisco Earthquake and Fire." *Architecture and Engineering*, 5/06.

Dosch, Arno. "Rudolph Spreckels: The Drama of the San Francisco Prosecution." 11/07.

"Earthquake—And Fire." *SP (Southern Pacific) Bulletin*, 4/56.

Edholm, Charlton. "Traffic in Girls and Work of Rescue Missions." Oakland, Calif., 1900.

Edwards, Clarence E. "San Francisco's Wonderful Building Operations." *Grizzly Bear*, 11/07.

Emerson, Edwin, Jr. "The Reconstruction of San Francisco." *Out West*, 3/07.

"Feeling the Earth's Pulse." *Harper's Weekly*, 4/28/06, 5/5/06.

Field, Charles K. "Barriers Burned: The Rhyme of the San Francisco Breadline." *Sunset Magazine*, 9/06.

Finley, Patrick. "Survivors: An 80th Anniversary Tour of What Stood Up to the '06 Quake." *Image*, 4/13/86.

"First-hand Account of Earthquake Havoc by Enrico Caruso." *Illustrated Digest*, 1906.

Fitzpatrick, F. W. "Fears Another Wooden City." *Architecture and Engineering*, 1/07.

———. "Notes on the San Francisco Fire." *Architecture and Engineering*, 6/06.

"For the Kingdom of California." *Harper's Weekly*, 5/23, 5/30, 6/13.

Funston, Frederick. "How the Army Worked to Save San Francisco." *Cosmopolitan*, 5/06.

Gilliland, John A. "Boyhood Memories: San Francisco Quake Changed Lives." *The Hartford World*, 4/85.

"The Great Fire of 1906." *Argonaut*, weekly from 5/1/26 to 8/20/27.

Hall, William Ham. "The Reconstruction of San Francisco." *Architecture and Engineering*, 5/07.

Hamilton, Edward H. "The Liberating of San Francisco." *Cosmopolitan*, 8/07.

———. "What San Francisco Has Done About It." *Cosmopolitan*, 7/11.

Hill, M. L. "San Andreas Fault: History of Concepts." *Geological Society of America Bulletin*, vol. 92.

"How the Mint Was Saved." *Sunset Magazine*, 8/06.

Howard, John G. "The Rebuilding of the City." *Out West*, 6/06.

"The Instrument That Records Earthquakes." *Popular Mechanics*, 6/06.

Jacobson, Pauline. "Jerome Bassity: A Study in Depravity." *San Francisco Bulletin*, 5/14/10.

Jennings, Rufus P. "Organization in the Crisis." *Out West*, 6/06.

Johnson, O. A. "Says Owners Are at Fault." *Architecture and Engineering*, 5/06.

Kalisch, Philip. "The Black Death in Chinatown: Plague and Politics in San Francisco, 1900–1904." *Arizona and the West,* Summer 1972.

Kennan, George. "Criminal Government and the Private Citizen: A Study of San Francisco." *McClure's*, 11/07.

———. "The Fight for Reform in San Francisco." *McClure's*, 9/07.

Kingsdale, Jon M. "The Poor Man's Club: Social Functions of the Urban Working Class Saloon." *American Quarterly*, 10/73.

Lafler, Henry Anderson. "My 60 Sleepless Hours." *McClure's* (Canada), 7/06.

Lathrop, Charles N. *The Sceptre*, 4/06.

Light, Ivan. "From Vice District to Tourist Attraction: The Moral Career of American Chinatowns, 1880–1940." *Pacific Historical Review*, 8/74.

Lipson, Loren George. "Plague in San Francisco in 1900." *Annals of Internal Medicine*, 1972.

London, Jack. *Collier's*, 5/5/06.

Lyman, Stanford M. "Conflict and the Web of Group Affiliation in San Francisco's Chinatown, 1850–1910." *Pacific Historical Review*, 11/74.

"The Man Who Saved San Francisco," *Sunset Magazine*, 5/28.

Mears, Winnifred. "Spending $9,181,403.23." *Overland Monthly*, 9/07.

Merry, Thomas B. "San Francisco's Future." *Grizzly Bear*, 10/07.

Morrow, William W. "The Phoenix of the Golden Gate." *The Red Cross Courier*, 1925.

Newman, W. A. "What the Earthquake Actually Did to California Federal Buildings." *Architecture and Engineering*, 7/06.

The New San Francisco Magazine, 5/06, 7/06 (entire magazine).

Nosnorb, James. "The Men of San Francisco." *Grizzly Bear*, 1/08.

Older, Fremont. "Shall Abe Ruef Be Pardoned?" *The Survey*, 9/2/11.

Orsi, Richard J. "The Octopus Reconsidered: The Southern Pacific and Agricultural Modernization in California, 1865–1915." *California Historical Quarterly*, Fall 1975.

Palmer, Frederick. "Abe Ruef of the 'Law Offices.'" *Collier's*, 1/12/07.

———. "San Francisco in Ruins." *Collier's*, 5/5/06.

———. "San Francisco Rising Again." *Collier's*, 5/19/06.

———. "A Stricken City Undismayed." *Collier's*, 5/12/06.

Paul, Rodman W. "The Origin of the Chinese Issue in California." *Mississippi Valley Historical Review*, 8/38.

Peddle, Jean Larson. "Pathfindings." *National Genealogical Inquirer*, Spring 1980.

Phelan, James Duval. "The Future of San Francisco." *Out West*, 6/06.

————. "The Regeneration of San Francisco." *The Independent*, 6/20/07.

Poehlman, H. E. "San Francisco, The Wonder City." *Grizzly Bear*, 9/07.

Polk, Willis. "The Reconstruction of San Francisco." *Architecture and Engineering*, 10/07.

————. "The City Beautiful." *Christmas Town Talk*, 12/22/06.

Pond, John E. "The United States Navy and the San Francisco Fire." *United States Naval Institute Proceedings*, 9/52.

Poore, Arthur C. "The Great San Francisco Fire and Earthquake of 1906." *The Argonaut*, Spring 1990.

"The Problem of the Earthquake." *Current Literature*, 6/06.

"Providence and the San Francisco Disaster." *Current Literature*, 6/06.

"The Purification of San Francisco." *Blackwood's Magazine*, 6/06.

Ransome, Frederick Leslie. "The Probable Cause of the San Francisco Earthquake." *National Geographic*, 5/06.

Ricards, Sherman L., and Gregory M. Blackburn. "The Sydney Ducks: A Demographic Analysis." *Pacific Historical Review*, 2/73.

Rucker, W. C. "Shutting Out Bubonic Plague." *Harper's Weekly*, 7/11/14.

"Rudolph, Spreckels: A Businessman Fighting for the City." *American Magazine*, 2/08.

Sandmeyer, Elmer C. "California Anti-Chinese Legislation and the Federal Courts." *Pacific Historical Review*, 12/70.

"San Francisco." *Collier's*, 3/30/56.

San Francisco Examiner, 10/21/06, whole issue.

"San Francisco the Marvelous." *Grizzly Bear*, 12/07.

"San Francisco—One Year After." *Sunset Magazine*, 4/07.

"San Francisco Rising from the Ashes." *Outlook*, 7/7/06.

San Francisco Today (entire issue on reconstruction), 1/08.

"San Francisco Yesterday, Today and Tomorrow." *The New San Francisco Magazine*, 5/1900.

Senate Special Committee on Governmental Administration. *Preliminary Study on Disaster Protection of Public Records, Sacramento, Calif.: Senate California Legislature, 1953.*

"Shutting Out Bubonic Plague." *Harper's Weekly*, 7/11/14.

Siegferth, Charles A. "San Francisco Yesterday . . . Personal Reminiscences of the Fire." *The Argonaut*, 4/13/56.

Smythe, William E. "The Ennoblement of California." *Out West*, 6/06.

Springer, Ralph. "Golden Gate Park." *Overland Monthly*, 2/17.

Steffens, Lincoln. "The Mote and the Beam," *American Magazine*, 11, 12/07.

————. "Rudolph Spreckels, A Businessman Fighting for His City." *American Magazine*, 2/08.

Stevens, James. "The San Francisco Disturbance." *American Mercury*, 3/39.

Strother, French. "The Rebound of San Francisco." *World's Work*, 7/06.

Voorsanger, Jacob. "The Relief Work in San Francisco." *Out West*, 6/06.

Walsh, James P. "Abe Ruef Was No Boss: Machine Politics, Reform, and San Francisco." *California Historical Quarterly*, Fall 1972.

Weeks, Charles Peter. "Who Is to Blame for San Francisco's Plight?" *Architecture and Engineering*, 6/07.

Wheeler, Benjamin Ide. "The Future of San Francisco." *The Century*, 8/06.

Wiltsee, Ernest A. "The City of New York of the Pacific." *California Historical Society Quarterly*, 3/33.

REPORTS, PAMPHLETS, AND OTHER DOCUMENTS

Burnham, Daniel H. "Report on a Plan for San Francisco." San Francisco, 1905.

The California Earthquake of April 18, 1906: Report of the State Earthquake Investigation Commission, 1909.

Earthquakes and Volcanoes, vol. 21, United States Government Printing Office, Public Documents Department, Washington, D.C.

Fire Officers of the San Francisco Fire Department. Reports on the fire of 1906. Bancroft Library, Berkeley, Calif.

Hazardous Buildings: Case Study, Seismic Retrofit of a Wood Frame Building, Bay Area Regional Earthquake Preparedness Project, Oakland, Calif.

House of Representatives Documents, 59th Congress, 1st Session, vol. 49, 1906.

Lane, Franklin K. *The Letters of Franklin K. Lane*, 1922.

"Living on the Fault." United States Geological Survey.

Marks, G.H. "Reminiscences and Lessons of the San Francisco Conflagration 18–21 April, 1906." Lecture to Birmingham Insurance Institute, February 26, 1909.

Pardee, George C. Manuscript Collection, Bancroft Library, Berkeley, Calif.

People of the State of California vs. Eugene E. Schmitz, San Francisco: James H. Barry, 1907.

Phelan, James Duval. Papers, Bancroft Library, Berkeley, Calif.

Records of the San Francisco Graft Prosecution. Bancroft Library, Berkeley, Calif.

"Reducing Earthquake Losses Throughout the United States." United States Geological Survey.

Reed, S. Albert. The San Francisco Conflagration of April, 1906: Special Report to the National Board of Fire Underwriters Committee of Twenty, 1907.

A Résumé of the Work Performed by the Committee for Housing the Homeless After the Destruction of San Francisco by Fire, April 18–20, 1906, Bancroft Library.

Richter, Charles F. "Our Earthquake Risk—Facts and Non-Facts." *California Institute of Technology Quarterly*, January 1964.

Rowell, Edward J. *The Union Labor Party of San Francisco, 1901–1911*. Manuscript, University of California.

San Francisco Board of Supervisors. "Report on the Causes of the Municipal Corruption in San Francisco, 1910."

San Francisco Chamber of Commerce. Records, California Historical Society.

San Francisco Early Documents Scrapbook. California Historical Society.

San Francisco Labor Council. Manuscript Collection, Bancroft Library, Berkeley, Calif.

San Francisco Merchants' Association. Minutes of board of directors, California Historical Society.

"San Francisco Municipal Reports for the Fiscal Year 1905–1906, Ending June 30, 1906, and Fiscal Year 1906–1907, Ending June 30, 1907." San Francisco: Neal, 1908.

San Francisco Relief Survey: The Organization and Methods of Relief Used After the Earthquake and Fire of April 18, 1906.

Scawthorn, Charles. *Fire Following Earthquake—Estimates of the Conflagration Risk to Insured Property in Greater Los Angeles and San Francisco, 1987.*

Thirty-Five Companies, Committee of Five. "Report of the Committee of Five to the Thirty-Five Companies on the San Francisco Conflagration, April 18–21, 1906."

United States Army, Pacific Division. "Earthquake in California, April 18, 1906, Special Report of Major General Adolphus W. Greely, U.S.A., Commanding the Pacific." Washington, D.C.: Government Printing Office, 1906.

United States Geological Survey. Fact Sheet 152-99, 1999 (likely quake by 2030).

Wallace, Robert (ed.). *The San Andreas Fault System, California.* Washington, D.C.: U.S. Government Printing Office, 1990.

PERSONAL STORIES AND INTERVIEWS

Alexander, W. E. Memoir, California Historical Society, San Francisco.

Baldwin, DeWitt C. Memoir, San Francisco Public Library.

Barker, Malcolm E. (ed.). Three Fearful Days.

Barrymore, John. *Confessions of an Actor.* New York: Arno, 1980, ch. 3 (no page numbers).

Bauer, William. Oral History, Bancroft Library, Berkeley, Calif.

Baumgarten, Edward (Etta Siegel's grandson). Interview.

Baumgarten, Juanita (Etta Siegel's daughter). Interview.

Berg, Halvor H. Letter to family, San Francisco Public Library.

Byrne, James W. Recollections of the Fire, San Francisco Public Library.

Carnaban, Melissa Stewart McKee. "Personal Experience of the Earthquake of April 1906."

"Charlie," letter to "Flora," May 8, 1906. San Francisco Public Library.

Cleary, E. W. Memoir, California Historical Society (soldier's story), April 14, 1971.

Conlon, J. J. Memoir, *Tale of a San Franciscan.* Bancroft Library, Berkeley, Calif.

Cook, Jesse. Memoir, March 1, 1925, San Francisco Public Library.

Crespi, Aurelio Delbert. Memoir, San Francisco Public Library.

Cross, Evelyn. Oral History, Bancroft Library, Berkeley, Calif.

Cunningham, J. C. Memoir, San Francisco Public Library.

Dickow, Henry W. Memoir, *My Early Life.* San Francisco Public Library.

Edwards, F. Ernest. Memoir, San Francisco Public Library.

Eyewitness to Disaster: Five Women Tell Their Stories of the 1906 Earthquake and Fire in San Francisco, National Society of the Colonial Dames of America in California, 1987.

Forvilly, Joan. Oral History, Bancroft Library, Berkeley, Calif.

Fraher, Teresa. Oral History, Bancroft Library, Berkeley, Calif.

Funston, Frederick. "How the Army Worked to Save San Francisco." *Cosmopolitan*, July 6, 1906.

Genthe, Arnold. *As I Remember*, New York: Reynal & Hitchcock, 1936, ch. 10.

Goerlitz, Ernest. Memoir, *Story of the San Francisco Earthquake and Conflagration as Far as It Affected the Conreid Metropolitan Opera Company April 18th, 19th and 20th, 1906*. California Historical Society, San Francisco.

Graves, Cliff. Memoir, San Francisco Public Library.

Greely, Adolphus W. *Reminiscences of Adventure and Service*. New York: Scribner's, 1927.

Grubb, Ethel McAlister. Oral History, Bancroft Library, Berkeley, Calif.

Gunn, James. Memoir, California Historical Society.

Hooke, Helen. Oral History, Bancroft Library, Berkeley, Calif.

Hopper, James. Memoir. San Francisco Public Library.

Kester, Frank. *Memories of the San Francisco Earthquake and Fire, April 1906*. California Historical Society.

Klauber, Lawrence M. Memoir, California Historical Society.

Lee, Lily. Oral History, Bancroft Library, Berkeley, Calif.

Leithead, Charles E. Memoir, California Historical Society.

Lesser, Sol. Memoir, *My Experiences During the Earthquake and Fire in San Francisco, April 18, 1906*. California Historical Society.

Levison, Alice Gerstle. *Family Reminiscences*. Judah L. Magnus Museum, Berkeley, Calif.

Livingston, Edward. *A Personal History of the San Francisco Earthquake and Fire*.

Lund, R. F. Memoir, San Francisco Public Library.

Mahoney, Margaret. Memoir, *The Earthquake, The Fire, The Relief*. San Francisco Public Library.

McArrow, Charles Drummond. Memoir, *The San Francisco Earthquake and Fire as Remembered by Charles Drummond McArrow*. San Francisco Public Library.

McCarrick, Marie. Oral History, Bancroft Library, Berkeley, Calif.

McGuire, John. Oral History, Bancroft Library, Berkeley, Calif.

Mangels, Carrie. Memoir, California Historical Society.

Nichok, William Ford. "A Father's Story of the Earthquake and Fire in San Francisco, April 18, 1906." San Francisco: s.n., 1906.

Page, Charles. Letter to son, San Francisco Public Library.

Perada, Rita (Etta Siegel's grandaughter). Interview.

Perrin, Helen Huntington. Memoir, *Early Years in San Francisco*, San Francisco Public Library.

Piazza, Dominic. Oral History, Bancroft Library, Berkeley, Calif.

Piper, Margaret. Oral History, Bancroft Library, Berkeley, Calif.

Power, Julia Gorman. Oral History, Bancroft Library, Berkeley, Calif.

Reiter, Victor. Oral History, Bancroft Library, Berkeley, Calif.

Reithead, Charles. Memoir, San Francisco Public Library.

Rosebaum, Sylvia. Oral History, Bancroft Library, Berkeley, Calif.

Ruef, Abraham. Memoir, *The Road I Traveled, San Francisco Bulletin*, April 5–September 10, 1912 (weekly).

Sharp, Doris. "Glimpses of Childhood in Early San Francisco." National Society of the
    Colonial Dames of America in California.
Siegel, Etta (Dulberg). Oral History. Bancroft Library, Berkeley, Calif.
————. Taped Memoir, author's possession.
Smith, Edgar C. Memoir, *Relief Work in San Francisco*. California Historical Society.
Spalding, Alfred. Memoir, San Francisco Public Library.
Stetson, James B. *Narrative of My Experiences in the Earthquake and Fire at San Fran-
    cisco*. San Francisco: Osborne, 1969.
————. Memoir, Bancroft Library, Berkeley, Calif.
Stewart, Jessie Harris. Oral History, Bancroft Library, Berkeley, Calif.
Surdez, Letitia. Oral History, Bancroft Library, Berkeley, Calif.
Thompson, Harry S. Oral History, Bancroft Library, Berkeley, Calif.
Tidell, Grover. Oral History, Bancroft Library, Berkeley, Calif.
Tyron, Tom. Letter to friend, California Historical Society (man hanged from pole).
Way, George P. *Story of the Earthquake As Experienced in San Francisco on April 18th,
    1906*. Detroit: G. P. Way, 1906.
Wilson, Jessy. Letter to friend, San Francisco Public Library.
Wing, Ng. Oral History, Bancroft Library, Berkeley, Calif.
Withering, Fred. Memoir, San Francisco Public Library.
Woods, Kate C. Letter to friend, April 22, 1906.

LIBRARIES, ARCHIVES, AND INSTITUTIONS

Allen County Historical Society and Funston Boyhood Home, Iola, Kansas
Asian-American Studies Library, University of California, Berkeley, California
Bancroft Library, University of California, Berkeley, California
California Genealogical Society, Oakland, California
California Historical Society, San Francisco
California State Archives, Sacramento
California State Library, Sacramento
Chinatown Library, San Francisco
Chinese American Citizens Alliance, San Francisco
Chinese Chamber of Commerce, San Francisco
Chinese Community Development Center, San Francisco
Chinese Cultural Center, San Francisco
Chinese Historical Society, San Francisco
College of Environmental Design Archives, University of California, Berkeley, California
Columbia University libraries, New York
De Young Museum, San Francisco
Doe Library, University of California, Berkeley, California
Ethnic Studies Library, University of California, Berkeley, California
Foundation for San Francisco's Architectural Heritage
Golden Gate Bridge Highway and Transportation District, San Francisco
Judah L. Magnes Museum, Berkeley, California

Legion of Honor, San Francisco
Library of Congress
Moffitt Library, University of California, Berkeley, California
Museum of the City of San Francisco
National Archives, San Bruno, California
National Archives, Washington, D.C.
National Maritime Museum, San Francisco
New York Public Library
Performing Arts Library & Museum, San Francisco
San Francisco City Hall Law Library
San Francisco Historical Society
San Francisco History Association
San Francisco Public Library
San Francisco Superior Court Archives
Society of California Pioneers, San Francisco
Sutro Library, San Francisco
United Irish Cultural Center, San Francisco
United States Geological Survey, Menlo Park, Calif.

Index

Adams, George C., xvii, 1, 175–76, 186, 247
Adams, May Hoffman, 176, 247
Adams, Will, 176
aftershocks, 40, 69, 176
Agnew's state insane asylum, 35
Ah Toy, Madame (prostitute), 57
alarm system, 96, 253
Alcatraz Island:
  federal prison on, 53
  federal troops dispatched from, 79, 92
Almora, 192
ambulance services, 66
American Hotel, 76
Angel Island:
  Chinese homeless deported to, 244
  federal troops dispatched from, 79, 92
animals:
  earthquake perceptions of, 31, 32–33, 37
  mercy killings of, 41, 43
  rescue of, 132–34
  stampede by, 47–48
Anza, Juan Bautista de, 2
arson, 17, 18, 97, 251
art treasures, 102, 103, 207
Atherton, Gertrude, 241–42
Aultman, Dwight E., xvii, 121

Baldwin, O. D., xvii, 216–17
Bales, Clifford, 130
Bank of America, xviii, 246
Bank of California, 109
Bank of Italy, xviii, 29–30, 141, 142–43, 171–72, 246
Barbary Coast, 5–6, 85, 160, 161–65, 214, 240
Barrymore, Ethel, 177
Barrymore, John, xvii, xviii, 12–13, 153, 167–70, 177–78
Barton, William Bon, xvii, 164–65
baseball, 236
Bassity, Jerome, xvii, 160–62, 163, 164, 165, 214, 240
Bekeart, Phil B., xvii, 133
Bell, J. Franklin, 79
Belvedere Ferry slip, fire beaten back at, 223, 225–26
Benjamin, Prince, 89
Berg, Halvor H., 130
Bermingham, John, xvii, 152
Berry, Fulton G., xvii, 206, 207
Bizet, Georges, 7
Black Death (bubonic plague), 58, 155–59, 232, 252
black marketeers, 182
Blanding, Gordon, xvii, 206–7, 208–9, 210

Blum's Candy Store, 137–38
Bohemian Club, 169, 209
Bowes, Thomas, xvii, xix, 105–6
Bowles, E. E., 139–40
bridges, 256
Briggs, Raymond W., xvii, 202
Brown, Jack, xvii, 144
Brunswick House, 105–6
bubonic plague (Black Death), 58, 155–59, 232, 252
building trades, in reconstruction effort, 252–53
burials, 119, 143, 252
Burke, William F., xvii, 198
Burnham, Daniel H., xvii, 5, 255

cable cars, 5, 100, 137
California:
    gold rush in, 3, 17, 58
    governorship of, xix, 100
    San Andreas Fault in, 33–35, 76, 254–55
California, University of, cadets from, 79
California Hotel, 72
California Wine association, 230
Call building, 95
Calvary Presbyterian Church, 245
Carmen (Bizet), 7, 9, 11
Carr, O. K., 117
Caruso, Enrico, xvii, xviii, 7–11, 37, 108, 109–12, 147–49, 232
Central Pacific Railroad, 59, 100, 109
Chase, George, xvii, 145–46
Chicago, Ill., 1871 fire in, 76–77, 229
children:
    births of, 44–45, 64, 120, 122, 234
    missing, 167
China, San Francisco racism protested by, 244
Chinatown, 56–62
    bubonic plague in, 58, 155–59
    in earthquake, 61–62
    1906 fire in, 150–55, 172–73, 244
    population of, 56
    vice activities in, 5, 56–58, 85, 240, 244
Chinese immigrants:
    assimilation resisted by, 59, 61
    businesses of, 59, 60, 153–54
    in disaster refugee facilities, 178–79, 232–33, 244
    immigration limits on, 60

photographs of, 209, 211
physical appearances of, 59, 61
prejudices against, 58, 59–61, 153, 178, 218, 232–33, 244
spiritual beliefs of, 60, 62
U.S. war vessel under command of, 216
in workforce, 58–60
chloroform, euthanasia with, 117
Christians, Jewish community aided by, 244–45
Chronicle building, 98
Chung Pao-hsi, 154
City Hall:
    earthquake collapse of, 52–55, 81, 82, 96, 98, 115
    fire damage to, 64, 118
    hospital patients evacuated from, 53–55
    reconstruction of, 252, 255
    treasury at, 91
Civic Center, 252, 255
Coffman, Bill, xvii, 162–63
Coleman, Le Vert, xviii, 194, 208
Collier, William, xviii, 168–69
Columbia Square Park, 183
Columbia Theater, 6, 21, 88
Committee of Fifty, xix, 94, 96
    end of fire reported to, 226
    federal militia withdrawal requested by, 237
    meeting locations of, 87–88, 90, 92–93
    membership of, 86, 87, 121, 203
    on plague as public health threat, 158
    refugee aid addressed by, 184
Compania, Antonio, xviii, 43, 66–67, 234
Comstock Lode, 3, 102
Congress, U.S.:
    discriminatory immigration policy of, 60
    San Francisco relief appropriation of, 231
Cook, Jesse, xviii, 32–33, 34, 35–36, 37, 40–42, 43
Cotillion Club, 9
Crespi, Aurelio Delbert (Del), xviii, 30–31, 49–50, 151, 172–74, 214, 222–23
Crocker, Charles, xviii, 99–100, 101
Crocker, Mary Ann, 101
Crocker National Bank, 98, 142
curfew, 31

Davis Street, 36
Delmonico's Restaurant, 131, 176
Denicke, Ernest, xviii, 135
Denman, William, xviii, 184
department stores, 98, 252
Devol, Carroll A., 135
Dewey, Guion H., xviii, 149
de Young, Mrs. M. H., 10
Dinan, Jeremiah, xviii, 77, 83, 85–86, 91, 103
Dobie, Charles Caldwell, 59
dogs, 31, 33, 132–34
Dolores Street, 194
Dougherty, John, xviii
    as acting fire chief, 83, 94, 96–97
    background of, 84
    Belvedere Ferry slip firefighting led by, 223, 225–26
    on creation of firebreaks, 84–85, 203
    leadership capability of, 19–20, 84, 191, 208, 223, 226
    on progress of fire, 83, 84, 190, 207
Dray, Charles Nicholas, xvii, xviii, 133
draymen, price-gouging by, 91, 130–31, 155
Drew, John, xviii, 177–78
Dulberg, Bernard, xviii, 44, 122–23, 180, 252
Dulberg, Etta, xviii, 44, 122, 180, 252
Dulberg, Rebecca, xviii, 44–45, 122, 180, 252
Dulberg family, 104, 181, 182, 220, 222, 229, 232, 233–34
Dwyer, Jeremiah M., xviii, 53
dynamite:
    evacuation prior to use of, 127, 201–2
    firebreaks created with, 85, 152, 193–95, 197, 201–5, 206–7, 208, 209–10
    forms of, 85
    resurgence of fire due to, 212–13
    sources of, 96, 201
    transport of, 66, 201, 202–3

Earth Dragon (Chinese deity), 62
earthquake of 1906, 32–55
    aftershocks of, 40, 69, 176
    epicenter of, 34
    fatalities caused by, 72, 248, 249, 250
    fire in aftermath of, see San Francisco, Calif., 1906 fire in

geographic range of, 34–35
onset of, 32–33
rescue attempts after, 39, 41, 45, 46–47, 53–55, 64, 248–49
reservoir conduits cracked by, 76
Richter magnitude of, 250
San Francisco effects of, 35–55, 61–62, 75, 79, 96, 97, 109–10, 250–51
suppression of reports on, 249–50
earthquakes:
    animal sensitivities to, 31, 32–33, 37
    building construction regulations and, 18, 250, 254
    of 1838, 33–34
    frequency of, 250
    of 1989, 254–55
    on San Andreas fault, 33–35, 76, 254–55
East Street, 96
electricity services, curtailment of, 91, 92
Emergency Hospital, xix, 53–54, 115
Emerson, George W., xviii, 1, 5, 39–40, 63, 66, 186–88, 247
    marriage ceremony of, xvii, 175–77
Emerson, Josephine Hoffman, xviii, 1, 5, 40, 63, 64, 66, 183–88, 247
    marriage ceremony of, xvii, 175–77
Emporium, 96, 98
entertainment, 6
    opera, 7–11
euthanasia, of hospital patients, 117, 118
Evans, Isabel, 132
Examiner building, 95, 229
Exclusion Act, 60
explosives:
    evacuations before use of, 127, 179, 201–2
    firebreaks created with, 84–85, 152, 175, 193–95, 197, 201–5, 206–7, 208, 209–10
    fire resurgence due to, 212–13
    guncotton, 203
    sources of, 96, 201
    storage of, 16, 103
    transport of, 66, 201, 202–3

Fairmont Hotel, 4, 92–93, 99, 103
Fenner, Max, xviii, 53–54
Ferry Building, 96, 186, 187, 228
    fire refugees gathered at, 64, 191, 225

Fichtner, Henry, 132
Field, Charles K., 215
financial district, 138
First Congregational Church, 1
Fisherman's Wharf, 82
fish market district, 43
Fitzsimmons, Bob, 115
Flood, James, xviii, 10, 102–3, 109
Flood, Mary Leary, xviii, 10
Flying Rollers of the House of David, 89–90
Fong Chong (Little Pete), xvii, 57–58
food distribution, 124, 182–84, 229, 230–31
food prices, 124, 182
Fort Baker, 79
Fort McDowell, 79
Fort Mason:
    commander of, 77
    emergency deployment of troops from, 78, 82
    fire threat to, 208, 224–25
    Funston's office at, 214, 224
    prisoners sent to, 53
    water pumped from bay near, 192
Franklin Hall, 93, 226
Franklin Street, 63, 206, 207, 208, 211
Freeman, Frederick Newton, xviii, 95, 215, 216
Fremont Street, 46
Fremstad, Olive, xviii, 7, 8–9
Fung Chow, 57
Funston, Frederick, xviii, 72–74, 75–80
    background of, 73–74
    evacuations engineered by, 214
    firebreak strategy supported by, 85, 96, 152, 175, 193, 194, 201, 202, 203, 213
    martial law instituted by, 76–80, 82, 92, 128, 135
    mint protection ordered by, 199
    on progress of fire, 190, 205–6, 208, 211, 224–25
    refugee provisions requested by, 182, 229
    Schmitz opposed by, 77–78, 83, 224, 225, 236–37
    Washington communications with, 79–80, 182

Gage, Lyman, 157
garbage wagons, 66
gas utility services, 91
Genthe, Arnold, xviii, 209–11
George & Company, 128
Giannini, Amadeo Peter, xviii, 29–30, 141–43, 171–72, 174, 246
Giannini, Attilio H., 246
Gimpy Bill (legless survivor), xvii, 45, 67, 144–45
Goerlitz, Madame (opera singer), 169
Golden Gate Bridge, 27, 256
Golden Gate Park, 5
    emergency hospital in, 116
    recreational facilities of, 180–81
    refugees in, 64, 125, 132, 145, 180, 181–82, 206, 220, 232
gold rush, 3, 17, 58
Gough Street, 63, 208
Governor Irwin, 215–16, 223
Graff, Edward, 104–5
Grand Hotel, xviii, 149
Grand Opera House, 6, 7, 8, 11, 108, 111
Grant, Ulysses S., 8
Graves, Cliff, xviii, 240–41
Greely, Adolphus, xviii, 74, 237
grocers, food distributed by, 50, 124, 182
Grunwald, George R., 136–37
Gubbins, Tom, 57
guncotton, 203

Hale, R. B., 252
Hall of Justice:
    city government relocated to, 78, 82–83, 87–88, 92
    earthquake damage to, 52, 82–83
    federal troops ordered to, 78, 82
    morgue facilities at, 118
    prisoners evacuated from, 53
    reconstruction of, 252
Ham and Eggs Fire, 63–64, 116, 118, 176
Hancock Grammar School, 151
hand laundries, Chinese, 59
Hansen, Gladys, 248, 250
Harrington, George, xviii, 120
Harrington, Ida McMahon, xviii, xix, 67–68, 120–21, 218–19
Hart, Edward, 69–70
Hartford Fire Insurance Company, 251–52
Hartmann, Gus, xviii, 125–26

Harvey, J. Downey, 86
Hayes Valley, 63
Hayward fault, 33
Hearst, William Randolph, 11, 24–25,
    229–30
Hearst Building, 98
Herbert, Victor, 6
Herstein, Marcus, 158
Hertz, Alfred, xviii, 110
high-rise buildings, 254
Ho, Jimmy, xviii, 178
Hoffes, Paul E., 167
Hoffman, Josephine, *see* Emerson,
    Josephine Hoffman
Hoffman, May, 176, 247
hog farmers, garbage wagons of, 66
Hopkins, Mark, xviii, 74, 99–100, 101–2
Hopkins, Mary, 101–2, 103
Hopkins Institute of Art, 102
Hopper, James, xix, 37–39, 226
Horace, 209
Horsburgh, James, Jr., 249
horses:
    earthquake onset felt by, 32–33, 37
    fire vehicles pulled by, 19
    mercy killing of, 41, 43
Horton, Amelia, xix, 13, 166–67, 181,
    246–47
Horton, George, xix, 13, 166–67, 181,
    246–47
hospitals, 53–55, 64, 115–18, 120
Hotaling's Whiskey, 214, 215
hotels, 4, 8, 51–52, 92–93, 103, 105–6,
    108–11
Huntington, Collis P., xix, 99–101

Ingham, R. Leonard, xix, 251–52
insurance industry, 251–52, 253
Iodoform Kate (prostitute), 161
Irwin, Will, 241

Jacobson, Pauline, 243
Jacoby, Josephine, 112
James Flood Building, 4, 98, 190
Jenness, C. K., 120
Jewish community, Christian support of,
    244–45
John A. Campbell, 34
Jones, Idwal, 197
Judson Powder Works, 96

Kane, Rose, xix, 54–55
Kester, Frank, 130
Ketring, Edna, xix, 105–6
Kohl, Mrs. Frederick, 10
Kwan Tai (Chinese deity), 62, 152, 172
Kwong Chow Temple, 172

labor movement, 21–22
Lake, J. W., xix, 230
landlords, rent profiteering of, 245
Lane, Franklin K., xix, 203, 206
laundry businesses, Chinese, 59
Laurie, Annie, 243
Lawson, Andrew, 249–50
Lawson, Charles, 130
Leach, Frank, xix, 200
Lesser, Sol, xix, 137–38
Levison, J. B., 87
Liang, Hugh Kwong:
    in earthquake, 61–62
    entertainment career of, 218
    family background of, 60, 61
    racial prejudice experienced by, 56, 58,
        60–61, 218
    as refugee from fire, xvii, 152, 155, 172,
        178, 217
    rescue of, xix, 217–18
    suicide planned by, xix, 178–79, 189, 217
Liang Kai Hay, 60
library, burning of, 118
liquor stocks, enforced destruction of,
    125–27, 230, 236, 240
Little Pete (Fong Chong), xvii, 57–58
Loma Prieta earthquake, 254–55
Lombard Street, 86
Long, Lieutenant, 78–79
looting:
    of Chinatown, 154
    in fire aftermath, 237, 239–40
    mint protected from, 199
    of relief aid, 239–40
    shoot-to-kill policy on, 86, 90–92,
        129–30, 134–35, 170–71, 177
    by soldiers, 127–28, 129, 154, 240
Los Angeles, Calif., 1906 population of, 3
lottery, 60
Lund, R. F., 134

McArrow, Charles Drummond, xix, 129
McClaren, John, 180

McDermitt, Mary, xix, 89–90
McEnerney, Garret W., 86
McIntyre, Dan, 167
McLean, John, xix, 54–55
McMahon, Ida, xviii, xix, 67–68, 120–21, 218–19
McMahon, John, xix, 67–68, 120–21, 218–19
McMahon, Ruth, xix, 68, 218–19
Macon, Clifton, xix, 90
Mahoney, Margaret, 105, 231–32
Manchu dynasty, 61
Mare Island Naval Shipyard:
    demolition team from, 201
    water pumped by vessels from, 95
Marina district, 255
Market Street, 4, 228
    earthquake damage on, 82
    fire damage on, 186, 190
    south of, 4, 8, 74, 75, 104–8, 121, 150, 176, 191–92
Mathews, Hazel, 167
Maxwell, Elsa, 11
meat market district, 43
Mechanics Pavilion, xix, xx, 54, 64, 115–18
Meese & Gottfried Building, 46
Meiggs, Henry, 82
mental patients, 35, 54–55
mercy killings, 41, 43, 117, 118
Merrill, Mrs. John F., xix, 203–5, 207
Metropolitan Opera Company, 6, 7, 11, 111, 148
Michelson, Charles, 11
Miller, Charles, xix, 116
Mint, U.S., 199–200
missing persons, 167, 218–19, 222, 235, 246–47
Mission district, 84, 191–92
Mission Dolores, 34, 191
Moller, John, xix, 47–48
Monterey, Calif., Presidio army base in, 79, 92
Montgomery, John Berrien, 3
Montgomery Block, 95, 197, 214, 215
Montgomery Street, 4
morgue, 118
Morris, Charles, xix, 77, 78–79, 85, 91
Mott, Frank, 85
Mount Vesuvius, eruption of, 7, 8, 111

Mount Zion Hospital, 122
"municipal cigars," 25
Murieta, Joaquin, 17
Museum of the City of San Francisco, 248
Mutual Bank, 98
Myers, Joseph, xix, 183–84

National Board of Fire Underwriters, 15–16
National Guard, 92, 154, 237
Nevada, silver discovered in, 3, 102, 109
Nevada House, 106–7, 112
newspapers, 220–22
New York American, 230
Nob Hill:
    Fairmont Hotel on, 4, 92
    fire on, 102–3, 176
    fire refugees and spectators on, 74–75, 172
    millionaire residences on, 86, 99–103
North Beach, 29, 30, 82, 99, 151, 213–14, 222, 246
Norton, Joshua A., 26–27, 256
Noyes, Henry E., 83, 125

Oakland, Calif.:
    earthquake damage in, 40
    fire refugee journeys to, 186–89, 191
Oakland Herald, 221
Oakland Tribune, 121, 221
Oberon Building, 98
O'Brien, Jack, 115
office buildings, 4, 69, 98
Older, Fremont, xix, 27, 28, 238–39
Old Flood Building, 96
Olema, Calif., earthquake effects in, 35
O'Neill, James, 76
opera, 7–11
opium, 56, 57, 58, 195
Orpheum, 6
Oyster Loaf, 12

Page, Charles, 242, 245
Palace Hotel, xix, 8, 11, 82, 108–11, 147, 149–50
Pan, Erica Y. Z., 62, 154
Panama-Pacific International Exposition, 256
Paper Mill Creek, 35

Pardee, George C., xix, 80, 92, 158, 224, 237–38
parents, missing, 167
Perrin, Helen Huntington, xix, 131
Perry, USS, 216
pets, 132–34
Phelan, James, xix, 27, 87, 158
Phelan Building, 75, 98
Philippines, U.S. conquest of, 73–74
photographers, archival negatives lost by, 209–11
plague, bubonic (Black Death), 58, 156–59, 232, 252
plate glass windows, 254
Plume, Edward J., xix, 53
Point Reyes, Calif., earthquake effects in, 35
police:
    chief of, 85–86
    civilian safety committees vs., 128
    corruption among, 25–26, 85
    courage and helpfulness of, 136–39
    evacuations handled by, 154–55
    looting prohibitions enforced by, 86
    military attacks on, 132, 136
political corruption, 18, 23, 25–28, 52, 85, 89, 161, 231, 138–39
Pond, John E., 95, 128, 136
Portola, Gaspar de, 2, 3
Portsmouth, 3
Portsmouth Square, 62, 82, 119, 152, 153
Post Office, U.S., 198–99
Powell, H. N., 51, 52
Powell Street, 99, 176, 190, 191
Powers, Laura Bride, 10
Preble, USS, 95
Prentice, Carol S., 255
Presidio army base:
    commander of, 77, 78–79
    disaster refugees at, 64, 178
    emergency deployment of troops from, 78–79
    end of fire celebrated at, 226
    explosives storage proposed at, 16, 84–85
    mental patients held at, 55
    Mexican establishment of, 3
Presidio Hospital, 116
produce district, 32
profiteers, 91, 130–31, 155, 245

prostitutes:
    of Barbary Coast quarter, 160–61, 164
    in Chinatown, 56–58
    in gold rush era, 17–18
    as refugees from earthquake/fire, 83, 199–200
prostitution, political kickbacks from, 25
Protection Committee, 224–25
Putnam, Osgood, xix, 195

rabies scare, 132
railroads, 4
    Big Four builders of, 99, 100–101
    Chinese labor on, 59
Ralston, William C., xix, 82, 108, 109
rats, bubonic plague carried by, 155–56, 158–59, 232
Red Cross, 117, 126, 231, 232, 239
refugee aid:
    Chinese immigrant persecution and, 232–33
    criticism of, 231–32
    federal appropriation of, 231
    food distribution to, 124, 182–84, 229, 230–31
    in Golden Gate Park, 64, 125, 132, 145, 180, 181–82, 206, 220, 232
    looting of, 239–40
    sources of, 229, 230, 231
    transport problems encountered in, 182–84
    on Van Ness Avenue, 12–23, 168, 180, 204
    water supplies and, 181–82, 229–30
Republican Party, 23
reservoirs, 76, 253
Reynolds & Company, 127–28
Rincon Hill, 95
Robertson, Myrtle, 155
Roosevelt, Theodore, 77, 79–80, 148, 221, 226, 231
Ross, William M., xix, 138–39
Rotary Rosie (prostitute), xix, 161
Ruef, Abraham, xix, 21–28, 85, 86–87, 161, 238–39, 244
Russell, Stephen, 223–24
Russian Hill, 35–36, 213, 222

safety committees, 128
sailors, shanghaied, 162–63

St. Francis Hotel, 13, 99, 147, 168, 169–70, 190
St. Ignatius Church, 64, 96, 116
St. Luke's Hospital, 115
St. Mary's Cathedral, 61, 153, 205
St. Nicholas Hotel, 64
San Andreas Fault, 33–35, 76, 254–55
San Bruno hills, disaster refugee escapes to, 64
San Francisco, Calif.:
  bridge connections to, 256
  bubonic plague threat in, 58, 155–59, 232, 252
  Burnham remodeling plan for, 5, 255
  criminality and vice activities in, 5–6, 17–18, 25, 26, 56–58, 83, 240–41
  cultural mixture in, 2, 50, 244–46
  current safety status of, 253–54, 255
  establishment of, 2, 16
  high society in, 9–10
  mayoralty of, 21–28
  Nob Hill mansions of, 99–103
  optimistic spirit of, 241–43, 246
  political corruption in, 18, 23, 25–28, 52, 85, 89, 161, 231, 238–39
  population levels of, 3, 17, 18
  port activities of, 4, 226
  under Spanish administration, 2–3, 5, 16
  successive fires in, 3, 16–17, 18, 19
  as trade center, 3–4
  waterfront landfill areas of, 36, 121
San Francisco, Calif., 1906 fire in:
  in business vs. residential areas, 15, 75–76, 176
  civilian efforts against, 196–98, 205, 208, 216–17
  debris cleared in, 130, 177, 180, 187, 196, 221–22
  destructive scope of, 251
  as divine punishment, 89–90
  earthquake before, 32–55, 61–63, 69, 72, 248–51; *see also* earthquake of 1906
  end of, 208, 211, 226–27
  evacuation activities in, 65–66, 70–71, 116–18, 121, 154–55, 177, 201–2, 204, 209–10
  explosives utilized in, 84–85, 96, 152, 175, 179, 193–95, 201–5, 206–7, 209–10, 212–13
  federal troops deployed in, 76–80, 82, 91, 92, 121, 123–35, 194–97, 216
  firebreaks bridged by, 190, 191, 205, 206
  heat generated by, 71, 83, 94
  ignition opportunities of, 63, 108, 131, 194
  medical treatment of victims of, 115–16, 122
  missing persons sought after, 167, 246–47
  official death toll and casualty figures of, 248–49
  photographs of, 209
  reconstruction after, 172, 226, 252–53, 255–56
  red sky in, 69–70
  refugees from, 64–66, 67–68, 121–23, 190, 199–200, 202, 229–34
  relief facilities in, 122–23, 124–25, 145, 178, 180, 181–82
  rescue efforts limited by, 64, 234–35, 248–49
  resurgence of, 213–17
  sightseers in, 75
  social class differences and, 75, 121–22, 232, 243
  spread of, 63–64, 69, 84, 92–96, 121, 150, 176, 190–91, 205–6, 213–14, 224–25
  state control vs. federal zones in, 125
  water resources for firefighting in, 14–15, 16, 76, 78, 83, 84, 95, 96, 191–92, 200, 202–3, 215, 225
  wind drafts produced by, 84, 95, 253
San Francisco Bay, discovery of, 2
San Francisco Bulletin, xix, 27, 221, 238–39
San Francisco Call, 10, 11, 220
San Francisco Chronicle, 10, 220, 221–22
San Francisco Daily News, 220
San Francisco Examiner, xx, 11, 25, 220, 221, 222
San Francisco Fire Department:
  earthquake damage to, 76
  establishment of, 16, 19
  firefighter fatalities of, 76, 97
  leadership of, 14, 19–20, 84, 94, 96–97, 192
  overwhelming task faced by, 76, 96–97, 206